The Andean Past

THE ANDEAN PAST

Land, Societies, and Conflicts

Magnus Mörner

Columbia University Press/New York/1985

Columbia University Press
New York   Guildford, Surrey

Library of Congress Cataloging in Publication Data
Mörner, Magnus.
   The Andean Past.

   Bibliography: p. 271
   Includes index.
   1. Peru—Economic conditions. 2. Peru—Social condi-
tions. 3. Bolivia—Economic conditions. 4. Bolivia—
Social conditions. 5. Ecuador–Economic conditions.
6. Ecuador—Social conditions. I. Title.
HC227.M645 1984   306'.098   83-23136
ISBN 0-231-04726-6 (alk. paper)

Printed in the United States of America

For Puck
Qanllapin sonqoy
Qantan rikuyki
Mosqoyniypipas.

Qanpin yuyani
Qantan maskayki
Ricchayniypipas.

My heart is beating for you only
And when dreaming
I see no one but you.

I think of you only
And, when awake, also
I am just looking for you.

Juan Wallparrimachi Sawaraura from Potosí
(1793 – 1814)

CONTENTS

LIST OF TABLES

LIST OF FIGURES

PREFACE

My purpose is to provide an up-to-date survey of the historical evolution of the three countries which once formed the Inca Empire. My work stresses social development but places it within an economic and political framework. It focuses, in particular, on the various ethnic groups of the Andean region — that is, human collectives defined in cultural rather than racial terms — beginning in prehistoric times. I have outlined their coexistence and conflicts and the complex process of acculturation through time. From the arrival of Europeans in 1492, the process of cultural mixture in Latin America often coincided with that of racial mixture. Yet, especially in the Andean region, miscegenation sometimes took place without acculturation. At other times there was acculturation without miscegenation. Also, the issue of structural change versus continuity runs like a red thread through our Andean story.

In a way, the present study is a regionally limited sequel to my 1967 book, *"Race Mixture in the History of Latin America."* It benefits from my experience and concerns related to research, for about a decade, on the history of the rural society of Cuzco, Peru from late colonial times until the present.

The many tables, graphs, and illustrations are closely integrated with the text. They serve to save words and to clarify concepts by making them more visible. The bibliographical suggestions at the end of each chapter are extremely selective. Naturally, works in English or translations into that language have been given preferential treatment. A short bibliographical note has been added to facilitate further study by providing references to the historiography and current state of research on the Andean past. The book as such, however, rests on a considerably wider basis of sources than either footnotes, bibliographical suggestions, or the historiographical essay can possibly specify. On the other hand, I do keep a personal record of such references. Direct observations during a long series of visits to the region helped to form my views. I have tried to be as fair and objective as possible in my judgments. At the same time, though, I am perfectly aware of the unavoidable impact of my own set of values, that is those of a Liberal, non-Marxist Swede, committed to the cause of social change and human rights in the poor countries of the world.

Many colleagues and friends have contributed to improve this book, whether they were aware of it or not. Let me thank especially Professor James F. Richardson, Department of Anthropology at the University of Pittsburgh, who read critically chapter 1; my Swedish fellow Latin Americanists Dr. Weine Karlsson and Roland Anrup for all their invaluable criticism; Dr. Heraclio Bonilla of Peru for many stimulating discussions; Professor Herbert Klein, Department of History, Columbia University, and Dr. Brooke Larson of New York, for their important observations. None of them should be blamed, however, for the many shortcomings that remain, nor, I should add, did I always take the advice of one or another of these distinguished friends. Finally, I want to thank Mr. Leslie Bialler, my skillful manuscript editor at Columbia University Press, for his splendid collaboration. Thanks are also due to Phillip Oxley for his diligence and patience in preparing the index.

Magnus Mörner
University of Gothenburg, Sweden
January 1985

The Andean Past

I.

The Vertical Dimension and the Growth of Andean Civilization

For forty million years, the giant Andean mountain chain (*Sierra*) has formed the warped backbone of South America. In Ecuador, the Republic so named for the Equator crossing it, the low coastal zone is rather wide. In Peru it narrows to a mere strip. Toward the east, the Sierra gradually descends to the Amazon Basin (*Selva*). The forested slopes which form the zone of transition are known as *Montaña* or *Ceja de montaña* ("Eyebrow of the Mountain").

a. The Geo-ecological Framework

The tropical location as such has had very limited influence on life in the Andean region. Strict limits for flora and fauna have been set primarily by *altitude*, from the beginning of human existence there, some 20,000 years ago, until today. Above 3900 meters or so humans can eke out a livelihood only on the basis of hunting or pastoral activities. Then follows a vertical range of other ecological zones, each of which lends itself to the breeding of particular animals or the cultivation of particular crops. In table 1.1, we illustrate this vertical scale in the case of a South Andean river valley which extends from the highland plateau down to the *Montaña*. The altitudinal limits of the zones are not the same everywhere. In Ecuador and Northern Peru the upper limits are somewhat lower.

TABLE 1.1
Ecological Zones in the Vilcanota Valley
(Department of Cuzco, Peru)

Altitude in meters	Name in Quechua	Native animals and crops
4340–3910	Puna	Ichu grass (for llama and alpaca grazing)
		Potatoes
3910–3300	Suni	Potatoes, oca, quinoa, cañihua, tarwi
3300–2400	Quechua	Maíze, guinea pig
2400–1500	Chaupiyunga	Subtropical starch crops
1500–1000	Yunga	Coca
1000–730	Ruparupa	Manioc, cocoa

SOURCE: Based on Gade 1975: 104.

On the Pacific coast, equally powerful constraints have been imposed by the Sea. Water off the coast of Ecuador is warm. On the Colombia border rainfall is heavy but declines as one goes farther south. The Santa Elena Peninsula is rather dry. However, the Guayas lowland, which extends inland from the Gulf of Guayaquil, is extremely wet and humid. But to the south of the Gulf, the transition from tropical rain forest to coastal desert is exceptionally abrupt. This natural desert continues all the way along the Peruvian coast reaching a climax with the Atacama Desert of northern Chile. This is so because of the cool waters of the Humboldt Current, which follow the coast northward up to the northern border of Peru. They efficiently cool off the prevailing southwesterly winds which pass over them on to the land. It is true that some fifty rivers cross the coastal desert on their way from the watershed on the crest of the mountain range down to the ocean. But half of them dry out and vanish from June through December. During this same season, though, the coast is covered by a thick fog, the result of the encounter of cold air and warm earth. Thanks to this humidity, in slightly higher, inland areas of the coast there are spaces with a sparse and seasonal vegetation known as *lomas* ("fog oases"). The basis of human existence on the arid coast is irrigation agriculture, made possible through history by the rivers, and spread along their valleys.

In the highlands, there is considerable variety from north to south. In Ecuador, the Andes form two neatly parallel cordilleras, which include some thirty active volcanoes. Between them there are a series of basins such as those of Quito, Riobamba, and Cuenca. There are also high plateaus, *páramos* as they are called. The highland basins are situated at about 3000 meters. Further south, in Peru, the mountain ranges are no longer continuous. The terrain becomes more rugged. Rivers, often flowing in a northward direction, at times cut deep canyons below the high level surface. The eastern slopes, in particular, form labyrinths of sharp ridges and ravines. Rains fall between October and April and less in the southern than in the northern Sierra. Basins of greater size are few, such as the Mantaro Valley of the central Sierra and around Lake Titicaca further south (3812 m.a.s.l.). Northwest of the Lake, the Andes divide. The western cordillera continues down to Chile. Once again volcanoes appear, like Misti above the present city of Arequipa. The eastern cordillera, on the other hand, runs north of the Lake into Bolivia. It branches out into several ranges to the east of the salt lake of Poopó. Between Titicaca and this smaller lake spreads the *Altiplano,* on a level of about 4000 meters. Beyond the Altiplano and the cordilleras the land descends towards the almost boundless lowlands, known in Bolivia as the *Yungas.* The overwhelming vastness of the Andean panorama is virtually beyond description: it must be experienced and felt. I vividly recall a trip by airplane, a small one, from Lima over the Andes down to the Selva town of Pucallpa. There were moments when, with an oxygen mask pressed against my face, I looked *up* toward the mountain peaks rather than down. The cross-section presented in Figure 1.1 shows the ups-and-downs of the land route between the very same places. The enormous Andean varieties in terms of altitude, temperature, and precipitation are illustrated in Figure 1.2.

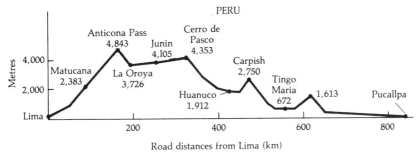

Figure 1.1. A Crosscut of the Terrain Between Lima and Pucallpa on the Ucayali River. (After: J. P. Cole 1975: 67.)

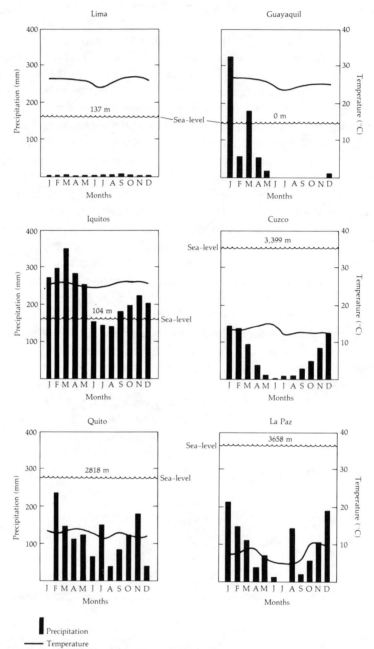

Figure 1.2. Contrasts in Altitude and Climate.

Both highland and coast live under the constant threat of natural disasters. The volcanoes have already been mentioned. In the highlands, the winter rains often produce landslides, sometimes of major proportions. In Peru, some eight major earthquakes can also be expected every hundred years. The city of Cuzco was destroyed in 1650 and again in 1950. In the beautiful valley north of Lima, Callejón de Huaylas, tens of thousands of people fell victim to the earthquake of 1970. In the highlands, droughts are sometimes prolonged and destructive, as in 1978 and 1979. Paradoxically, on the coast occasional rainstorms constitute a threat. They happen when, for a change, a warm Pacific counter-current from the north hits the Peruvian coast at Christmas. This phenomenon is known as *El Niño* ("The Child"). It destroys the otherwise abundant plant and animal life of the sea as well as coastal agriculture. Major disasters of this type occurred in 1891, 1925, 1972, and 1983. Even under normal circumstances, existence is often difficult: the coastal fog can be depressing; life in the Selva presents a countless number of hardships. By comparison, the pure and transparent air of the Sierra is a delight. But those who climb toward higher altitudes are, one after another, struck by the sickness known as *soroche*, related to the lack of oxygen. Pressure decreases rapidly from 760 mm on the sea level to 526 at 3000, 462 at 4000 and 405 at 5000 meters. The lack of oxygen as well as the cold constitute major stresses. Although they are more acutely felt by outsiders, they also affect the existence of permanent dwellers. In the course of time the natives have adapted marvelously, both physiologically and culturally, even to altitudes above 4000 m. But the move from one biotopical extreme to another is always risky. The highlanders descending to Lima easily fall victims to respiratory diseases. Women newcomers to the highlands often prove infertile.

For all the problems they present, Coast and Sierra have provided an immensely fruitful challenge to human inventiveness, tenacity, and social collaboration. We do not yet know to what an extent the inhabitants of the Montaña have taken part in the complex process of Andean cultural creation. In whatever case, so far the Montaña has remained marginal to Andean societies. The population is, and always has been, scarce. The exuberance of tropical vegetation merely hides a thin layer of vulnerable, acidic, and mostly meager soils. Political and intellectual leaders of the Andean countries have often dreamed about the immense tropical inlands as a reservoir for future development. Unfortunately such dreams are largely devoid of reality. Thus, the enormous size of the land surface of the Andean countries (2.7 million kms²) is rather illusory. In present Peru, only 2 percent of the land surface is arable; another 23 percent or less is usable for pastures. In Bolivia, the arable surface is 2.8 percent. Only Ecuador has a share well above the Latin American average — 13.4 percent. However, although they are overexploited and limited today, the natural resources of Coast and Sierra will continue to remain the basis for human existence.

In the cosmic version of the ancient Andeans, the Earth Mother, *Pachamama*, played a crucial role. She continues to do so in the minds of present Indian peasants. Pachamama unifies time and space. She gave rise to the past and the present and will bear the future. Humans, their animals, lands, and crops, all spring from Pachamama and to her they will eventually return. For most of the year, Pachamama is passive, generous, receptive, and productive. People may sow her, cultivate her, and reap their harvest without hurting her. But during some festive occasions every year, Pachamama also becomes a living woman. She is happy or angered, talks or weeps; she is ready to punish or reward. She needs peace and love. People must then abstain from working the soil, and had better offer her food and drink. In the words of a contemporary Cuzco peasant, "Pachamama cares for us, cares for all the animals and the folks. Like our own mother does. She gave life to all her children, even the Incas."[1]

The sad truth is, however, that the Andean Earth Mother of today has been crudely exploited and raped. On the Peruvian coast, the share of irrigated, highly productive soil, always very limited, has been greatly reduced in recent years in favor of sterile, poorly planned urbanization. Also, in the course of time, salinization has often followed in the wake of irrigation, destroying previously productive land. The forests and savannahs, which to some extent still remained along the arid coastal strip as late as in the early twentieth century, have all vanished. Their disappearance has opened the way for erosion, thus preventing the regeneration of humus. A yellow layer of air pollution reinforces the natural coastal fog above Lima. In the highlands, extensive methods of cultivation, overgrazing, and extreme fragmentation of ownership have been reducing the yields of many crops. At the same time, the terraces constructed by the ancient Andeans, with a view to increasing both area and yield by combining them with irrigation, have partly been abandoned, notwithstanding the accelerating population pressure. Indeed, the future survival of Andean populations can only be based on renewed respect for the integrity of limited natural resources.

b. Early Societies

The desert-like Peruvian coast is an archeologist's paradise. Here, all kinds of human remains — even artifacts made of textile or wood — have survived for many hundreds of years. The highland areas of Peru, Bolivia, and Ecuador offer less ideal conditions and they have been far less explored. On the Ecuadorean coast, climatic conditions do not allow the preservation of perishable goods and only a few archeologists have been active there. Thus, our present knowledge about prehistorical times is very unevenly distributed. Also, as often happens in archeology, almost every interpretation of the data is of a controversial and hypothetical nature. In whatever case, the empirical basis is expanding at an impressive speed thanks to increasingly sophisticated research techniques. (See table 1.2)

The first humans in the Andean region almost certainly arrived from the north via the Isthmus of Panama. In which ways they spread and settled down we do not know. The earliest traces of human activities so far have been found in caves in the area around Ayacucho in the Central Peruvian highland. According to Carbon 14 estimates, the sloth bones found in one of these caves, believed to have been worked by humans date from almost 16,000 years ago. The game of these early hunters also included such other now extinct species as mastodon and wild horses. In the so-called *Lauricocha* caves in Callejón de Huaylas, points and knives of stone have been dated to about 7500 B.C.

If hunting provided the main food supply in the highlands, nutrition on the coast was more varied. The plankton-rich Humboldt Current has an abundance of fish and other sea food. But the early sites ex-

Table 1.2
Prehistorical Chronological Divisions

Date	Division	North Peru	Central Peru	South Peru/Bolivia	Ecuador	Culture
1530	Contact					
1476–1530	Late Horizon	Inca Expansion	Inca Expansion	Inca Expansion	Inca Expansion	
1000–1476	Late Intermediate					Integration
600–1000 A.D.	Middle Horizon	Chimu	Early Pachacamac	Tiahuanaco	Manteño	
200 B.C. – 600 A.D.	Early Intermediate	Moche		Nazca	Bahia	Regional
900–200 B.C.	Early Horizon	Chavin	Chavin Influence	Paracas	Chorrera	
1800–900	Initial Period	Kotosh				Formative
2500–1800	Preceramic Period 6		El Paraiso			Valdivia
4500–2500	Preceramic Period 5				Real Alto	
6000–4500	Preceramic Period 4		Lauricocha caves			Preceramic
8000–6000	Preceramic Period 3					
9500–8000	Preceramic Period 2					
12,000–9500	Preceramic Period 1		Pikimachay cave			
pre-12,000						

SOURCES: Based on Bankes 1977: 55 and Meggers 1966: 25. The recent site of Real Alto has been added.

plored so far are situated at some distance from the coast line. Crude stone tools have been uncovered dating from about 10,000 B.C. Early clusters of pre-farmers apparently chose to live in a more or less sedentary fashion in the *lomas*. They brought there huge amounts of mollusks from the ocean, some 12 to 14 miles (19 to 23 km) away. On the site, fresh water as well as land snails and edible plants were at their disposal.

As shown by recent research, the crucial transition from a gathering/hunting/fishing economy to one based on agriculture and breeding of animals took place in very remote times. The bones of guinea pigs and llamas appear in such an abundance in some highland cave abodes from between 7000 and 4000 B.C. that they suggest that these animals must have been at least semidomesticated by then. To the extent that the "sources of wild protein" became more scarce, conscious domestication presented a way out from this crucial dilemma. In the Old World, herding, on the whole, followed agriculture; in the Andean highlands, agriculture appears to have emerged as merely a supplement to pastoral pursuits. By 1000 B.C. both guinea pigs and cameloids, including llamas as well as alpacas with their excellent wool, were clearly domesticated. The New World fauna had almost no other species to offer for the purpose.

On the coast, interestingly, cotton and gourds, both for industrial usage, were among the very first plants to be cultivated. But gradually, as the population grew, the maritime food basis must have proved less than sufficient. Thus, little by little, the cultivation of food crops like squash, beans, yams, sweet potatoes, and yuca took on greater importance. Some of them were obviously of Montaña origin. Some years ago, cultivated common beans, too, were found in the northern highlands at a site dating from as long ago as 4000 B.C.

To return to the coast, there are also traces of villages and cemeteries. The oldest village has been unearthed at La Paloma just south of Lima. In 1981, carbon dating showed this settlement to be no less than 7700 years old, thus making it as far as we now know the oldest one in the Hemisphere.

The first attempts to systematically use the water resources for cultivation took place when people planted their seeds on the river beds inside damp silt after the summer floods had receded. But they also used "sunken gardens," created through the removal of earth with a view to coming closer to lenses of subterranean water deposits. Yet, for a long period of time, a wide range of sea food continued to supply coast dwellers with the principal portion of their diet. In the highlands, on the other hand, Lake Titicaca seems to have been the only place where fishing was of any consideration. It was practiced from the reed boats which are still in use.

The first signs of a more complex Andean social organization appear on the Ecuadorean coast north of the Gulf of Guayas. The rectangular plaza at *Real Alto*, found in 1971 near Chanduy, suggests a ceremonial center, in use from 3400 to 1500 B.C. This agglomeration may have housed as many as 2000 people. Pottery appears, rather suddenly, at the *Valdivia* site further north on the coast by about 3000 B.C. It comprises both vessels and human-shaped figurines. Similarities with pottery of the contemporary Jōmon culture of Japan made some archeologists suggest some accidental trans-Pacific voyage 5000 years ago as the likeliest explanation. The pattern of currents would make it feasible even though the shortest distance is as much as 8200 nautical miles (15,186 km). This explanation may underrate the creativity of the ancient inhabitants of present Ecuador, however. In any case, their links with both the peoples to the north and to the south seem to have been weak.

On the Peruvian coast, the oldest traces of more complex societies uncovered so far belong to the period between 2500 and 1800 B.C. In distant Egypt, Pharaoh Cheops had built his famous pyramids by 2600. The large structure excavated in the 1960s at *El Paríso* near the mouth of the Chillón river near Lima is much more modest. Yet it is remarkable in view of the apparently simple and unsophisticated material basis supporting that society. At *Kotosh*, Huánuco in the Central Sierra, the first temple identifiable as such was excavated, not long ago, by Japanese archeologists. Dating from about 2000 B.C., it is known as the Temple of the Crossed Hands, after a decorative motif on one of the walls. In Central Peru, in particular, recent excavations are revealing a great number of sites from the same era. On the Peruvian coast, unlike that of Ecuador, pottery was not widespread until 1800 B.C.

The time and place of the domestication of maize has been the subject of much scholarly discussion. Most likely it spread from Meso-America

(Mexico plus Central America) to South America between 2500 and 1800 B.C. At Real Alto, however, a type of corn with eight rows of large kernels was cultivated long before that. Maize also soon appears both at a coastal Peruvian site and in the Ayacucho caves. The domestication of maize implied a much higher productivity per acre than earlier plants. Maize was also more resistant against drought and permitted greater food reserves. After what may have been times of conflict and crisis, by the first millennium B.C. a wide ranging productive change set in. Pottery, textiles, even ornaments in gold, appear in abundance, as do the traces of nets of irrigation canals. According to one estimate, the construction of 40 km of long lateral canals in the Cañete valley made the cultivable area there jump from 500 to 1500 hectares.

Organized religion took the lead. In 1943, a great stone temple was found at *Chavín de Huántar* in the North Peruvian interior at an altitude of over 3000 meters. It dates from about 800 B.C. Its most striking feature is a feline head, probably a jaguar, with snakes as eyebrows and the mouth formed in an awesome snarl. This feline deity can also be recognized on a great many artifacts from both highland and coast before 400 to 300 B.C. Thus it is not too far-fetched to think of a cult consciously spread by missionaries or in some other way. Nothing is known for sure, however. As with the so-called Chorrera "horizon" (a favorite term among archeologists) in Ecuador, Chavín seems to have been related both to the spread of maize cultivation and to that of manioc. The latter domesticate is clearly of tropical lowland origin. Neither is there any consensus among archeologists as to the roots of Chavín culture. Were they mainly domestic or external? Striking similarities can be found with Meso-American cultures. Some archeologists have also hinted at the possible role of Valdivia as a "bridge" between Chavín and Southeast Asian cultures. Nor do we know what caused the rather abrupt cease of Chavín culture and possible religious and/or political domination in the northern half of present-day Peru.

During the very last centuries before Christ, the Peruvian coast returned to a fragmented cultural pattern. This state of affairs would prevail for more than a thousand years. Major irrigation systems were built in each river valley. At times, these systems were also interconnected by long canals. According to a well-known theory, large-scale irrigation here and elsewhere gave rise to stratified, urbanized societies and centralized political power. The causal relationship seems to be more complex, though. So far, anyway, the empirical data do not suffice to adopt the "hydraulic power" thesis. In fact, strong political power seems to have been slow in emerging. With respect to technology, the use of copper for the fabrication of tools and arms was a major innovation of this era. The first construction of terraces (*andenes*) for cultivation is also believed to have taken place around 500 B.C. At *Paracas*, in Pisco south of Lima, enormous numbers of mummies wrapped in exquisite textiles have been found. Beyond burial customs, though, these findings give us few clues as to the character of society.

Also the polychrome pottery of *Nazca*, on the Southern coast, with highly stylized motives, provides only occasional glimpses into what life was like. The predominance of elaborate grave materials does suggest an emphasis on ancestral worship. The famous Nazca "lines," large complexes of designs, visible only from the air, not unexpectedly were the point of departure for sensational "theories" about Andean contacts with outer space. Most likely they actually represented a sort of agricultural calendar or other astronomical device. On the northern coast, the imaginative pottery of *Moche*, with its welter of figures representing human beings, animals, and plants, is considerably more generous in providing details about life in a highly stratified, artistically sophisticated society. Modelled Moche pottery conveys the portraits of individuals engaged in work, lovemaking, or leisure. The faces bear individual expressions, sometimes harried by anguish or disease. But in the absence of any writing, despite its lively human image, the historical development of Moche society remains hidden to our eyes. The massive, truncated construction of *Huaca del Sol*, dating from the Moche period, is the largest mudbrick pyramid of the Americas. In some ways, probably, Andean prehistoric cultures never reached a higher level than during this first millennium after Christ. The population maximum was probably now reached in the coastal valleys. With respect to that of Virú, it has been estimated that the cultivable area was probably 40 percent larger than today, supporting some 25,000 people. The superior level of irrigation-agriculture and the massive constructions of andenes probably reflected population pressure. The level of craftsmanship attained during this period seems to have been unsurpassed.

Around 500 B.C., the Ecuadorean archeology presents a puzzling though strictly circumscribed phenomenon, the *Bahia* "phase" figurines, in their characteristic sitting position, possibly depicting priests in the act of prayer. Once again, some occasional trans-Pacific contact in the form of a drifting craft has been forwarded as an explanation.

In Ecuador, as in Peru, this period was one of varied regional development. Yet, once again, unifying influences marked a new stage in the evolution of the Andean world. The main site is *Tiahuanaco* at an altitude of about 4000 meters on the eastern shores of Lake Titicaca. There are several huge temple complexes lying in ruins there. Most famous is a doorway made from a single block of hard stone, about 3 meters high, known as the "Gateway of the Sun." In the center of a carved frieze a human figure emerges with a staff in each hand and decorated with the heads of pumas, eagles, and condors. Oral tradition gathered by a Spanish chronicler has it that this figure was Viracocha, Creator God of the Andean universe.[2] Tiahuanaco dates from the early centuries of our era, but seems to have exerted its strongest influence in the Andean space before 900 A.D. It was probably a great center of trade where products of the Sierra, Costa, and Montaña were exchanged. No doubt it was a great religious center like Chavín. The many artifacts found that relate to the use of hallucinogenic plants suggest that a "drug culture" formed an important ingredient of worship. The impact of Tiahuanaco religion and culture spread all over highland and coast. *Huari* in present Ayacucho is one strongly "tihuanacoid" site that later would become a political center in its own right, an "empire" as it is usually termed. The influence of Tiahuanaco is also visible at *Pachacámac*, the enormous temple structure near Lima, which remained the seat of a famous oracle as late as the arrival of the Spaniards. It has been suggested that the emergence of the Tiahuanaco – Huari "Empire" was as a response to a deterioration of the climate, and that the same would be true, later, about the concentration of power under the Incas.

Around 1200 A.D. the forces of regional diversity obtained ascendancy once more. Within the confines of Moche tradition, the *Chimú* (or Chimor) realm emerged as a leading power on the northern Peruvian coast. Other such realms were being formed, for instance, around Cuzco in the southern highlands and at Chincha on the southern coast.

Oral tradition was still strong enough at the time of the Spanish conquest to provide us with a few names from Chimú history. According to one myth, two stars had given birth to kings and nobles, while another two stars produced common people. There was, apparently, a wide and unbridgeable gap between social classes. Commoners had only one wife; kings and nobles often had harems. But marriage ceremonies stressed the equality of both sexes. The social order was maintained by an elaborate and harsh legal system.

Artisanship turned to mass production while still maintaining considerable quality in pottery as well as metal work. The large Chimú gold masks are particularly striking. The huge city of Chan Chan served as the capital of the Chimú realm. It is estimated to have covered some 20 km². The central area consisted of a number of "citadels" or rectangular compounds encircled by walls with easily controlled narrow entrances. Apart from dwellings they comprise storages and water reservoirs. They have caused considerable speculation. Was each of them inhabited by a specific lineage (that is, descent group) or other social group? Recently, it was persuasively proposed that they were, in fact, the palaces of the subsequent kings. The platforms on which they were buried served as objects of continuous worship by the groups of their descendants. In whatever case, unlike the Aztec and Maya cities with their central temples, or, for that matter, the medieval – colonial city with its cathedral, in the farflung city of Chan Chan no single structure imposed its authority over the entire agglomeration.

c. The Inca Empire

As we have just seen, recent research has pushed the beginnings of Andean prehistory into an ever more remote past. The duration of the last stage, that of the Incas, thus continuously shrinks in relative terms. Also the originality and significance of the Incas is becoming increasingly subjected to questioning and debate. Yet one fact can never be overcome: Our entire knowledge about pre-Spanish times, insofar as it is not based on archeological evidence, rests on the observations made by the Spanish newcomers of Inca institutions and on the testimony they gathered from former subjects of the Inca rulers. Thus, the conditions of the Inca period unavoidably constitute our frame of reference while their possible pre-Inca antecedents can only be hypothesized.

Until very recently, a long series of Spanish chroniclers were believed to be our only noteworthy sources of knowledge. Admittedly they provide extensive but often contradictory information. Unfortunately, however, there was no one among the Peruvian *conquistadores* endowed with the curiosity and literary talent of a Bernal Díaz del Castillo, to whom we owe so much in the case of the Aztecs of Mexico. At that time, it would still have been possible to observe the Inca Empire in its pristine forms. The earliest qualified observers, Pedro Cieza de León and Juan de Betanzos, wrote their remarkably objective accounts some twenty years later. The later, more frequently quoted chronicles exhibit a glaring bias, for or against. Inca Garcilaso de la Vega (1609), the offspring of a Spanish captain and an Inca princess, expresses pride for his maternal ancestors while Pedro Sarmiento da Gamboa (1572), in keeping with the policy of his taskmaster Viceroy Toledo takes a very negative view of "Inca despotism." The curious chronicle of an Indian, Guamán Poma de Ayala (1613), with its abundant drawings represents an intermediate position. The author belonged to one of the ethnic groups subjugated by the Incas and he was much aware of a glorious past before Inca rule.

The Incas possessed no scripture. Thus the first Spanish chroniclers had to depend on Inca oral tradition. Later, the chroniclers copied one another, usually without acknowledgment and in often confusing fashions. To be sure, the Incas had a staff of chroniclers of their own, specialists in preserving a "controlled" official tradition. (In the case of quantities, at the least, they also disposed of the intricate knot records [*quipus*] which constituted mnemonic devices.) But the Spanish chroniclers appear to have relied much more on the personal reminiscences of Indian informants. Such oral tradition is necessarily much more short-lived than tradition learned by heart ("controlled"). Also the Spanish chroniclers naturally present an image colored by the ethnocentric European concepts of their times. They interpreted what they saw or heard according to their own set of values.

At times, the words of the Indians themselves can be heard, however, expressed in their own tongue, as in the case of the Huarochirí tales, written down around 1600. A grammar and dictionary in the Quechua

language were prepared as early as the 1550s by a Spanish friar. They
can provide useful clues for historical analysis. But much less material
in the native tongue has been preserved than in the case of Meso-
America.

More recently, however, the scholarly search has focused on long
neglected records of Spanish officials: legal and administrative records
from the early times of colonial administration. Indian witnesses were
often heard on issues of land tenure and the like. These sources yield
considerable new information which broadens our understanding of
conditions during Inca and possibly also earlier times. Archeological
research, naturally, also contributes to our knowledge but can seldom
provide more than approximations for this short period.

The duration of the Empire, for instance, appears to have been so
short that archeological dating can hardly settle the chronological problems surrounding Inca territorial expansion. As recorded by the chroniclers, tradition lists twelve or thirteen Inca rulers along with their
respective exploits. The founder, Manco Capac, and his wife, Mama
Occla, are said to have been created by the sun on an island in Lake
Titicaca in order to bring civilization to mankind. They eventually
chose Cuzco as their headquarters. Most other rulers on the list are also
described merely in mythical terms. The territorial expansion that
transformed a tiny city-state of the ordinary Andean model into a
farflung empire is ascribed to three rulers only — Pachacuti, his son
Topa Inca Yupanqui, and Huayna Capac. The latter's death occurred
just a few years before the Spanish Conquest. According to the well-
known chronology, elaborated by an American archeologist, John
Rowe, the expansion took only some ninety years. But, as shown by a
European historian, Åke Wedin, this chronology is based on deficient
data. The expansion may very well have lasted longer.

Cuzco tradition also possibly ignored the contributions of earlier
rulers. Apparently, Pachacuti starts a new cycle in Inca tradition. Thus,
everything before his reign could have been consciously reduced to
myth. Recently, it has been suggested, also, that the whole list of rulers
should be arranged into pairs under the assumption that two reigned
at the same time. It is clear, anyway, that the succession was normally

secured through co-optation of one of the Inca princes by his father. In this way, for example, Topa Inca was the co-regent of Pachacuti, and it is hard to separate their achievements.

Inca armies first conquered the region around Lake Titicaca that contained the Aymara realms of the Lupaqa and the Colla. Subsequently, the central and northern highlands up to Quito fell into their hands. Then they swept the coast from the north of Peru down to Rio Maule in central Chile. The most important state absorbed was that of Chimú. But more modest opponents, such as the Cara of the Quito area, sometimes put up more tenacious resistance. In present Ecuador, archeological remains suggest a rather uneven spread of Incaic influence. Spread especially by Inca settlers from the nuclear areas, the Quechua language of the Incas there, as everywhere, was imposed as the common tongue. Only the Aymara speakers of present Bolivia have been able to retain their language. (see Figs. 1.3 and 1.4).

Though often neatly outlined on modern maps, the borders of the Empire were probably rather blurred. The little hilltop settlement of Machu Picchu, nowadays the greatest tourist attraction in South America, is just one of several traces left by Inca agricultural colonization in a vague Montaña border zone. Yet the Incas did not go far in colonizing the lowlands because they were justifiably scared of the virulent infectious diseases (such as leishmaniasis) rampant there. Indian societies in northwestern Argentina and northern and central Chile were probably only loosely associated with the Empire. As far as the Indians on the Island of Puná, in the Bay of Guayaquil, were concerned, one of the Spanish conquistadores asserts: "They only offered recognition and certain tribute and nothing more. But from Tumbez [on the Northern shore] southward all were vassals and very obedient."

Nevertheless, Inca tradition records a great number of local uprisings that the indefatigable armies had to put down as the Empire's external boundaries expanded. Huayna Capac had turned his headquarters in Ecuador at Tomebamba (near Cuenca) into a kind of counterpart to Cuzco. When he died (probably a victim of a smallpox epidemic of Old World origin which preceded the Spaniards around 1527), succession, always a moot issue, rather logically turned into civil war. One of his

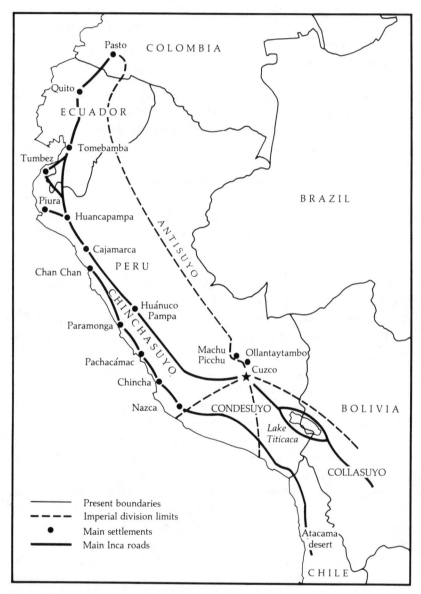

Figure 1.3. Pre-Spanish Settlements and the Inca Empire, with Its Main Divisions and Roads. (Based on Cobo 1979, map 12; Morales Padron 1975: 98, and Morris 1976: 63.)

A

B

C

Figure 1.4. Inca Expansion and War Through the Eyes of Guamán Poma de Ayala. **A.** Fighting the Ecuadorean "Barbarians." **B.** A young Inca draftee contributing to "Head Count." **C.** A Colla rebel is being punished. As shown by his dress, he is not a "Barbarian."

sons, Atahualpa, supported by the Ecuador-based army, succeeded in defeating his Cuzco-based half-brother Huascar. These very last events of Inca history are, of course, the ones about which our knowledge is most certain and detailed.

Population estimates for the Inca Empire have differed widely, from three to sixteen or even thirty million. However, the most careful recent research into this tricky question makes it likely that the population of Inca Peru reached about six million people. By comparison, present-day Ecuador and Bolivia probably held a much smaller population.[3]

Until recently, the Inca Empire has been represented as a very rigid and uniform structure in time and space. It has been analyzed in the West as being a "welfare state" or "socialist" or "communist." This has been so because the local variations were unknown or underrated and because the short duration of most parts of the Empire was not realized. Yet there is no doubt that the goal of the Inca rulers was extreme centralization. They claimed to be of divine descent, sons of Inti, the Sun God. As in the case of the Pharaohs, royal incest was the logical consequence of such pretensions, but the rulers also surrounded themselves with harems of lesser rank. Thus, the descendants of each ruler soon formed a numerous lineage or kin group, *ayllu,* similar to those which formed the basis of society all over the Andes. Each Inca ruler built a palace of his own in the capital, which became the center of his ayllu or *panaca.* This aristocracy, the "Big Ears" (so-called because of the ear plugs that marked their status) were the Incas in the strict sense of the word. They monopolized the highest offices of the state. But Pacha-cuti already is said to have extended the Inca status to all the Quechua-speaking ayllus living in the surroundings of Cuzco. In that city there were also a number of shrines (*ceques*). The lines which connected the ceques with each other seem to have determined a distribution of religious and public service duties and preferential marriage patterns. More importantly, the pattern of the major division of the city, into four parts (*suyos*) which met at the central plaza, also ran through the entire Empire. For this reason it was called *Tahuantinsuyo* (or *Taguansuyo*), the four parts. *Chinchasuyo* extended toward the northwest, and thus became the largest portion; *Condesuyo* extended toward the Southwest.

Collasuyo extended southeast toward Lake Titicaca and present Bolivia; *Antisuyo* extended northeast, over part of the sacred valley of Uru-bamba into the Montaña.

Each pair of suyos was also related to the division of the Inca capital into a superior upper half (*Anan*) and an inferior lower part (*Urin*). This division is visible also today in many Andean communities. During Inca times, the administration of each suyo was the responsibility of a high functionary (*apu*), subordinate only to the ruler himself. Each suyo was divided into a number of provinces with their respective governors. In their turn, these Inca governors controlled a number of members of the local elite, *curacas* (in Quechua) or *mallkus* (in Aymara). In accordance with a famous decimal division, one curaca was respon-sible for 10,000 heads of households, other lesser cuaracas for every 5,000 or 1,000 units (*huaranga*) down to only 100 (*pachaca*), 50, and 10. This division seems to have derived from the Chimú realm. It has also been related to military obligations. Anyway, it marked a norm rather than a reality, and should not be taken as literally as is often done. The fact that the elite of the local ethnic groups were in charge of adminis-tration on lower levels was an important feature of Imperial organiza-tion, however.

On the grass-roots level, population was broken down into sex-and-age groups related to different functions to be performed. The married men between about 25 and 50 years of age, *hatunruna*, were especially important to the state. They periodically had to perform public work (*mita*) and were also taken out to fight in the wars. Thanks to the Quipus and administrative efficiency, numerical population data were kept at the disposal of Cuzco leadership. As Guamán Poma explains, there was no taxation or tribute in the proper sense. "The individual's obligation to the State was only expressed in the form of work and service." The fields for the subsistence of the hatunruna and their families were redistributed regularly by the ayllu according to family size and needs. The measure used was that of *topu*, the extent of which shifted according to the crop and land quality but was considered enough for the needs of a normal size family. Llama and alpaca herds were at the disposal of the various ayllus.

There were other types of property as well. A three-tier partition of land between ayllus, state, and "church" is usually mentioned. The fields set aside for the latter two purposes were worked by the hatunruna as a part of their obligations. But there were also lands acquired by the ruler in a personal capacity which after his death passed into the possession of his panaca. These appear to have been cultivated by *yana*, members of a category of individuals living outside the ayllu organization: "perpetual servants," as Cieza de León calls them. Yana herders also cared for the increasing state-owned herds of alpacas and llamas. They occupied positions of trust at the service of the elite.

According to recently found records, even the yanas disposed of special subsistence parcels of land. There were also other "specialist" categories in the Empire, like the priests, the *aqlla* (chosen as young girls to be trained at the temples and usually destined to become wives or concubines of the elite, the so-called "Virgins of the Sun"), and the *mitmaq*, colonists sent out from Cuzco to spread Inca customs and the Quechua language and to strengthen by their presence internal security in faraway territories of the Empire. In the same way, parts of the subjugated population of the periphery were obliged to settle down in or around the Imperial Capital. The last years of the Empire probably witnessed a trend toward increased Inca reliance on yana labor, on mitmaq colonization, and mita service.

Recent research emphasizes that the principles of *reciprocity, redistribution*, and *verticality* pervaded Inca, and indeed all Andean society, on all levels. Reciprocity ran through community life in all respects. It still does. Talking about the *ayni* variety of reciprocal labor, a contemporary informant from Cuzco declares: "This form of ayni help does not only apply in farming. It is everywhere. You marry. They will help you through ayni. When somebody of your family dies, ayni will help burying him. . . . But, of course, all ayni services you have to return with your full heart."[4]

Though not necessarily symmetrical, reciprocity also characterized the relations between the hatunruna and the Inca state. Indians on mita service as well as their families back home were taken care of at public expense. Within the economy, redistribution from above to a very great extent took the place of barter and trade. Thus, the alpaca and llama wool from state herds were handed out to the adult women who had spinning and weaving as their main working obligations. Their task done, cloth was redistributed by the state according to regional needs. Naturally, the systems of reciprocity and redistribution were both related to the varied pattern of productive capacity and human needs dictated by the vertical range. Anthropologist John Murra has made the term of "vertical control" a household word among Andeanists. He showed that, during Inca times, a large-sized subjugated ethnic group like the Lupaqa in the Titicaca region had virtual colonies as far as a ten-day or more journey from the Altiplano (that is, in the Montaña and the coastal desert respectively) to ensure a more varied supply. Reciprocity regulated the exchange of goods between the nuclear area and these outlying settlements or, "islands," as Murra calls them. The same ambition, though on a somewhat smaller scale, can also be discerned among the Chupachos of Huánuco in the Central Sierra. The frequency and relative importance of such cases of *macro verticality* remain to be assessed, however. *Micro verticality*, that is, the use of the vertical range within a lesser, contiguous area was probably even more important. It can often be observed today as well. In the remote district of Q'eros in Cuzco, the native community controls a range from 1400 through 4800 meters above the sea level. The length of their land is 60 km. and they spend about a fifth of their time just moving from one ecological niche to another in order to make full use of the varied resources.

Inca policy apparently tolerated the existing vertical patterns already established on the provincial or local levels. It was, however, regional redistribution that was the Incas' main concern. A system of state warehouses and a remarkably efficient network of communications made, in fact, the principle of redistribution work. In Huánuco, for instance, some 500 warehouses have been found with a combined storage capacity of no less than 10,000 m.[3] They were apparently used to store grains and tubers brought from elsewhere for the subsistence of the people of the town. They, on the other hand, were kept busy producing textiles in some forty workshops. No trace of a marketplace was found. Yet, state redistribution probably did not completely exclude marketing and trade. Merchants have been found active in Northern Peru as well as Ecuador in Inca times. Also, verticality did not have the same range in Ecuador as in the Southern Sierra. The mountains are lower and the highest zone too humid to suit llama herds.

The principal paved Inca roads went parallel in a northwest–southeast direction in the Sierra and along the coast. But, of course, there were also roads connecting Cuzco and other inland centers with the coast. All goods were transported on the back of men or llamas. The elite were carried on litters. The many rivers and gorges were crossed on daring fiber-rope suspension bridges. Even today, one or two continuously reworked bridges of this type still exist. A system of posthouses (*tambos*) and of messengers (*chasqui*) made it possible for the government to get news quickly. No less than 1980 km. separate Cuzco from Quito, but a dispatch transmitted by chasqui runners could be forwarded in no more than eight days. This is what it usually takes today for an airmail letter sent from Europe to reach the United States.

By far most of the population of the Inca Empire lived in small scattered rural settlements of a modest character. But also, apart from the capital city with its many temples, markets, and palaces, there were numerous more or less urban settlements spread out across the Empire. Most were probably of pre-Inca origins but some were founded by Incas to serve military and/or economic needs. The town of Ollantaitambo on the Urubamba-Vilcanota River has preserved a cluster of streets crossing each other at almost right angles with houses almost entirely Incaic. Also, Ollantaitambo, like many other Andean towns, possesses a huge, fortified complex on a hill overlooking the population and on the top of a set of terraces designed for the support of the garrison. The mortarless stone masonry used in the highlands in Inca times is simply perfect. On the coast, Inca engineers like earlier and later constructors had to use instead sun-dried mudbricks (*adobe*), much less durable and resistant, of course.

The Incas naturally were interested in maintaining and if possible extending irrigation networks. The impressive terracing that we can now observe, for instance, along the Urubamba–Vilcanota River, were clearly a result of their engineering skill and systematic approach to problems of material improvement. Before Inca times, terraces were much smaller, the product of cooperation on the village level only. Near Lake Titicaca, the traces of another rather advanced agricultural technique used by the Incas and perhaps even earlier can still be observed (see fig. 1.5). These ridged fields served to protect cultivation from excessive moisture in certain areas. The foot plow, *chaquitaccla*, was probably invented or at least widely spread throughout the Andes in Inca times. More efficient than the digging stick, it is used for the sowing as well as harvesting of tubers by two or three people moving rhythmically together. It is still widely used, in particular on hillsides and slopes.[5] Inca artisanry naturally comprised pottery, the making of copper and bronze tools and arms, weaving, and other crafts as well. On the whole, however, the products did not match the quality reached by pre-Chimú societies. In this respect, previous Andean societies fulfilled the same mission as ancient Greece, whereas Inca greatness, as in the case of ancient Rome, lay in the administrative, economic, and military spheres, not in cultural creativity.

Inca mentality appears to have been harsh. They imposed strict, sometimes almost puritanical norms of behavior on the masses. The system of justice stressed corporal punishment. Those guilty of theft, robbery, or insulting the ruler were thrown into caves filled with poisonous snakes and other dangerous animals. Couples guilty of adultery were stoned to death (see fig. 1.6). For the masses, traditional religion, focusing on local shrines, probably filled the most important function. The ancestor of each ayllu was often preserved in a mummified state and made the subject of worship. The ayllu also tended toward endogamy. On the state level, the sun, Viracocha and the Inca ruler himself were worshipped. Sacrifice played an important role in religious activities on various levels. While human sacrifice did occur in addition to that of beasts, its extent was apparently much less than among the Aztecs. Naturally, regional differences were also reflected in this type of worship. Guamán Poma tells us that in Chinchasuyo, people sacrificed cottons, coca, fruit and maize spirit to Pachacámac. In Condesuyo, gold, silver-colored shells, raw meat, and blood were also offered at the shrines. In Collasuyo, llamas, dried potato (*chuño*), and fish caught in the Lake of Puquina were among the offerings; in Antisuyo, that is the Montaña, the jaguar was the object of worship. Snake-fat, maize, coca, and the feathers of various birds were burnt as

TRAVAXO
ZARA TARPVMITAN

A

TRAVAXA
ZARACARPAIIACOMVC

B

TRAVAXO
ZARACALLCHAIARCVIPA

C

TRAVAXA
ZARAPAPAAPAICVIAIMO

D

sacrifices. The Spanish conquistadores were surprised to find confession and prayers widespread. Divination was a task fulfilled by the priests. The Incas believed in the existence of an "Upper World" as well as a "Lower World" after death. But the elite were destined for the former whether their behavior had been virtuous or not. Only by virtue, could commoners reach the same pleasant place.

The kinship units of Meso-American and Andean societies, ayllus and *calpulli,* were very similar and both Aztec and Inca societies functioned on a roughly similar material level. Yet the differences are probably more enlightening. Tenochtitlán, capital of the Aztec federation, absorbed booty and tributes from all parts of Mexico. It was the center of a wide network of trade. It may have housed as many as a million inhabitants. Cuzco, on the other hand, received only a minor share of the accumulated wealth of the Inca Empire. The redistribution was a nationwide leveling mechanism. The city probably had only around 100,000 inhabitants. Also, because of *mitmaq* (population exchange), the Cuzco population comprised different ethnic groups. That of Tenochtitlán, on the other hand, was homogeneously Aztec. This helps to explain not only vigorous resistance it could put up against

E

Figure 1.5. Agricultural Production Through the Eyes of Guamán Poma de Ayala. **A.** Maize planting with the help of the chaquitaccla in irrigated land starts the agricultural year in September. **B.** In November, irrigation takes place. **C.** In May, the maize crop is ready for harvest. **D.** Crops are being brought to storage. Both beasts and men are used as carriers. **E.** The ruler himself inspects the warehouse. The anxious official presents his quipus for checking.

A

B

C

D

the Spaniards, but also why the conquest of Tenochtitlán was in effect that of the realm. In the Andes, Inca resistance would continue long after the fall of Cuzco.

However, comparisons with other civilizations on a similar material basis developed outside the "Eurasian" cultural tradition may be even more enlightening for our understanding of Inca society. In fact, the Inca concepts of state, city, redistribution, stratification, mobilization, and rights-in-land have more or less close parallels in the old kingdoms of Black Africa. Inca society does not, as is so often believed, provide a model for an egalitarian, socialist society. But Incas knew how to coordinate the use of the scarce surplus produced by an economy based on the input of direct human energy. For this they deserve our admiration.

E   F

Figure 1.6. Women In Inca Society Through the Eyes of Guamán Poma de Ayala. **A.** A little girl, on all fours, usually watched by an elder sister... **B.** But here the nine-year-old girl also picks flowers for dyes. **C.** The pretty girl ready for marriage is spinning... **D.** The middle-aged one is weaving. **E.** At eighty, she is finally permitted to rest... **F.** But adulterous love leads to untimely death at the hands of justice.

II.

Conquest:
New People, Animals, Plants, and Diseases

The growth and expansion of the Inca Empire had been a process of conquest. One after another, proud lords of ethnic groups were forced to accept the authority of the rulers of Cuzco. From that perspective, the violent imposition of Spanish domination appeared to be merely a second conquest of the Andean space. But as the perspective changed, there could be no doubt that the Spanish Conquest was of another, different kind. The gates of the isolated Andean world were thrown open. Under the forceful impact of European values and techniques, the Andean cosmos collapsed, the creative potential of the Andeans vanished; with the linkage to the Atlantic world, the dynamics of commercial capitalism replaced a regionally circumscribed economy based on the principles of redistribution and reciprocity. The biological vigor of the Andean peoples themselves was sapped by demographic decline — of catastrophic dimensions in certain areas. For all the nostalgic dreams of later Andean generations, the Conquest could never be undone.

Yet, the Conquest was triggered by a small band of men engaged in activities that have the sound of a thriller rather than of verified historical facts. Therefore, the Conquest of Peru makes for a first-rate novel, as discovered by William H. Prescott in the 1840s. John Hemming has recently written a most successful book, which contains all those exciting, gruesome, at times "heroic" details. The reader so inclined is urged to consult it. I shall include here just the most important of the long series of events, and stress instead the various aspects of structural change taking place in the wake of military actions.

a. The Events

The Conquest was a step-by-step process, eagerly watched and supervised by the Crown. Every new expedition was preceded by the building up of a base which could provide the supplies needed. The dynamics of Conquest, however, derived from individuals who combined the martial qualities acquired by Spaniards in the course of centuries of warfare against the infidels on their own soil with the entrepreneurial spirit of capitalism. They secured the capital needed for the purchase of arms, horses, and rations in the form of partnership. They recruited their men on the basis of personal loyalty and a share in the booty. Last but not least, they had to obtain from the Crown in advance the governorship of the province to be conquered. The right of disposing over Indian wealth and labor loomed as the foremost prize of success even though the Crown never relinquished its superior rights in these respects.

In the same way as Hispaniola and Cuba were the bases from which the conquest of Mexico was launched, the Isthmus of Panama (crossed by Vasco Nuñez de Balboa in 1513) and Nicaragua served as the base of the Peruvian Conquest. An old and frosty conquistador, Pedrarias Dávila, had Balboa executed in 1519—long before he could extend his explorations southwards — but he also improved the base for future advance. The shipyards he set up were crucial, as the jungles proved practically impossible to cross. Among the eager Spaniards who flocked in Panama and heard the rumors of a gold-rich realm down south called Biru were Francisco Pizarro and Diego de Almagro, both in their forties. They made two expeditions southward along the coast in the mid-twenties. On the second one, they reached the town of Tumbez, on the southern shore of the Gulf of Guayaquil. This provincial outpost of the Empire made it clear that an impressive new civilization had been found.

Pizarro now quickly returned to Spain to ask the Crown for a *capitulación*, or contract, to conquer the mysterious realm for Spain and Christianity. He succeeded in this purpose, got some advice from Hernán Cortés, conqueror of the Aztecs, and recruited men, among them four tough half brothers from his hometown of Trujillo in Extremadura. In late 1530, Pizarro set out from Panama with the first part of the expedition. He proceeded slowly and cautiously at first. Following normal procedure, he founded a little town on the coast, San Miguel de Piura, as a local base. Already informed about Atahualpa's recent victory over Huascar, he boldly crossed the Sierra with 62 horsemen and 106 foot soldiers to visit the Inca at his headquarters at Cajamarca. On November 16 1532, the all-powerful monarch was in his hands. One of the young Spaniards describes the coup in a letter to his father eight months later:

The lord came... to see the Governor and what kind of people we were, with about 5,000 men all dressed in his livery, and him in a litter covered with gold... and all of them singing in unison, and when he arrived where we were, the Governor rushed out with all his men and we attacked them and seized the lord and killed many of his people.... with him prisoner, a man can go by himself 500 leagues without getting killed, instead they give you what ever you need and carry you on their shoulders on a litter.[1]

Nothing could be more similar to the techniques of terrorism of the late twentieth century. Atahualpa's panic-stricken subjects paid a huge ransom in gold for his release, but in vain. But by converting to Christianity at the least he was mercifully strangled instead of being burnt at the stake.

Now the Spanish forces marched against Cuzco on the excellent Inca roads. After a battle Cuzco fell into their hands. Here, a heir of Huascar, Manco Inca, was installed as a "puppet" monarch in December 1533. But a Spanish municipality was also founded there. At the same time, one of Pizarro's lieutenants, Sebastián de Benalcázar, left for Quito, which, after defeating the local leader, Rumiñavi, he occupied in June 1534.

While Francisco Pizarro had been rewarded with the governorship of "New Castile" (including the bulk of Tahuantinsuyo), Almagro had to carve out a territory for himself further south. While, in 1535, Pizarro took the momentous decision of founding the Spanish capital on the coast, far from Cuzco (he called it the "City of Kings," but it was later known as Lima), Almagro, his men and Indian auxiliaries set out for the South. Manco Inca chose this moment to escape the Spaniards, who had been pestering him to reveal even more gold treasures and insulting him continuously. Manco Inca raised a sizable army, which laid siege to Cuzco in 1536. The Spaniards set up a desperate and skillful defense, though, but in a counterattack, Juan Pizarro fell. Meanwhile, Almagro and his men, bitterly disappointed with the hardships suffered in the desert of Atacama, came back. Manco Inca now withdrew into the Montaña with his remaining warriors. Instead, Almagro now seized Cuzco (which as he claimed belonged to his jurisdiction) from Hernando Pizarro in 1537. But only a year later he was himself defeated and put to death by the Pizarristas. The war against Manco Inca, now entrenched at Vilcabamba to the Northwest of Cuzco, was taken up again. In 1538 Hernando and Gonzalo Pizarro took time to conquer what is now Bolivia. The city of La Plata/Chuquisaca was founded in the same year.

From Quito, an expedition also set out toward the lowland interior. Eventually, a handful of participants, on a raft, reached the mouth of the Amazon in 1542. Meanwhile, the Almagro – Pizarro vendetta continued. Diego Almagro Jr. saw to it that the old Marquis Francisco Pizarro was cut down in his palace in Ciudad de los Reyes in 1541. But now a high Spanish official was on his way to bring order in restless Peru. He defeated Almagro and had him executed in 1542.

The moment had arrived when the Spanish Central government decided to do something drastic to strengthen Crown authority overseas and to curb the ruthless exploitation of the Indians by the Conquistadores. In Peru, the *Encomienda* or repartition/trusteeship of Indians to meritorious Spaniards meant virtually unrestricted right to their goods and labor and that for two generations of holders. The New Laws of 1542 forbade personal service under the Encomienda. Also, the Encomienda was to revert to the Crown with the current holder's death. Entrusted with the application of this new, unavoidably unpopular legislation, a viceroy was sent to Peru. Once he made public the new laws, open rebellion broke out, led by the remaining Pizarro brother, Gonzalo. The laws were seen as a royal breach of the promise to recompense the conquistadores for invaluable services rendered. The Viceroy was defeated and killed in 1546. But a couple of years later, a skillful new crown representative, Pedro de la Gasca, saw to the defeat and execution of Gonzalo Pizarro as well. There was one final Conquistador rebellion in 1553–54, but it was also suppressed.

La Gasca installed an *Audiencia* — a court of appeals — invested also with high administrative functions, at Reyes/Lima and a second viceroy, previously in Mexico in the same position, arrived in 1551. Normal Spanish administration began to function also in the chaotic ex-Empire of the Incas, but the Peruvian civil wars had demonstrated how easily the forceful individualism of the Conquest could degenerate into a sanguinary and destructive split. Among the veterans of the Cajamarca coup, sixteen died in action against the Indians; but almost as many, fifteen, died at the hands of their compatriots. Also, during the wars, abuses against the Indians were tolerated by both parties.

Yet the Indians were unable to turn the feud of the Spaniards to their advantage. It is true that Vilcabamba continued to form a bulwark of a so-called Neo-Inca state until 1572. It was mostly on the defensive, though, and often traded with the Spaniards and received missionaries. Indeed, the Neo-Incas adopted Spanish military techniques and the ruins of Vilcabamba itself were recently identified thanks to the Spanish-type tiled roofs. Finally, in 1572, the last Neo-Inca ruler, Tupac Amaru, a nephew of Atahualpa was seized and converted. At the Plaza of Cuzco he eloquently asked his countrymen to abondon pagan religion. "After he finished his address," as a Spanish chronicler put it, "his head was cut off; this caused the Indians incredible pain..." The cycle of 1532 was closed.

To understand the speed and success of the Spanish conquest of the Inca Empire, several factors have to be kept in mind. First, the timing practically coincided with the Atahualpa-Huascar feud, which Francisco Pizarro took advantage of with great skill; second, at the outset the Incas fatally underestimated their opponents and ignored the possibility of their receiving reinforcements; third, was the sheer military superiority of the Spaniards, with their horses, gunpowder, iron harnesses, and swords. Finally, the Spaniards formed alliances with several anti-Inca ethnic groups, who supplied warriors, carriers, and supplies. The first to join the Spaniards were the Cañaris of Ecuador, who had just been brutally punished by Atahualpa for siding with Huascar. Even their women and children had been slaughtered. The Cañaris surely must have enjoyed the events at Cajamarca. Another important ethnic group loyal to Pizarro were the Huancas of Huamanga. In general terms, both the centralistic, autocratic ambitions of the Incas and the factual variety and bitter ethnic divisions barely hidden under the officially uniform surface facilitated the Spanish triumph. (See fig. 2.1)

b. Structural Changes

The most immediate effect of the Conquest was of a psychological nature, and it left lasting scars. I do not refer so much to the problem of identifying, at first, those strangers who came, as it were, from outer space. Years later, an Indian noble explained that the Inca army at Cajamarca surrendered so easily because they thought, on the Spanish side, "man and horse were the same and that the tail of the horse was what killed the Indians... and that both gun and sword were parts of the horse." But the first shock of surprise was soon overcome. Even though, to this day, whites are sometimes known as *wiracochas* in the Quechua tongue, it was soon realized that they were not Gods, just evil men. The death of the sun — the strangulation of the Inca — was a more profound shock, reinforced later on by the beheading of Tupac Amaru. Until present times, popular dances about the subject of Atahualpa's death have continued to reflect the "Trauma of Conquest."

Related to that psychological effect, a new religion was imposed. Indeed, Christianity may have been received more readily at first than usually supposed simply because the Conquest appeared to prove the superiority of Christian deities and because the divine Inca had vanished. Instead, during the first decades after the Conquest, local shrines, the *huacas,* experienced a kind of revival. Not until a systematic program of eliminating pagan rites was launched in the early seventeenth century would the persistence of traditional religion, under a thin veil of external Christianity, be seriously challenged.

Yet even the rather few direct contacts with the new lords of the land were enough to build up deep frustration in the Indian as a religious

CONQVISTA CAPITALVISDEAVA LOSDEAIALA

A

CONQVISTA ENLOSBANOSESTAVA ATAGVALPAINGA

B

CONQVISTA ATAGVALPAINGACIVDAD DECAXAMARCA·ENSVTRONOVSNO

C

CONQVISTA PRESOATAGVALPAINGA

D

being. By and large the temples were already being looted and destroyed in the 1540s as reported by Cieza de León. Also, the missionaries, backed up by Spanish force, tried to destroy the Andean kinship systems as being incompatible with the Christian faith. Forced labor for the Spaniards implied much more than just that. In Andean tradition, all work was marked by ritual and festival occasions and performed in ceremonial forms. For the Europeans, work and worship belonged to different spheres, and they considered labor degrading. Among the Indians, consumption of intoxicating drinks used to be confined to ceremonial occasions. Now, alcoholism became one way of expressing frustration and has so remained. Thus, less than a generation after the Conquest we find a widespread movement aiming at return to an already idealized past. The *Taqui Onqoy* of the Central Sierra was anti-Spanish as well as anti-Catholic; it rejected Spanish food, dress and names. Yet the prophet of this Messianic or millenarian movement had an Indian Virgin Mary and a Mary Magdalena at his side. It probably had no links with the Neo-Inca state, which still persisted; it never produced action and was quickly suppressed. But the dreams persisted. In the Andes of modern times the myth about Incarrí has been repeatedly told in different versions:

Figure 2.1. The Conquest Through the Eyes of Guamán Poma de Ayala. **A.** The fact of Conquest. **B.** Atahuallpa on his litter meeting Hernando Pizarro and his men. **C.** The Spanish friar Valverde, a key figure in the Cajamarca coup, before the Inca. **D.** Atahuallpa as a Spanish captive. **E.** Atahuallpa put to death. In fact, he was strangled.

According to one of these, Incarrí was born to a savage woman but begetted by the Sun. Having grown up, he shut up the wind and tied his father the Sun. He did so to make the time and the day last longer so that he could do what he wanted. He then founded the City of Cuzco. But the Spanish "Inca" seized Incarrí, his equal, and nobody knows where he put him. People say that only his cut off head is left but that it is growing from inside, growing towards the feet. Once his body has become complete, Incarrí will return.

Also, as revealed by oral tradition gathered in Huamanga in 1981, there are Indian peasants who still retain a religious vision of the world that is clearly dualistic in ethnic terms. While Jesus Christ was brought from somewhere by the *misti* (= non-Indians), he is adored by the Indians as well but never helps them. For assistance and guidance, Indians have to turn to Tayta Wamani. From his abodes in the high mountains, Wamani is always ready to listen to the peasants and he rules on what matters most to them: animals and crops.[2]

The instrument of control over Indian populations as well as the means of extracting surplus from the rural Indian economy to support the Spaniards was the encomienda. Thus, the centralization of the Inca Empire in reality broke down into a number of loosely connected units, identified by the chief curacas assigned, with their subjects, to each Spanish encomendero. At first, the Peruvian encomiendas were very large, comprising some 5000 to 10,000 Indian heads of household and, in the case of more prominent conquistadores, many more. The total number of encomenderos in the former Empire reached a maximum of 500 around 1540. Early military merits and/or distinguished social background determined who received them, and the great majority of adult Spanish males in Peru never did. There were some 5000 of them in 1540. Some served as the stewards of the encomenderos. Others functioned as their chaplains, as one of the obligations of the encomenderos was to convert the Indians. But the main collaborators of the encomenderos were the curacas. Insofar as they could produce the tribute in goods and labor service the Spaniards wanted, thanks to their traditional authority, the encomenderos had every reason to favor them in their turn. Not until 1549 was there a serious effort to regulate the obligations of the Indians. The norms imposed by La Gasca in one highland district have survived; they show how encomendero exploitation was reduced (table 2.1).

At the same time, the encomenderos, in their capacity of *vecinos* (burghers), were also the elite of the newly established towns. The surplus they extracted made it possible to establish and maintain these towns, which were planned on the gridiron model of the Renaissance. They became centers of administration and markets, where scarce high-cost imports, products of local artisanship, and Indian-made necessities were offered for sale. The frontal attack against the encomienda by virtue of the New Laws had to be given up. But in one respect the Crown remained adamant, from 1549 onward. Indians could no longer be obliged to perform personal service to their encomenderos,

Table 2.1
The Population and Tributes in the District of the Chupacho Indians, Huanuco, Central Peru in 1549

Population

In 1532: 4 *huarangas* with very approximately 4000 heads of family

Depopulation since then severe: a third of the abodes empty. Great imbalance of sexes though part of the men might have fled rather than died.

1549: 1200 tributaries (= heads of family discounting curacas, yanas, old and sick people)

Distribution into 143 villages or hamlets.

Tribute in kind

	As levied by the encomendero	As revised in 1549
2400	cotton cloths	1920
960	pairs of sandals	720
480	sacs of agave fiber	480
360	baskets of coca leaves	320
288	pitchers of honey	240
1200	wax cakes	1200
1200	breads of barley(!)	1200
1040	"fanegas"(1 = approx. 100 kgs) of maize	780
520	"fanegas" of potatoes	520
3650	chickens(!)	2190
104	llamas	104

Personal service (still exacted at the time of the *visita* of 1549):
To be rendered by 181 persons, among them

66 artisans

30 collectors of coca

10 farm hands to cultivate wheat, maíze, cotton and to raise pigs

29 yanaconas for domestic service

SOURCE: Helmer 1955: 1-50.

just pay them their tribute. Furthermore, judges of the Audiencia set out on inspection tours (*visitas*) to determine the amounts to be paid in each district (*tasa*). In this way, the encomenderos were gradually transformed from a privileged and largely entrepreneurial group — who used their Indians profitably in cultivation, transports, and mining — into an aristocracy of *rentiers*. The encomenderos were never granted perpetuity to these grants, but they were made inheritable for three generations. More important, though, the rent they produced steadily shrank as a consequence of the decline of the Indian population.

The Andes of the mid-sixteenth century witnessed increasing numbers of Indians on the move. Former *mitmaqkuna* returned to their home grounds. Others left their villages to escape from their various duties to curacas and encomenderos, their stewards and their priests. The *yanas* of Inca times thus saw their numbers increased by people outside the ayllus and more often than not on the move. But the encomenderos often tied them to their service; the yana, on the other hand, had seen the Spaniards as the redeemers from their usually degraded status in Inca society. They escaped the payment of tribute.

Drastic population decline was a basic feature and consequence of the Conquest in the Andes as everywhere in the New World. It was brought about primarily by the epidemic diseases of the Old World carried by the Spaniards and their Negro slaves. Against such diseases — smallpox, measles, typhoid fever, malaria — the autochthonous populations, because of their age-old isolation, had built up no biological resistance. The disease that killed Huayna Capac was probably the prolongation of the first great wave of smallpox that hit the Spanish West Indies in 1518, coincided with and greatly facilitated the Conquest of Mexico, and then killed off about a third of Central America's population.

We have no idea how many of the Inca's subjects had already followed him to the grave before the Conquest, but the Indian population of present Peru seems to have dropped from about 9 million to 700,000 between 1532 and 1625 (see table 2.2). On the densely populated open coast, the decline was even more drastic than in the highlands. The number of Indian tributaries of the central coast valleys dropped from some 85,000 to merely 3441 in 1575 — that is 4 percent of what it used to be or a decline at a 7 percent average. It is true that the relation of the number of tributaries to total population is always a tricky problem and that we ignore the percentage of deserters. Yet the fact of demographic disaster is beyond doubt. On the coast it may have been also related to the destruction of irrigation works. Warfare and Spanish cruelty, so eloquently conveyed in the drawings of Guamán Poma de Ayala, surely played a lesser demographical role than traditionally believed. Yet the age pyramids (fig. 2.3) which have been put together by students for some highland populations for dates some 30 to 35 years after the Conquest show a tremendous imbalance of sexes among those who were young adults at the time of Pizarro. This does suggest the impact of military action. At the same time, though, the severe reduction of those between 10 and 19 suggests the heavy — indeed, decisive — impact of epidemic disease or excessively high child mortality in the wake of Conquest.

Indian population decline provides the backdrop of a long series of phenomena in Andean history until the nadir was reached at some point during the eighteenth century. It undermined the encomienda system, caused a rationing of the labor force in the external form of Incaic *mit'a*, led to the concentration of Indian population within urban settlements, *reducciones*, and caused the labor-intensive terrace systems to be partially abandoned. It produced a vacuum in the holding and cultivation of land, which was filled by Spanish landowners, *hacendados*, and more humble elements, poor mixed-bloods and others who settled down among the Indians and tilled their land.

Table 2.2.
Indian Tributary Population of Peru's
Southern Sierra

	Southern Sierra	Total	Percent of Total
1570	121,584	260,544	46.7
1580	108,738	222,570	48.8
1590	97,944	195,017	50.2
1600	88,611	171,834	51.6
1610	80,500	152,424	52.8
1620	73,462	136,235	53.9

SOURCE: N.D. Cook, *Demographic Collapse*, p. 101

A

B

C

Figure 2.2 The Suffering of the Indians Through the Eyes of Guamán Poma de Ayala. **A.** If the Spaniards threaten the Indians with daggers... **B.** Why should not their women hit and abuse the Indian women? **C.** This Indian is being flogged at Spanish orders by a Negro. Their mutual hatred was in the interest of the whites.

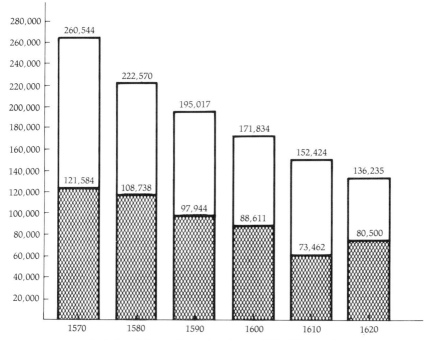

A. Indian Tributary Population of Peru, 1570–1620. Based on estimates by Cook (1981), p. 118. Shaded parts of columns refer to the Southern Sierra.

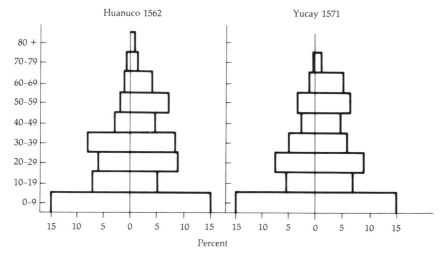

B. Age Pyramids for Two Sierra Districts

Figure 2.3. Indian Tributary Population and Two Indian Age Pyramids After Conquest. (Source: N. D. Cook 1981:101, 118.)

The tiny number of conquistadores engaged at Cajamarca in 1532, there were just 168 of them—is so well known that the swelling size of Spanish immigration is easily underrated. 15,000 to 20,000 people in the former Inca empire before 1560 is a reasonable estimate, with another 50,000 to 60,000 arriving before 1600. Before 1540 this immigration was almost entirely male, but during the 1540s women constituted about 16 percent of all migrants to the Indies, and by the 1560s and 1570s, they made up almost a third. Half of them were married or widowed.

This modifies our traditional view of early Spanish American society: If the quest for gold, glory, and power made Pizarro's warriors endure incredible hardships and dangers, migrants followed in their wake. They, like other ordinary migrants, just wanted to improve their material conditions somewhat in peaceful ways. About a tenth were artisans representing a variety of trades, many others were merchants. In fact, the wars may have stimulated some of these activities through the demand for arms and supplies. But there were also, in keeping with the traditional view, numerous members of the small gentry (*hidalgos*), especially among the conquistadores in the strict sense. They formed a third of the 168 "Men of Cajamarca," others were, as the specialist on the topic puts it "upper plebeians."

Remarkably, out of this sample as many as 76 were functionally literate while 41 were clearly not. No less than 74 eventually returned home with their savings, while the final destiny of 36 is unknown. This was probably an exceptionally high share of returnees.

Those who came with a lower degree of ambitions and had a less striking success were probably satisfied to remain. The artisans and merchants could ask more for their goods than in Spain; they also easily acquired Indian and Negro slave assistance for all the hard jobs. To whatever degree that Indian or slave women helped to satisfy the sexual needs of Spanish males, the wives of encomenderos as well as artisans strongly contributed to the reproduction on American soil of Spanish-type homes, material, and spiritual civilization.

During the first two decades after the Conquest, while the former subjects of the Incas were not formally enslaved, great numbers of Indian slaves were shipped to the Peruvian coast from outside. Most of them came from Nicaragua, once densely populated but ravaged as few other areas by the conquistadores. But on the Peruvian coast, where native Indians were dying away with such a terrifying speed, they were soon replaced by Negro slaves. In the early sixteenth century, African slaves were a very common sight, particularly in Southern Spain. Already Spanish-speaking, acculturated *negros ladinos* were actively participating in the expeditions of Conquest. The Pizarro brothers alone asked the authorities for license to import a total of 258. Encomenderos placed them as foremen, *calpisques,* in the villages of their Indians. They were used as servants, artisans, and farm-hands on the truck farms being formed around the Spanish towns. They were used as fighters on both sides in the civil wars. Increasingly, they were imported directly from Africa (*negros bozales*). Yet, on the whole they were more easily acculturated in this alien environment than were the Indians. Once they had learned the tongue of their masters, and by virtue of their price, their actual position became superior to that of the Indian masses, even though the Peruvian Indians were legally free. More African slaves were men than women, but the latter often became more numerous in urban areas. Total slave imports in the sixteenth century may have almost matched that of Spanish immigrants. A relative frequency of manumission — whether free of cost, e.g., as a reward at the death of the owner, or by self-purchase — characterized slavery in the Spanish possessions. Thus, a free sector of Negroes and Mulattoes largely urban, soon emerged. According to court records they seem to be an unruly lot; through the pages of notarial records, though, they appear as remarkably thrifty, enterprising individuals, relegated to the lower strata only by their origin and dark skin.

Everywhere in Spanish America, Conquest was, not least, the conquest of native women. They were taken forcibly at times, but probably they more often complied docilely with the conquistadores' desires. They were at the free disposal of the whites; they were legally either slaves, serfs, (yanaconas) or free servants. Cieza de León reports from Cuenca in Ecuador that the Indian men sent their wives and daughters to carry the luggage of the whites. They were, he says, "beautiful, and not a little lascivious and fond of the Spaniards." But as soon as Spanish women were available for marriage, the men rejected their Indian spouses or lovers. This also happened to an Inca princess such as the mother of Inca Garcilaso de la Vega. A purely Spanish lineage was to be preferred. Even so, Indian concubines hoped that their children would be accepted as "Spaniards," members of the new Andean elite.

In the beginning, such expectations appeared to be fulfilled. The first generation of mestizos, growing up to adulthood by mid-century, were largely considered "Spaniards," insofar as they had not been raised in isolation by their mothers. Though few of these mestizos were legitimate, many were belatedly recognized by their fathers. Only later, as they became more numerous, would the mestizos form a transitional socio-racial group of their own. Apart from illegitimate birth, mulattoes and Zamboes (being the mixture of black and Indian) would always suffer from the stigma of slave origins. They were for these reasons relegated to the lower social strata.

While the period of *indirect colonial rule* through encomenderos and curacas lasted for a generation after the Conquest, direct Spanish contact with the Andean masses, still an overwhelmingly great majority, remained limited. On the coast, the Spaniards were surrounded by Nicaraguan and African slaves. In the highlands, Spaniards settled only in key basins like those of Cuzco, Quito, Jauja, Huamanga, and Chuquisaca. The mountain slopes and Puna areas were left virtually untouched by the Europeans. In numbers these were still very few, even though surprisingly many of those unable to obtain encomiendas or unwilling to take up jobs are reported to have lived as vagrants. They were called characteristically *soldados;* at times, they did join some military expedition.

Despite the small extent of the Spanish sector, however, because of the demand for familiar food and other essentials, it quickly triggered a profound change in terms of ecology as well as production. On the coast, the lomas were largely destroyed as a result of overgrazing. At the same time, the growing of wheat, olives, and wine on the irrigated fields surrounding the Spanish cities grew up in direct response to urban demand (see fig. 2.4). In the highlands, naturally, Old World animals and plants had to be inserted in the appropriate niches of the vertical ecological range. To take our previous example of the Urubamba–Vilcanota River Valley, above 3900 meters the hardy sheep were able to join native llamas and alpacas. Between 3900 and 3300 meters, three Old World crops—wheat, barley, and broad beans—found their places side by side with potatoes and quinoa. Between 3300 and 2400 meters, maize remained the dominating crop but it was supplemented with a great number of Old World vegetables, fruits, and animals. In the warm highland valleys, for instance in Apurímac, below 2400 meters, imported sugar cane proved a great success. In the Montaña, between 1500 and 1000 meters, the native coca experienced great expansion for a specific reason. The use of coca, under the Incas, had been the privilege of a small elite, and was also used for rituals and bartering; now the chewing of coca, a powerful stimulant that reduces the effect of hunger, thirst, and hard labor, spread to the Indian masses. Thus it became a profitable Spanish business, carried out in disregard of the sufferings of the coca-leaf-collecting labor force in the jungle. Indian workers from the highlands did not just succumb to the unfamiliar hot and humid environment. In particular, they contracted the dreaded *espundia* disease (leishmaniasis) and "with their noses eaten

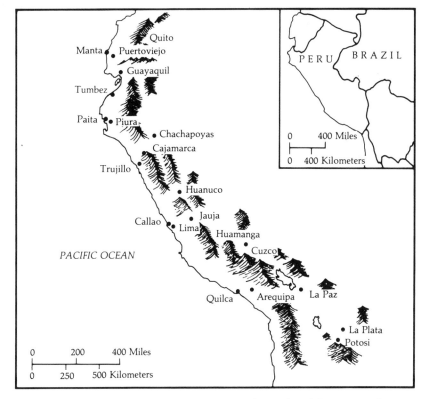

Figure 2.4. Spanish Centers in the Andes in the Wake of Conquest. (Source: Lockhart 1968:7. Reproduced courtesy of the University of Wisconsin Press.)

away" many died. The Incas used to get their coca instead through barter with less vulnerable local tribes.

On the whole, the middle levels of the vertical range were those most affected by Old World animals and plants. European cattle thrived, for instance, on the Andean altiplano around Lake Titicaca. Logically, as a chronicler reports, prices were lowest there, highest in Lima. Cattle breeding caused the early introduction of alfalfa. But at higher altitudes, the access to enormous llama herds helped the Aymara to resist the impact of European invasion. Some were not even subjected to encomiendas. On the whole, a remarkably harmonious coexistence was established between the flora and fauna of the New and the Old World, even though it is true that, for example, Europeans let cattle and horses extend on terrains more fit for the cultivation of grains.

Cultivation techniques suffered much less of a change after 1532, largely for the simple reason that they were good as they were. Improved merely with an iron share, the footplow, *chaquitaccla,* is still the most rational way of plowing steep slopes. On flat lands, however, the ox-pulled Spanish scratch-plow was introduced. But the Spanish waterwheel was never adopted, as the ways in which Andean water supply was channeled into the fields were efficient enough. The attitude toward the crops suffered a change, however. In Inca farming each plant received individual attention with the help of the hoe, while groups of plants were the subjects of European-type farming.

In the beginning, naturally, Europeans as well as Indians essentially clung to their traditional food. Thus, the Spaniards considered themselves dependent on a ready supply of white bread, meat, olives, and wine while the Indians continued to rely on maize, chuño, and the occasional animal protein provided by llama meat and festive guinea pig meals. But, little by little, both parties learned to appreciate selected products from the other "world." Indians, for example, adopted Old World chickens and pigs—the latter, incidentally, of basic importance to the conquistadores as moving, live, food supplies. In the long-term perspective, it can hardly be denied that the introduction of Old World animals and plants was an overwhelmingly positive consequence of the Conquest. It increased the food basis of Andean populations, of both Indian and European stock. Like potatoes would in Europe, the new animals and plants would considerably increase nutritional security.

III:

The Impact of Silver and Mercury on Andean Society

The Viceroys of Peru until the early eighteenth century administered the whole of Western South America from the Caribbean coast to the straits of Magellan. The subdivisions, that corresponded to the former Inca Empire, were the jurisdictions of the High Courts (*Audiencias*) in Lima, Los Charcas, and Quito. That of Lima, both coast and highland, was known as Lower Peru, that of Charcas as Upper Peru. Apart from present Bolivia, the Audiencia of Charcas also comprised the far-flung territories of the River Plate. Likewise, the Audiencia of Quito stretched to the North of the present Ecuadorean borders.

a. The Viceroyalty and its Function

As compared with the other Spanish Viceroyalty, that of New Spain (which included Mexico, Central America, the West Indies, and Venezuela) Peru suffered the handicap of longer distance to Spain and Europe. Furthermore, the crossing of the Isthmus also made transportation more complex. While New Spain was able to export a wider range of goods, the export capacity of Peru was reduced to goods combining small volume with a high price. This is why from the outset, the extraction of precious metals spurred all economic activities in the Andean region after the Conquest. Especially in Upper Peru, huge deposits of silver coincided with great population resources that could be mobilized for the extraction.

In the course of the sixteenth and seventeenth centuries, Spain fought a valiant struggle first to obtain, then to defend a West European hegemony. Everywhere and at all times, money constitutes the chief requirement of wars. Also, for the crude variety of mercantilist theory prevailing at the time in Spain, the accumulation of bullion was a boon *per se*. Consequently, the production of silver and gold became the first priority of the Peruvian Viceroyalty, particularly the two Perus. This became the central theme of three centuries of Andean history.

The output of precious metals can be roughly estimated because there was a special tax, the Royal Fifth (*Quinto Real*), on every amount produced. Between 1533 and 1536 great quantities of gold and silver were put listed in the accounts, but this was the result of looting. Not until the mid-forties did the production curve rise once again. The cone of Potosí, at an altitude of 4000 meters on a barren high plateau to the south of Huiquisaca, was found to be loaded with silver ore. At first, production was largely entrusted to the Indians. They extracted and ground the ore in their own ways and also smelted it in small clay furnaces (*guairas*) of a traditional type.

The surface strata were so rich that the production curve rapidly rose, but by the 1560s these thin layers were depleted. Production at Potosí now faced a crisis (fig. 3.1). At this time, also, the whole Viceroyalty was beset with problems even though the civil wars had finally ceased. The Indian population was declining; at the same time, a restless class of poor mestizos and jobless *soldados* was emerging, which caused grave concern. There was a lack of direction that the first Viceroys and high officials were unable to provide. This is what makes the long tenure of office by one exceptionally strong and energetic Viceroy, Francisco de Toledo (1569 – 81), a point of departure for, in some sense, all subsequent Andean history.

Toledo's actions cannot be judged in terms of "good" or "bad." Everything depends on the length of the historical perspective chosen and on the essentially "pro-Western" or "pro-Indian" viewpoint of the particular observer. He efficiently imposed direct colonial rule on the Indians, still an overwhelming majority of the population. The main instruments were the *Corregidores de indios*, who were put in charge of levying an Indian head tax (*tributo*) to be paid in money or possibly specified goods. In this way, the Indians, to some extent, were integrated with a Western type money economy. At the same time, Toledo subjected the Indians of the districts surrounding the mines to fixed periods of forced labor at low wage rates at the respective mine. The Incaic term of *mita* was retained to design this exploitation for the benefit of an Atlantic-based economy. As *mitayos* or as voluntary mining workers at a higher wage rate, Indians earned the money to pay their tribute. Toledo also undertook the "Westernization" of the production process of silver mining. Above all, he introduced the refining of the ore by means of amalgamation with mercury, the so-called *patio* process, first used in the 1550s in New Spain. Thanks to this and the abundant mita labor supply Potosí production soared from the 1580s onwards.

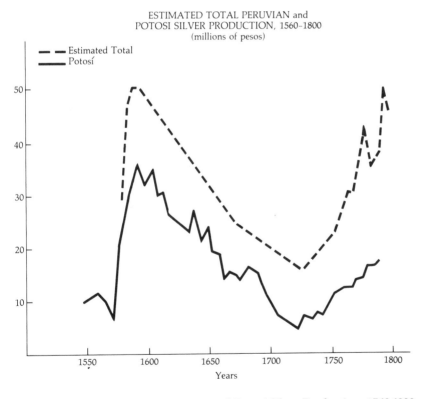

Figure 3.1. Estimated Total Peruvian and Potosí Silver Production, 1560-1800 (millions of pesos) (Source: Brading and Cross 1972:569.)

The Viceroy also carried out a massive resettlement of the Indian population. Instead of living in scattered small hamlets, they were forced to settle down in new European-type agglomerations, *reducciones*. This facilitated, at the same time, direct colonial rule, their economic exploitation, Christianization and partial westernization, and their separation from other elements of population. In this way, it was believed, the Indians would suffer less abuses from outsiders. Toledo also strongly imposed viceregal authority on the judges of the Audiencias and other bureaucrats as well as on the ecclesiastics. State supervision of the Church in Spanish America, the so-called *Real Patronato*, was accepted on principle by the Papacy from the beginning of colonization. But in Peru Toledo was the first one to make these rules work. He exercised strict state control over ecclesiastical appointments. Priests and friars were obliged to collaborate with the State, above all as missionaries and parish priests.

Toledo also undertook a fight against the Inca past. His chief propagandist, Sarmiento de Gamboa, blackened their rule; the head of the last neo-Inca monarch, Tupac Amaru, was cut off. Apart from the greatest Inca rulers and Francisco de Pizarro, no single individual has played a greater role for shaping, for good or bad, Andean society than Francisco de Toledo. Yet, the proud Viceroy, true to the colonialist character of his mission, was an obedient servant of his cautious, suspicious royal master. Phillip II recalled him in disgrace in 1581. Toledo died shortly afterwards "of a broken heart" (fig. 3.2).

By then, colonial administration was so firmly rooted in the Viceroyalty that the personal qualities of Toledo's successors and other high functionaries no longer mattered as much. Some were quite able. The Duke of La Palata (1681–89) strengthened the defense of Lima against sea attacks and made a thorough study of the Indian situation. The Marquis of Castel-Fuerte (1724–36) valiantly fought smuggling, and the corruption of bureaucracy and clergy. The Count of Superunda reconstructed Lima after the ruinous earthquake of 1746. (Incidentally, the enclosed wooden balconies have been typical of Lima since that time.) Other viceroys and high administrators were mediocre or even poor, but Colonial peace was maintained, and the system laid down by Toledo continued to function, even if far from smoothly, until the period of change during the last quarter of the eighteenth century. It should

BVENGOBIERNO
DONFRANCISCODETO
LE DO SE NIV RIO EN CASTILLA

Figure 3.2. The Viceroy in disgrace as imagined by Poma.

From Francisco de Toledo's final report to the King: "With the punishment I ordered to take place in the cities of La Paz, Huamanga and Cuzco [the execution of Tupac Amaru], everything remained smooth, without any disquiet or unrest."

Poma on the pleas to save Tupac: But...Toledo was extremely annoyed about a remark which Tupac Amaru was reported to have made....the Inca, with youthful candour, had said that he could not comply with an order from the servant of another master.

Toledo: I encouraged the miners [of Huancavelica] sharing out and giving them Indians of the district with good order, religious instructions and wages I fixed.

Poma: Once [the Indians] inhale the mercury..., they contract asthma and gradually their bodies become as thin and dry as sticks. They cannot find any peace, either by day or night, until death comes to free them from their sufferings.

Toledo: As it was not possible to teach these Indians Christian doctrine or make them live a civilized life without pulling them out from their lurking places, they were...settled down to towns and public places where streets were opened by blocks according to the patterns of Spanish towns.

Poma: Some of [the new settlements] were in suitable areas and others in wholly unsuitable ones, depending on the luck of the draw. In no case were the Indians consulted and some of them found themselves far away from the homes and sources of food.

be kept in mind, however, that in political reality the Viceroyalty of Peru was continuously shrinking. The dependency of Chile on Lima, mainly for money and soldiers to fight the Mapuche Indians to the south, diminished greatly in the course of the seventeenth century. The Audiencia of Quito was placed under a newly named Viceroy in Bogotá in 1717. After a return to the old arrangement, it became a part of the new Viceroyalty of New Granada in 1739. The Governor of Buenos Aires, a province thriving on contraband trade, made himself increasingly independent of both the Viceroy and the Audiencia of Los Charcas.

For practical reasons, the present and the following chapter will focus on the mining-urban sector and rural society respectively. It must always be kept in mind, however, how closely interconnected the activities of the two sectors were.

b. Mining and Draft Labor

Mining requires the input of capital, technology, and labor. In legal theory, the Spanish Crown claimed ownership of all sub-surface resources. This was the basis for the levy of the Royal Fifth. Yet, Peruvian silver mining was actually in private hands, even though the history of capitalization is not at all clear. Around 1585 there were more than 600 individuals who owned "mines" and shafts within the cone of Potosí. With the introduction of the amalgamation process in 1572, however, the small group of owners of refining mills (a guild of 75 *azogueros*) and the still-smaller group of silver merchants became the real force behind Potosí mining. But, at the same time, because of the great advantages of amalgamation over other forms of refining, the Crown held the key in its hands. There were only two noteworthy deposits of mercury at the disposal of Spanish American silver mining. One was Almadén in Spain, the other Huancavelica in the Central Andean Sierra. While, on the whole, Almadén would be reserved for Mexican mining, Huancavelica would assure the supply of Potosí and other smaller Andean mines. Both mercury mines were the property of the Crown, while usually worked on lease; thus, the price, of crucial importance for the miners, was set by the State. The rugged terrain made the transportation of mercury to the Upper Peruvian mines a complicated affair (fig. 3.3).

Mining technology, both at Potosí and Huancavelica, long remained on a sixteenth-century European level. The excavation at Potosí faced special problems because of the fragmentation of ownership, but visitors were most impressed by the huge system of water supply that provided hydraulic power for grinding the ore and for various extractive and refining operations.

Mining was a very dangerous occupation, of course. Indian workers, climbing long, steep ladders, brought out the ore on their backs. At Huancavelica work was particularly lethal, however, because of the poisonous fumes. Gunpowder was tried for underground blasting at Huancavelica as early as 1631 but without success. Manpower remained paramount.

According to the mita system as devised by Toledo, sixteen provinces surrounding or to the north of Potosí had to keep roughly a seventh of all their adult Indian males available at the mine at any time. That meant 13,500 men. Similarly, Huancavelica would have a supply of 3280 men. The *mitayos* served for four-month periods, but travels absorbed much additional time. A procession of mitayos, usually accompanied by their families and flocks of llamas, took about two months to go from the shore of Lake Titicaca to Potosí. At the mine, they were divided into three shifts of about 4500 men each. Each shift worked as mitayos one week out of three, some inside the mine, some at the refining mills or at other tasks at the low wage rate fixed. During their "free" weeks, the Indians would hire themselves out as *mingados* at a rate twice as high to earn money for the tribute and their high living expenses. Many remained mingados permanently. Thus, the mita system forced the Indians to Potosí, and reduced labor costs somewhat.

Mita service, in whatever case, was bitterly resented by the Indians from the beginning. It contributed to the desertions of Indians from the districts obliged to *mita minera*. In the area of Huancavelica, according to a report from 1657, mothers would cripple their children to save them from the horrors of mita service. The extreme shortage of males and the grievances unanimously voiced by the parish priests in the districts subjected to the mita at Huancavelica toward the end of the seventeenth century suggest the proportions of a genocide.

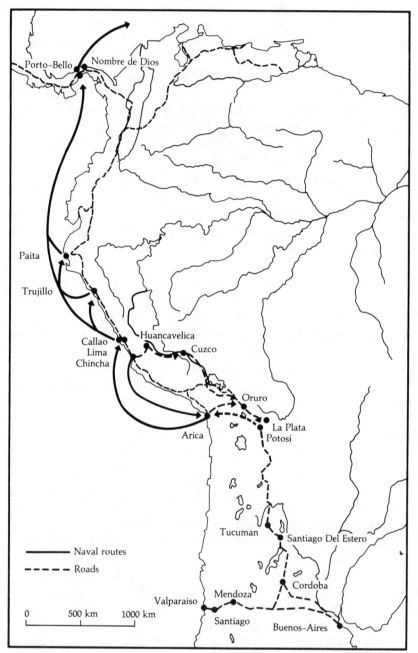

Figure 3.3. Main Trade Routes of the Peruvian Viceroyalty. (Based on Jara 1966: 72, 84.)

To be sure, the mita system was also used for other tasks, for public works or to provide private entrepreneurs with cheap labor. The percentage of Indians on service out of all adult Indian males varied. In the Audencia of Quito, it was by as much as one-fifth. But the mita at Potosí has remained particularly famous (or infamous). As time went on, the mita quota fixed by Toledo could not be fulfilled. Increasingly, miners instead accepted redemption in cash from the Indians, even though substitute labor became increasingly difficult to hire. On the other hand, occasional recommendations from the Crown that Negro slaves be employed in Andean mining never produced results. The cost of purchase was too risky an investment considering the probability of early death in the chilly Potosí environment.

The Royal Fifth was supposed to be levied rigorously on all precious minerals produced. At Potosí there was a Royal Mint where money for internal Spanish American circulation was coined. But the bulk of the royal share and quantities in individual possession destined for Spain were to be sent down to the Pacific on the backs of mules. The cargo was then to be forwarded to the Isthmus of Panama by ship. From Puerto Bello on the Caribbean coast it was to be taken to Spain by what was in theory an annual convoy fleet. However, by the 1730s the fleets ceased to exist altogether. Both in the Pacific and the Atlantic, Spain took great care to defend its silver cargoes against pirates or hostile fleets. It seldom lost them. Backed up by merchant monopolies at Lima as well as at the Spanish end, Seville/Cadiz, the system functioned remarkably well for awhile, despite all problems.

Increasingly, however, the whole mining economy suffered a change caused by the steady decline of Spain's economic capacity. The trickle of contraband silver via the officially closed harbor of Buenos Aires became a wide stream by the late seventeenth century. The extra-legal commercial exchange with other European powers, which had slaves and many other articles needed, threatened to bypass trade with Spain. Smuggling also spread on the Pacific. Under these circumstances, the exact figures of silver production and export will never be known. The peak was reached, anyway, in the late sixteenth century (fig. 3.4), the bottom in the early eighteenth century.

As a chronicler who visited Potosí in the early seventeenth century put it, "although this site is desert, it is nevertheless the largest settlement in the Indies." He talks about a population of 80,000 Indians "not counting women and children." There were more than 4000 Spanish residents plus transients and elements known as *soldados honrados* "and the truth is that many of them are lost souls." Some 800 professional gamblers were busy as well as 120 prostitutes, many of them high class.

Virtual civil war broke out in the giant mining camp during the 1620s. It split the white population along both economic and ethnic lines. A group of Basques controlled most mills and mines. Other European-born and American-born "Spaniards" set their mutual differences apart to fight them. Considering the cruel and vicious character of Potosí society, it appears awkward when the characteristic cone is sometimes represented on religious paintings as the Virgin's gown (fig. 3.3). But Potosí had become the symbol of Spain's whole power, and, in the minds of contemporaries, that power served above all to sustain the fight against the heretics and other enemies of true Christianity.

As we shall see in the next chapter, Potosí and other mining camps of lesser size played a crucial role as consumer markets for all kinds of artisan and agricultural production. Characteristically, the richest

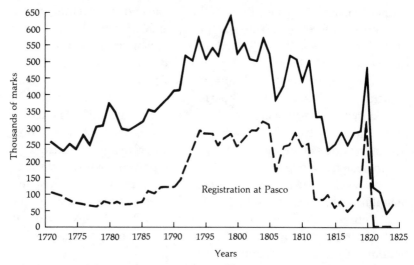

Figure 3.4. Registered Silver Production in Peru, 1771-1824 (Source: Fisher 1975:27.)

"miner" in the history of Potosí succeeded in creating a vast, integrated enterprise, comprising the marketing of products partly derived from his own lands. The ups and downs of silver production in time naturally affected both the numbers of inhabitants of the mining camps and their purchasing power. In turn, this would affect wide areas of rural and urban suppliers.

The impact of Spanish American silver in Spain and Europe has been very much discussed by scholars. We leave this topic aside here. On the other hand, the impact of mining on Andean society still remains to be systematically assessed, but economically it was surely a stimulating one.

c. Taxation and Resettlement of the Indians

There had been local counts of Indian *tributarios* before Toledo. His great inspection tour (*Visita general*) lasted five years, however, and provides global data. In Upper and Lower Peru there were a quarter of a million tribute payers, that is, men between 18 and 50 years. They were distributed in 614 districts (*repartimientos*). On the basis of information on the population and productive capacity of each district the amount and nature of tribute was fixed (in cash but also in kind; for an example see fig. 3.4). It was enforced vigorously and was imposed on the Indians as a collective unit until reassessed. Such a *retasa* might be put off for a long while. Thus, population decline could make it increasingly difficult for the Indians to fulfill their obligation. Before Toledo, the yanaconas had been free from tribute; now they were included, but at a lower rate. The curacas/mallkus and the members of Indian municipal councils that were being introduced enjoyed exemptions from tribute. The new officials, *corregidores de indios*, were responsible for the levy of tribute, whether destined for an encomendero or for the Royal treasury. They, in turn, relied on the curacas for assistance. We have only to keep in mind that the corregidores usually acquired their positions by purchase, to understand that the levy of tribute was also used for their own enrichment.

Until the reforms of the late eighteenth century, the numbers of tribute payers and the revenues from this source continuously dropped, as illustrated by table 3.1. The share accruing to the encomenderos also fell until these grants were finally abolished in 1720.

The urbanization of the Indians into special towns of Mediterranean type to facilitate their Christianization had been outlined as a policy in 1503. It was implemented with success in the wilderness of Northwestern Central America some thirty years later. In the 1560s, both the Second Council of the Peruvian Church and Judge Juan de Matienzo, later Toledo's adviser, urged that the program be carried out in the Andes, where the Indians so far lived in scattered areas. In the *reducción*, the priest as well as the Corregidor would keep them under close watch, see to it that a municipality on the Spanish model, *cabildo*, functioned and that the Indians fulfilled their obligations to State, Church, and their own community.

The land belonged to the community but most was divided into family parcels. The produce of the rest of the land, kept for the collective use of Indians, should be reserved for the care of the sick and old and other common expenses. No land should be allowed to pass into non-Indian hands and a belt of land surrounding the village was strictly inalienable. After a period of transition, usually ten years, under missionary tutelage and with exemption from tribute, the reducción became an ordinary Indian parish, but the norms for its organization remained in force. Non-Indians were strictly forbidden to settle down among the natives. As the many repetitions of these laws and decrees suggest, they were disobeyed with great frequency.

The reducción expressed the dualistic aims of Spanish policy in America. At the same time it should serve to imbue the Indians with Western Christian and urban values and to make them more easily disposable for the purposes of the State. As implemented by Toledo and his successors, the reducción program implied a drastic, often traumatic, change in Indian life. They were forced to leave familiar grounds, where ancestors were buried and huacas asked for devotion. The new settlements were often located halfway between valley bottoms and highland pastures, naturally a rational solution. Roughly ten ayllus, that is an Incaic *huaranga*, might be concentrated there. A royal official mapped out the lands and boundaries, a gridiron town plan

TABLE 3.1

I. Estimates of Tributary Indians

A. *Present Peru*	1540	443.997
	1550	365.315
	1560	306.207
	1570	260.533
	1580	222.577
	1590	195.025
	1600	171.841
	1610	152.432
	1620	136.243
	1630	122.686
B. *Huánuco, Peru*[b]	1578–83	31.255
	1591–92	28.523
	1615	27.415
	1754	11.366
C. *Cochabamba, Upper Peru*[c]	1573	3.599
	1683	2.179
	1737	1.718

II. Tribute and production in an Andean district: Ccapi, Paruro, Cuzco (Altitude: 3.150m.) [d]

1570–75   Population: 31 tributarios (1 curaca)
4 old men
26 boys
80 women of different ages
141 persons

            Tribute: 150 *pesos de plata ensayada*
105 of which in cash
45 = 16 *fanegas* of maíze
10 *fanegas* of wheat
48 chickens

To be deducted from the sum: 52 pesos for the religious instruction of the Indians, for the curaca and legal consultants of the Indians. The rest, incl. the articles, for the encomendero.

1689   Population: 2782 Indians distributed in three *pueblos* and 792 families, 144 of which of *forasteros*, probably tied to the Haciendas; 17 "Spanish" families scattered in 14 Haciendas, a total of 62 persons. Average Indian family size: 3.51; Spanish family size: 3.65.

            Production: 4.000 *fanegas* of wheat, maize etc. on the Haciendas; 1000 *fanegas* of grains and potatoes on Indian land. One of the haciendas dedicated to the production of sugar. No llamas, nor sheep but oxen both of haciendas and pueblos.

[a]SOURCE: Cook 1977: 41.
[b]SOURCE: Mörner 1970: 288.
[c]SOURCE: Larson 1978: 344.
[d]SOURCE: Tasa 1975: 197; Villanueva Urteaga 1982: 426-32.

was laid out with a plaza where the church was eventually constructed by the Indians and essentially at their expense. Most, but far from all, reducciones sooner or later took root.

Subject to incessant demands for labor and tribute, in the seventeenth century, the reducciones lost much population through desertions. In many cases, however, population increased in the eighteenth century. As middlemen between the Indian peasants and the authorities, the *caciques* (as the latter called the curacas and mallkus) found themselves in a far from easy position, which, however, many of them knew how to exploit for their personal enrichment. Rich caciques sometimes posted bond for tribute dues. In this way, they felt justified in extending their control over community assets. Also, at least to judge from a recent study on the Spanish-type religious brotherhoods (*confradías*) in the Valley of Mantaro, the caciques both helped to increase these funds for the financing of fiestas in honor of saints and for other ritual purposes, and managed to turn the administration of the funds to their individual profit. The former reducciones have become today the centers of Andean rural life, especially full of life during the weekly (often Sunday) market or religious festivals. They may still retain an "Indian" character in language and customs or, at some point, became instead Mestizo.

However unintentionally, the establishment of reducciones—which from the mid-seventeenth century onward was also pursued among the nomadic or seminomadic tribes of the Montaña, by missionaries in Chiquitos, Mojos, and along the Amazon River — probably had an adverse demographic effect. Uprooted and crowded, the Indians became easier prey for epidemic disease than they would otherwise have been. The typhoid plague of 1585–91 proved especially destructive in the Andean region. Sources will never allow us to reconstruct the biological (or demographic) decline with precision. It is clear, however, that the Indian population continued to drop. The nadir was reached after another widespread plague in 1718–21. In some parts of Upper Peru which had included some 160000 inhabitants in 1573, population had fallen by 42 percent in 1683. It should be noted, however, that the fall in the numbers of tributarios was even more drastic (57 percent). But finally the remaining Indian population of the highlands had acquired some biological resistance and, despite all their sufferings, a will to survive. In the case of the Diocese of Cuzco we know that, notwithstanding the great 1718 plague, the *average* annual population growth from 1689 through 1786 ascended to 0.4. But for the Indians the rate was only 0.3 as compared to 1.6 for the Spanish-Mestizo minority. In the fertile Cochabamba Valley the general growth rate for 1683–1786 was 0.7. It is not at all clear, though, to what an extent the decline and recovery of the Indians was conditioned by cultural factors. How many Indians simply escaped Indian status by leaving their communities and adopting Spanish speech and customs? They could do so by settling down in a Spanish town or by entering the service of a landowner or miner as a common worker, *peon*.

In present Andean society the usually derogatory term of *cholo* is often heard but proves hard to define. Yet it probably emerged as an expression of the suspicion that an individual claiming Mestizo status was merely an Indian trying to escape his own oppressed condition. In whatever case, the growth rates of the various racial groups certainly differed. White and Mestizo families appear to have been larger. A sample from seventeenth-century parish records for Lima shows that the mortality of the Indians (mostly immigrants from the highlands and thus also vulnerable to climatic changes) was three times as high as that of the "Spaniards." The mortality of the Blacks lay in between. The European and African sectors of the population were, of course, also affected by immigration. Our knowledge about this aspect of demographic history after 1650 is practically nil at this point, however.

Most likely, the process of race mixture was especially intensive in the Spanish towns and in the mining districts, where racially different elements met. Sexual proportions were often imbalanced on this level and priestly vigilance less than in a stable rural parish. In a Lima parish (1562–1689) more than a third of Spanish and Mestizo children were born out of wedlock; the vast majority of Indian, Black, and Mulatto babies also were. The growth of the racially mixed population was especially great in the coastland, be it in Peru or Ecuador. In the north of Ecuador, Esmeraldas, slaves from a stranded slave ship mingled with still unsubdued Indian tribes. These warlike Zamboes only accepted the nominal sovereignty of the King of Spain. To the south, the Ecuadorean *montuvio* of the coast absorbed the three stocks. Inland, the process was slower. In the Cuzco area, Mestizos became numerous in some of the districts closest to the city during the late seventeenth and eighteenth centuries. More remarkable, though, they increased even more strikingly in some remote, isolated districts. As one parish priest put it in 1689, these Mestizos "have no possessions, [are] modest people who sow in the lands left idle by the Indians, pay rent to the Indian mayor." Some were mule-track drivers, *arrieros*, an Andean occupation which evolved around the relatively long-distance supply of mining camps, plantations and towns. (See also figs. 3.5 and 3.6.)

d. Spanish Towns

When not formed around mines as in Potosí, the early Spanish towns were founded mainly for administrative and security reasons. Later they also arose to absorb a roaming non-Indian population or simply gave an existing settlement formal status, as in the case of Ibarra, founded in Northern Ecuador in 1607. The first residents with recognized burgher rights (*vecinos*) might be encomenderos, or landowners with reasonable numbers of yanaconas at their disposal, or wealthy miners. When the rights were gradually extended to other, more humble elements, the former became established elites who shared the municipal offices among them. The offices sometimes became inheritable, more often put up for sale. In terms of power, little by little, though, the mayors (*alcaldes*) were pushed aside by governors (*corregidores*) named by the Viceroy or the King.

Toledo, in particular, put constraints on the freedom of the cabildos to regulate their own affairs. Originally, the jurisdiction of each Spanish town was often very large. With the introduction of the Corregidores de indios, however, the factual districts of the cabildos were practically reduced to the town itself and its immediate surroundings. The Spanish cities and towns housed only a small part of the total Andean population. Most "Spaniards" and perhaps Negro slaves resided in them, however. In Lima, in 1613, slaves, free Mulattoes, and Negroes formed half of the population. Also, many Indians resided in the Spanish towns, although they were supposed to be confined to special quarters (*barrios*). El Cercado in Lima housed many Indians, some of them owners of African slaves.

The growth of the urban population of Spanish America, 1580–1630, has been roughly estimated on the basis of the data of two chroniclers (tables 3.2, 3.3). The rapid growth of the Audiencia de Los Charcas in this regard was, of course, due to mining. The towns of the Audiencia of Quito were surrounded by Indian populations, subject to a lesser decline than elsewhere.

Some of the towns, like Lima, were surrounded by a belt of truck-farms that assured the bulk of their food supply. They constituted the

Figure 3.5. Mining Society Through the Eyes of Guamán Poma de Ayala.

With the Spanish miners behind him, a corrupt judge would rob even an Indian Curaca of his goods. Notice the Spanish dress of this member of the Indian elite.

main markets of their respective rural district. But they could also serve as depots for long distance trade. Each city or town formed the basis of a superstructure the size of which was determined by its function within the civil or ecclesiastical administrative hierarchy. This is how a probably clandestine Jewish observer starts his description of Lima around 1620:

Figure 3.6. Rural Society Through the Eyes of Guamán Poma de Ayala.

"Not much," the assistant of the Corregidor de indios says when looking at what the Indian has to offer. The Indian's sandals *(ojotas)* are of the same type as today. Otherwise, the Indian masses of the early seventeenth century were still using dresses from Inca times.

Table 3.2
Urban Growth, 1580-1630

Audiencia	1580		1630		
	Number of Vecinos	Number of Spanish towns	Number of Vecinos	Number of Spanish towns	Growth rate
Quito	874	15	5283	11	6.0
Lima	5.018	19	16.966	24	3.3
Los Charcas	1.445	8	10.000	20	6.9

SOURCE: Hardoy & Aranovitch 1970, based on the works of Juan López de Velasco and Antonio Vázquez de Espinosa. For 1580, data on another 6 towns are lacking; for 1630, data on another 38 towns.

Table 3.3
Centers of Growth in the Andes in the Seventeenth Century

Regions and areas	Degree of economic diversification according to 85 criteria around 1628	Income from alcabala in the late seventeenth century
Quito-New Granada		
1. Center Quito	69	12.000
2. Intermediate zone		
New Granada	51	
Popayán	43	
		No data
3. Periphery		
Cartagena	40	
Santa Marta	36	
South Andean region		
1. Centres		
Los Charcas/La Paz/Santa Cruz	62	33.000
Lima	61	45.000
2. Intermediate zone		
Cuzco-Puno	62	22.500
Trujillo	47	6.700
Arequipa	45	7.000
Periphery		
Tucumán	40	No data
Huamanga/Huancavelica	37	8.500
Huánuco	28	4.000

SOURCES: B. Slicher van Bath 1979; R. Escobedo Mansilla, 1976: 14.

The City of Reyes is the head of the whole Kingdom of Peru. It is the residence and Court of the Viceroys. It houses the Royal High Court (*Audiencia*) and the Archbishop who is great and rich also lives here. It is also the seat of the Inquisition, feared and loathed by everybody, and of the heads of the Mendicant orders. The officers of the Royal Treasury are to be found here .... It is the residence of the Postmaster of the Indies, and also of the Tribunal of the Merchant Guild.[1]

The lesser the towns, the lesser the dignitaries, of course; but all towns exhibited the same inclination for a display of power and magnificance. Visitors, of whatever status, should be duly impressed. Our anonymous witness found Lima ladies to be " the most beautiful and well-shaped in the world," and expensively dressed, too. Most of the Limeño Spaniards, while elegant and courteous, impressed him as being very clever merchants. Their American-born (*criollo*) sons were prodigious and apt to lie, fond of fooling around with Black women. They always went on horseback to make believe they were of noble birth. These are stereotypes, often repeated in similar terms. They do reflect, however, the rigidly stratified character of Spanish American colonial urban society, the so-called *Régimen de Castas*.

   Basically, this pattern of stratification derived from the transfer to the New World of the hierarchical, estate-based, corporate society of late medieval Castile that was imposed upon a multiracial, colonial situation. The social reality of Spanish America, simultaneously, was characterized by two deep cleavages and by the miscegenation between the opposite groups. The descendants of the conquerors and of the vanquished were set against each other. There was a sharp division between masters and servants or slaves. Yet they all mingled. A dualist, socio-racial hierarchical system enjoyed legal sanction, but as shown by table 3.4, the ranking in social reality differed in some important respects. Though theoretically superior to halfbreeds, the Indian masses undoubtedly formed the lowest social stratum, in urban as well as rural areas. Unlike the slaves, their lives were not safeguarded by price. Also, even the poorest of halfbreeds, free Blacks, and slaves knew Spanish and were able to reflect the authority of their white masters in dealing with the Indians. In general these were regarded as inferior beings, fit only for servile tasks. Nevertheless, despite all their handicaps, some Indians did succeed in becoming "social climbers." Also, some "Indian nobles" and curacas were able to maintain a longer or shorter social distance to the mass by showing off their Spanish ways. Racially, too, this group gradually became Mestizo.

In very broad terms, Peninsulars and Criollos fulfilled the function of an aristocracy. To begin with, this was especially true of the encomenderos. But the economic basis of the encomiendas dwindled with the decline of Indian population. By 1630, the encomendero rentier class formed less than one percent of all "Spaniards" of greater Peru. They still enjoyed a great prestige, but in Lima high-ranking bureaucrats and wealthy merchants also formed parts of the elites. The encomiendas were abolished in 1720. If the claim to elite status was primarily based on "illustrious blood," it could only be sustained with money. For this reason, the composition of the actual elites of the viceregal capital in particular underwent constant change. In the case of a provincial town (Lambayeque), behind a façade of conspicuous consumption and grandiose ways, the landowner elite has been found to strive above all toward economic profit. At all levels, though, for all the roles that money played, the disdain that imbued society was based on ethnic grounds. The Peninsular bureaucrats and merchants looked down at their Criollo colleagues or, if they married in America, at their relatives or even offspring. The criollo landowners and municipal aldermen looked down at the Mestizo tenants, artisans, and shopkeepers; these felt superior to the Mulattoes and Negroes, who in turn considered themselves "rational persons" compared with the Indian "dogs." In similar ways, as in Europe of those times, the various groups in society were separated by their dress. Many squabbles arose on this

Table 3.4
Schemes of Social Stratification During the Colonial Period

Legal Status		
Republic of the Spaniards	*Republic of the Indians*	*Social Ranking*
Spaniards	Nobles	Peninsulars
	Indians	Criollos
Mestizos		Mestizos and curacas
Free Negroes, Mulattoes,		Mulattoes, zamboes, and
Zamboes		free Negroes
Slaves		African Slaves
		Indian majority

Based on Mörner 1967:60.

account. A seventeenth-century viceroy forbade Negroes and Mulatto women from wearing any kind of silk. If they were caught a second time, they were to get 100 lashes with a whip, and be expelled from urban limits. There were also many kinds of socio-racial discrimination. The universities, the Church, the guilds of merchants (*consulados*), and the more distinguished artisan guilds tried to exclude all those of suspect birth from membership. Religious brotherhoods (*cofradías*) were established for the respective ethnic groups. But the pride of lineage was not a monopoly of the Whites. Guamán Poma admonished the curacas not to marry their daughters to lower class people " but only to their equals to produce people of good family in this Kingdom."

e. Spread of Culture

The towns were the centers and bulwarks of Spanish culture in the New World. The University of San Marcos in Lima, modeled on that of Salamanca, started its teaching of theology and law in the 1570s. Missionary needs prompted the foundation of a chair in *quechua*. In Lima and other towns, the religious orders opened schools (*colegios*) for secondary education. There were special schools for the sons of the curacas to promote the formation of a hispanized, loyal Indian elite. In general terms, higher education served to train officers of the State and Church. The spirit of neoscholasticism, which inspired great minds in sixteenth-century Spain (such as Francisco de Vitoria in international law), continued to pervade the intellectual atmosphere of the overseas possessions until the mid-eighteenth century. But the intellectual curiosity of the Renaissance can also be detected in the natural history of Father José de Acosta (1590). One hundred years later, a limeño savant, Pedro Peralta y Barnuevo, was vacillating between the findings of science and the dictates of Christian dogma until he finally opted for the way of mysticism to the Faith. Learned lawyers studded their treatises with quotes from religious texts. Also the satirical genius of the poet Juan del Valle Caviedes expressed obsession with death, disdain for the humbugs of this world. The gentle nun, Santa Rosa, Lima's special saint (can. 1711) became famous for her mortifications of the flesh.

For all its dedication to the enhancement of God and concern with Death, the Spanish American Baroque also expressed an exuberant vitality and dramatic energy. Composer Tomás de Torrejón y Velasco was not only a composer of sacred music, he also composed the only opera to be written and produced in the New World during the colonial period (1701). Along with the splendid façades and altars of the cathedrals, the sacred sculpture and paintings, the Baroque style also expressed itself in life. The pomp displayed on the arrival of a new Viceroy or in the course of religious festivities diffused the Baroque values widely. There is a profound paradox in the culture of this era. It was exclusivist, Court-centered, learned, overwhelmingly European in conception and expression — even when the artists are known to have been humble Mestizos and Indians. Only in more remote rural areas, like that around Lake Titicaca, did Indian artisans leave more distinct traces of their own artistic tradition and the motifs of New World fauna and flora.

Yet even the illiterate Indian masses were reached to a lesser or greater extent by the Baroque and Counter-reformation conception of the world and afterlife. It may have had to do with the successful result (from the missionary point of view) of the vigorous campaign launched by the Church around 1610 to extirpate the remaining traces of paganism that is, the cult of the huacas. The deep religiosity of the Andean Indians now turned increasingly toward the symbols of Catholicism. The Indian cofradías became widely diffused after 1650, with their main function of subsidizing religious festivities. The Christian liturgy blended with traditional Quechua dancing, which became legitimized in the process. Likewise, European polyphony fused with the apparently pentatonic native musical scale to produce the folkmusic of later times. European instruments such as the harp and the mandolin (*charango*) were adopted by the Indians. The Virgin of the Upper Peruvian sanctuary of Copacabana had been carved by an Indian as early as 1576. The large chapel where the Indian pilgrims gathered to pay her homage was not completed until 1678, however. The *Cristo de los Terremotos*, at the Cathedral of Cuzco, was associated with miraculous powers after its escape (though it was blackened by fire) from the earthquake of 1650. These symbols and others, in the eyes of the Indians, replaced their old divinities. They thus wholeheartedly joined in the rituals pervaded by the West European Baroque.

IV:

Land and Labor in Colonial Andean Society

As we have seen, from the mid-sixteenth century onward, the population of the Spanish towns swelled. Thus, food demand increased, especially for articles not yet readily supplied by Indian farmers, such as meat, wheat, sugar and wine. Encomenderos and other vecinos now asked the cabildos for land grants, usually modest in size, in the district of the town to set up production units of their own for cultivation or grazing. A variety of laborers were used, mitayos, free Indian farmhands and, on the coast, African slaves. Even more extraordinary was the demand triggered by mining centers, especially that of Potosí. The concentration there of probably more than 100,000 people at a time, gave rise to this huge need for food, water, clothes (most necessary in this chilly climate), stimulants (wine, liquors, coca leaves, *yerba mate*, or Paraguay tea), fuel, construction materials, and beasts, as shown by figure 4.1.

a. Land Tenure and Rural Labor

The growth of commercial agriculture and stockraising and the patterns of land tenure must, or course, be seen against this backdrop. The large estates (*haciendas*) emerged as integrated units within the regional markets that were taking shape. At times, however, the decline of such a market adversely affected the units of commercialized agriculture already established. Then, the haciendas could take on the look of self-sufficient manors. In other cases, they expanded rapidly, but not necessarily with a view to acquiring more land to exploit. Rather, the aim often was to discourage competition from other landowners or forcing the Indians, when deprived of their own lands, to supply cheap labor needed. Yet, in colonial times, average hacienda size appears to have been modest with just a handful of Indian or other workers with their families.

On the Peruvian coast, the importance of Lima as a market grew steadily. In 1610 there were some 25,000 people; in the 1680s, 80,000.

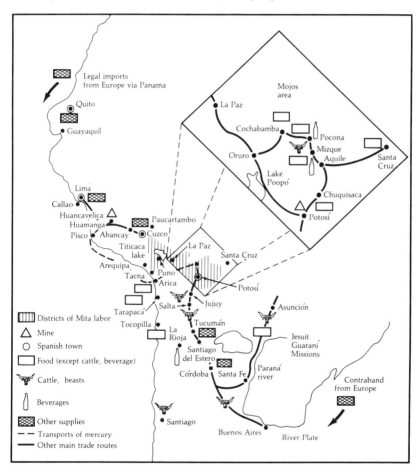

Figure 4.1. Potosí: Supply of Labor and Merchandise in the Early Seventeenth Century. Based on Sanchez-Albornoz 1974:87; Larson 1978:63.

Truck farms were set up in the neighboring valleys with a view to supplying Limeño needs. In the northern valleys, urban market stimulus was much less significant. Large units arose devoted to ranching or the cultivation of cotton or sugar for distant marketing. They absorbed the lands left by a vanishing Indian population. Side by side with secular landlords, ecclesiastical holdings increased, as in the valley of Jequetepeque north of Trujillo (owned by Augustinians). The Jesuits possessed no less than eleven sugar haciendas in the northern and central valleys at the time the order was expelled in 1767. On the southern coast, properties tended to be smaller but more profitable than in the north. The great cash crop was grapes for wine. At first Arequipa enjoyed an especially good location for diversified agriculture, finding itself on the route from Lima to Potosí. In the surrounding valleys, encomenderos set up prosperous estates. But later, from the 1570s onwards, the Upper Peruvian trade was channeled from Lima to the more southern port of Arica, and a labor shortage also contributed to Arequipa's decline. Whenever they were available at reasonable prices, African slaves formed the bulk of the coastal labor force. The Jesuits in 1767 employed a total of 5224 slaves, 62 percent of whom were occupied on sugar plantations, 30 percent in the vineyards. Slaves were often provided with parcels of land on which to grow their own food. So were the permanent Indian workers (*agregados*). Little by little, the share of free Negro, Mulatto, and Mestizo labor also increased.

In the interior of Northern Peru, where Indian population from the 1570s onward, declined more rapidly than elsewhere in the highlands, sheepraising, with its low demand for labor, gave rise to numerous ranches (*estancias*). As on the coast, Spanish estates grew at the expense of Indian lands. Indians, at the same time, provided the main labor force of both the ranches and textile sweatshops (*obrajes*) that were set up. At the same time, non-Indian population steadily increased. In the Central Sierra, Huancavelica was surrounded by haciendas. Unlike most other areas, though, these served as labor reservoirs for the mines rather than for the production of supplies. These were obtained from the coast. Further South, highland Indians appear to have suffered a lower rate of decline. Here, the ratio of Spaniards to Indians was especially low, while the impact of European disease appears to have been less lethal at these high elevations. Cuzco produced textiles, sugar, and coca for the Upper Peruvian mines. At the same time, such a large city formed an important market by itself. It was surrounded by truck farms and haciendas from early times.

In 1689, there were 705 haciendas in the region of Cuzco; in 1786, the number had decreased slightly to 647. Most were situated along the road, *Camino Real*, which despite many difficult passages connected Cuzco with Lima and Potosí. In 1689, a fifth of them were owned by gentlemen entitled to be addressed as "Don," 15 percent by women (often widows) and no more than 7 percent by the Church and Orders. Ecclesiastical estates, though, included some of the largest and most profitable ones. The Jesuits owned the most important sugar estate, Pachachaca, located in a hot valley of Abancay, as well as the large obraje-hacienda of Pichuichuro in a more elevated, chilly part of the same province. Both were centers of networks of farming and ranching units the function of which was to supply the provisions needed by sugar and textile workers. The ecological diversity clearly facilitated this type of economic integration. It also existed in the case of some huge entailed estates (*mayorazgos*) such as that of the Marquis of Vallehumbroso. But most "haciendas" were probably quite modest and small. In 1689, a labor force of some 15 to 20 adult Indians seemed to have been the norm on Cuzco haciendas. Furthermore, most Indians lived in their communities. The non-Indian population of the Cuzco region increased rather slowly, from 5.7 percent in 1689 to 17.4 in 1786.

In the cold region of Puno around Lake Titicaca, Indian communities raising llamas and sheep were the main feature of rural society, though there were also scattered Spanish ranches. In Upper Peru, the valley of Cochabamba was one of the main granaries of Potosí. According to a seventeenth-century chronicler, the haciendas here were large; later on, when market conditions deteriorated, fragmentation increased. The labor force of highland haciendas comprised several categories. The mitayos of the communities served by turns in the same way as they did in the mines. The yanaconas, especially numerous on the Spanish haciendas which covered most of the Cochabamba Valley, producing grains for Potosí on a large scale, formed a servile labor force. They were provided with the usufruct of tiny parcels of land for their subsistence, but were not paid. From the late seventeenth century onward, when Potosí became much less important as a market, the rural society in the valley also changed. Landowners let tenants take over most of the production and marketing of grains to reduce their own costs and risks. In the course of the eighteenth century, everywhere in Upper Peru, haciendas stopped growing. In combination with the Indian demographical recovery which now set in, this meant that Indian communities tended to house a growing share of the Indian population.

The Audiencia of Quito requires special comment. Unlike Peru, its Indian population started to increase in the late sixteenth century, and reached a high by 1690 (fig. 4.2). At that time, epidemics began reducing the Indian population drastically. In explaining the demographic rise until then, one may suggest that Quito Indians enjoyed a better food supply than those of Peru and that they lived more dispersed; the reducción program appears to have been less successful than farther south. With the virtual absence of mining, the economic life of Quito was geared to two major products, the cocoa of the tropical province of Guayas and the woolen textiles prepared in the highlands. On the coast cocoa gave rise to slave-based plantations. In the Sierra both haciendas

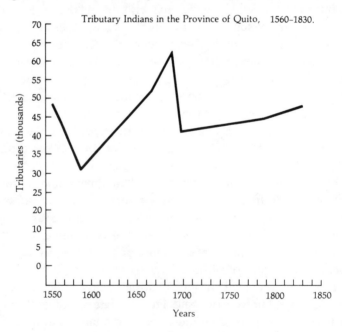

Figure 4.2. Tributary Indians in the Province of Quito, 1560-1830. (Based on Tyrer 1976:81.)

and to a lesser extent the Indian communities tried to combine subsistence agriculture and sheepraising with textile production. As in Peru, rural labor derived from yanaconato and mita. But in Quito, the yanaconas practically vanished during the seventeenth century. Instead, mitayos formed the bulk of the rural labor force. There was no competition here with mining needs. Through the concession of usufruct parcels (here called *huasipungos*) and in other ways, hacendados finally bound as much as half of the total Indian population to their estates. Their status came to be similar to that of the earlier yanaconas. Around 1740, two Spanish travelers give a graphic account of this process underway in grain-producing haciendas, cattle, and sheep ranches respectively. The shepherds are presented as possibly the least abused even if much worse off than their counterparts in Spain. The Indians tied to the estates were known as *conciertos*, a somewhat ironic term because it means "by contract." Later, they would be called *huasipungueros* and they continued to be known as such until very recent times.

At the end of the colonial period, the Province of Quito had 1182 haciendas, often comprising obrajes, housing 20,613 Indian taxpayers with their families. Yet less than 6 percent of this labor force worked on haciendas that employed more than 50 resident laborers.

According to the contemporary account referred to, the conditions of the Indians set to work in the obrajes of Quito were by far the most awful. The workers were locked up at night at their quarters to prevent their escape. The obrajes employed a variety of labor such as mitayos, hired — usually indebted — dayworkers, penal labor, and yanaconas. Despite the abusive treatment of this labor force, mortality was apparently not excessive. After all, the era of greatest textile production, the seventeenth century, was also that of the long-term growth of the Quito Indian population. Also, it should be noted that there were obrajes of various categories, those of individual owners, of the Crown and also those set up by the Indians themselves in their communities to get money to pay the tribute. From 169 obrajes in 1700, the number in the Province of Quito had dropped to 125 in 1780. By then, all but 18 were situated in the countryside.

Individually owned obrajes were probably often profitable. As in mining, these enterprises were often integrated within a complex of other activities. The founder of a huge obraje in Huamanga in the Central Peruvian Sierra was, at the same time, an encomendero, the owner of various haciendas complementing each other in terms of production, a miner and a merchant. He was a member of the cabildo and spent some of his money founding two monasteries.

The large estates were formed in many ways: land grants, purchases and acquisitions of land through marriage, as well as through encroachments on the lands of neighbors—Indians more often than not. The legalization of this de facto situation took place as a consequence of the growing financial needs of the Crown in Europe from the 1590s onward. After due inspection and, above all, the payment of a fee, landowners were confirmed in hitherto questionable property rights (*composiciones de tierra*). This procedure obviously legalized many shocking abuses but it brought some order to a chaotic situation.

As we have noted, the Church, in particular religious orders such as the Jesuits, formed a conspicuous element among landholders. The driving force behind Jesuit land acquisition was the need to ensure a regular income for the upkeeping of colleges and other urban activities. The process was facilitated by gifts in land as well as cash from members of the elites. At times, acquisition could also be the consequence of individual landowners being unable to meet their financial obligations to some ecclesiastical body—the main sources of rural credit. The land acquisition policy of the Jesuits was strikingly systematic, so that properties specializing in different products complimented each other. Rural properties of the Church were not overly numerous (7 percent of all estates of Cuzco in 1689; 8 percent of those of Trujillo in 1710), but they covered a great part of the best lands and were situated within convenient distance to main markets.

Among secular landholders, some entailed their estates (*mayorazgos*), others managed to see to it that somehow the estates passed from generation to generation without major divisions. But the opposite phenomenon of frequent changes taking place in ownership by purchase appears to have been much more frequent. Such changes were facilitated by the often high level of indebtedness. By assuming the payment of the obligations, the buyers of estates sometimes had to pay a small sum in cash only. The obligations could consist of mortgage loans as well as self-imposed promises to the Church to pay for masses or other religious services to help the owner in the afterlife (*capellanías*).

In the Andean highlands as a whole, by the mid-eighteenth century, Indian communities, notwithstanding hacienda expansion, must have retained the largest part of the cultivable areas. They, too, to some degree, became integrated within the emerging regional markets. Because of the Indian population decline, discrepancies between the diminishing number of resident Indians and their legally inalienable landholdings often arose. In these cases, humble non-Indian elements — regardless of legal prohibitions — quickly settled down among the Indians to cultivate part of their lands. At the same time, Indians left their communities to form new clusters of population around the haciendas along with Mestizo, Black, and Mulatto workers. This process was confirmed when many of the larger haciendas were made vice-parishes with chapels of their own.

At the same time, some former reducciones were transformed into Mestizo parishes populated by owners of small or medium sized property. The originally dualistic pattern of rural settlement had partially broken down. However, especially in the southern Sierra, many former reducciones, albeit weakened, retained their corporative Hispano-Indian character. They would become the *comunidades* of modern times.

b. Patterns of Production

The organization of production, in the case of the highland communities, followed pre-Columbian patterns, only slightly modified by the introduction of Spanish municipal forms. On the European-owned estates, naturally, European patterns prevailed. Labor relations were more or less paternalistic. Whether legally free or not, workers depended entirely on their masters' will. Basically their compensation consisted of free supplies and usufruct rights — that is, they were within the framework of a "natural" economy. Because of the low level of technology, capitalization, and management, the sheer input of manpower was the main determinant of production. There were also extractive activities requiring special, usually even simpler, varieties of productive organization. Stimulants like cocoa were gathered in peripheral areas by Indians forced to do so by the entrepreneurs, often under very severe and dangerous conditions. Production for sale in the Montaña missions was authoritatively organized by the missionaries.

Little is known about the volumes of production, especially over time, even less about the rates of productivity. Also, if they are to be meaningful, data of this kind must be related to similar data from other areas, inside or outside Latin America, from the same time. Two-ninths of the tithes (*diezmos*) were entered into the records of the Royal Treasury, but it is very risky to estimate volumes of production on the basis of the monetary figures found in these accounts.

On the coast, whether of Ecuador or Peru, the change of production was particularly profound. Two main crops, sugar and wine, as well as domesticated animals, agricultural techniques, and the majority of producers and consumers came originally from abroad. The growing of grapes (and the resulting production of brandy and wines) was concentrated in Ica and Moquequa on the southern Peruvian coast. Ranching comprised the whole range of domestic animals of the Mediterranean. Fodder such as oats and alfalfa were also grown on a large scale. White settlers preferred wheat to maize. It was grown in huge quantities despite a less than ideal climate. Trujillo specialized in rice, Lambayeque in cotton. The earthquake of 1687 is said to have produced widespread sterility of the earth, thus bringing about a deep agricultural crisis. The destruction appears to have been limited to the surroundings of Lima, however. The effects were probably only temporary.

In the 1740s Lima was surrounded by "gardens, producing all the herbs and fruits known in Spain, and of the same goodness and beauty, besides those common to America," the two travelers already quoted write. The extensive olive orchards, also, produced an "oil... much preferable to that of Spain... " Besides irrigation, by no means abandoned though perhaps less extensive than in Incaic times, guano from the Chincha islands was still being used as a fertilizer, though this has often been denied. The great variety and richness of tropical lowland production in Guayas and in Esmeraldas, farther north, did not fail to impress our travelers. First of all, there was the cocoa tree, producing "its fruit twice a year, and in the same plenty and goodness." Also, the fertile but fever ridden lands yielded cotton, tobacco, sugar cane, bananas, coconuts, yuca, peanuts, and many other fruits.

In the Andean highlands much more of pre-Columbian production patterns were retained. A seventeenth-century chronicler underscores that in Upper Peru, the Spanish scratch plow pulled by oxen and the native chaquitaccla were used side by side. The same blending of two different agricultural traditions was expressed by the dichotomies of maize and wheat, broad beans and potatoes, coca and sugar, llama and sheep, each within its respective ecological niche. There was also an element of disruption, though, when Spanish cattle invaded terrains hitherto used for farming. Also, the networks of complementary production units on different levels of altitude held by Indian groups, were often destroyed. On the other hand, the largest of the emerging Spanish estates often succeeded in incorporating different kinds of terrain in order to secure for themselves a wide range of products. Terracing and irrigation continued to be used, though to a lesser extent than in Inca times. Unirrigated tracts (*temporales*) gave inferior yields. No overall picture of highland production can be obtained at the present time.

We have a series of data for the Cuzco area in 1786 (table 4.1). Production per capita compares favorably with present conditions, in particular in terms of tubers and maize, a result of obsolete techniques, overpopulation, erosion, and other factors. Yet the seed ratio in eighteenth-century Cuzco seems to have been low even in terms of the times. It is worthwhile to notice that in the province of Calca y Lares, in 1786, about a fourth of the wheat was grown by Indian communities, which also kept a third of the horses and half the cattle. On the other hand, haciendas produced 60 percent of the maize and almost 30 percent of the tubers. Apparently, the process of acculturation in terms of rural production was advanced.

The oscillations of this production were often violent due to shifting weather conditions in a harsh environment where margins were always narrow. Droughts, early frosts, or inundations would lead to starvation and broaden the way for epidemics which, by turn, caused crucial shortages of labor. As we have already seen, textile production based on sheep and also alpaca wool was important in many parts of the highlands, from Quito to Cuzco. Apart from the obrajes situated in the towns, this production was closely integrated with the rural economy, be it that of the haciendas or that of the communities. Where mining did not develop, textiles or at times sugar or coca production provided the dynamics of Andean economy.

c. Trade and Regional Dynamics

After the introduction of the corregidores de indios in the 1560s, the so-called *reparto* or forced sale of merchandise by these officials to the Indians and poor Mestizos of the countryside became a most important form of internal trade. In the Peruvian highlands, mules from the River Plate and textiles from Quito and Cuzco constituted the main items of this trade. The repartos have recently been considered as more important mechanisms of transfer of Indian labor output to the "Spanish" sector of economy than either the payments of tribute or the mita obligations. Repartos implied a massive redistribution of Andean products like textiles and coca from producing to nonproducing areas, in

Table 4.1
Population and Production in an Andean Province: Calca y Lares, Cuzco, 1786

	Population	Production		Measure	Percentage on Haciendas
8	Ecclesiastics	Maize	12.130	*fanegas*	59.8
230	"Spaniards"	Wheat	2.794	*fanegas*	73.2
424	Mestizos	Potatoes	10.358	*cargas*	27.1
9.200	Indians				
9.682	*Total*				
		Livestock			
		Horses	551		69.9
		Mules	534		38.0
	Haciendas:	Cattle	5.482		51.4
	38	Sheep	26.403		36.8
	Parishes:				
	5	*Lares*:			
	All situated in the temperate zone (about 2.800 m.) except that of *Lares* in the ceja de montaña.	coca	230	*cestos* =	1.380 kgs
		Production per inhabitant			
		Maize 1.2 *fanegas*		Approx. 120 kgs	
		Wheat 0.3		30 kgs	
	An "average" hacienda: Viccho	Potatoes 1.1 *cargas*		440 kgs	
	24 Indian Farmhands	Cattle 0.6			
	Maize 170 fanegas	Sheep 2.7			
	Wheat 110 fanegas				
	Horses 63				
	Mules 18				
	Cattle 69				
	Sheep 380				

SOURCE: Mörner 1978: *passim*

this respect not so unlike the Incaic distribution system. The corregidores, who of course greatly benefited from this trade, and got a bad reputation from it, were probably rather the straw men of professional merchants.

The usual business form was the *compañia*. Two or more individuals contributed capital and/or labor for a specific venture for a certain time to divide profits afterward.

The purest type of consumption center was the mining town. At Potosí virtually all commodities had to be brought there from outside. The cheapest and bulkiest articles were produced as near to the city as possible; those of higher value per size entered from a greater distance (figure 4.1). The greatest administrative center, Lima, with a population of 25000 in 1610, consumed yearly some 24,000 *fanegas* of wheat, 25,000 of maize, 3500 heads of cattle, 400 sheep, 69 tons of rice, and 200,000 bottles of wine. These products arrived from distant as well as nearby parts. Fruits and vegetables were grown nearby. Wood, timber, and charcoal had to be brought in from much greater distance, as Chilean wheat, which had been imported even before the earthquake of 1687 and thereafter in greater quantities.

Overland transportation, always difficult, became virtually impossible during the rainy season. Also, in the Sierra, steep grades did not allow for the use of the carts and wagons of the plains. Muletracks had to be used. Problems were compounded in the case of agricultural produce, usually bulky. Thus, distance, or rather the time of journey to centers of Spanish population was a crucial factor for the value of land and produce. When a mining boom subsided or a city lost population, the surrounding rural area was adversely affected. Grievances were often voiced that certain tracts could no longer be kept in cultivation because of lack of market. On the other hand, specialized production of small-volume–high-price items like wine and sugar lent itself to long distance trade and could provide considerable profits. Also, the transportation of live animals, though slow, could provide a long-distance undertaking. Water transports, finally, wherever feasible, greatly reduced the problem of bringing produce to the market. They were preferred even between different points along the flat Pacific coast — sea currents permitting — despite the existence of a long coast road. It proved more expensive to make shipments by pack animals than by ship. On the other hand, the existence of a great many excises and internal customs duties always hampered long distance trade in comparison with the production costs of producers closer by.

Price movements, which remain to be explored, probably exhibited great local differences. They must also have been modified by the existence of a very large subsistence and barter sector. Especially on the municipal level, efforts to regulate prices in the interest of urban food consumers and artisan producers were constantly made.

In economic terms, the former territories of the Inca Empire were little by little split up during the colonial period. The Audiencia of Quito was more oriented toward New Granada — present-day Colombia. It also had a significant Amazonian dimension, as illustrated by the populous and temporarily prosperous Indian missions established in the early eighteenth century along the higher reaches of the Amazon river (Marañón) by the German Samuel Fritz and other Jesuits. With respect to Lower and Upper Peru, the latter was also closely related to Northwestern Argentina, then the Province of Tucumán. Even the distant Moxos missions in easternmost Upper Peru, by forming part of the well managed, economically centralized Peruvian Jesuit Province, were linked commercially and financially to Lima and the Pacific coast.

A road connected Cali, Popayán, and Pasto in New Granada with Quito, Cuenca, and Loja whereas the vital branch road to Guayaquil was bad and hazardous. To go overland from Loja to Piura in northernmost Peru was also difficult. Most travelers and cargoes from Panama, New Granada, and Guayaquil went farther south, to Paita, thence to Lima. Currents were adverse. In Lower and Upper Peru the main routes were those of Inca times, more or less. It is worthwhile to note that by the late seventeenth century, the share of navigation and trade between Lima and Panama had declined considerably. This not only reflected the drop of silver production and of net transfer of Treasury funds from the capital of the Viceroyalty to Spain. It also demonstrated a higher degree of self-sufficiency by means of intercolonial Spanish American trade on the Pacific. The maritime defense was less impressive here than in the Caribbean. Despite a constant threat ever since the unexpected appearance of Francis Drake's tiny ships in 1579, and occasional attacks by foreign fleets against harbors like Guayaquil, it was never put to a severe test, however. The shipyards of Guayaquil remained of essential importance to Pacific navigation.

According to a recent analysis, Spanish America comprised an archipelago of "islands." These were centers of administration, ecclesiastical institutions, population densities, and economic activities. The centers naturally differed in importance and were surrounded by intermediate and peripheral zones. On the basis of carefully elaborated data for the period 1574 – 1628, and by establishing the degrees of diversified economic activities, population concentration, and ecclesiastical presence, Quito was found to be the center of a region comprising New Granada as an intermediate zone with the Atlantic coast of present-day Colombia as a periphery. Within the other huge region, the Potosí – Chuquisaca – Chuquisaca – Santa Cruz complex and Lima were both identified as centers. Puno, Cuzco, Trujillo, and Arequipa were found to form an intermediate zone, while Tucumán, Huamanga, and Huánuco were peripheral. In terms of incomes of bishops and cathedral chapters, around 1628, the dioceses of Los Charcas and Lima ranked far above the rest. Cuzco was a poor third with half as much while the remaining dioceses, including that of Quito, each had between a third or fourth of the income of Lima or Los Charcas. Not surprisingly, cathedral constructions, in quality as well as size, reflected roughly the same rank of order. Data on crown income from *alcabala*, a sales tax, from the end of the seventeenth century, can be arranged according to the same pattern of classification as in table 4.1. These data, while representing only a single variable, suggest the relative growth in trade of Lima and its Sierra hinterland (Huamanga) at the expense of both Los Charcas and Quito, which also fits with other pieces of information that we have.

Toward the middle of the seventeenth century, silver production began a steady decline in Potosí as well as Oruro, a more recent mining district to the north of Lake Poopó, exploited with free wage labor. In turn, smaller silver output led to the rapid decline of urban population, in Upper Peru at least. By 1750, the population of Potosí had dropped from more than 100,000 to 30,000. The whole widespread supply net of

Land and Labor in Colonial Society

the Upper Peruvian mining populations was naturally affected adversely and hacienda expansion generally came to a halt. In Upper Peru both Chuquisaca and Cochabamba suffered a decline. By contrast, La Paz, less dependent on Potosí, had by 1750 become the largest city of Upper Peru, with some 40,000 inhabitants, as a commercial and administrative center of an area with a growing Indian population. In Lower Peru, too, the decline of the population of Lima from some 50,000 by 1650 to 27,000 a hundred years later reflects the falling economic trend. Thus, both the earlier growth poles of two Perus were weakened and the economic integration of the Andean space loosened in favor of trends toward subsistence and external forces such as River Plate contraband trade.

V.

Indian Revolt, Reorganization, and Collapse of Colonial Rule

From the mid-eighteenth through the early nineteenth century, the Western world underwent a process of profound cultural, economic, social and political change. Even though Spanish America was a marginal area of that world, the culmination of Spanish colonialism and its ensuing collapse both took place within this general framework.

Under the Bourbon dynasty, in foreign policy Spain regularly lined up with France in its lengthy struggle against Britain for hegemony. This was a crucial option because the English held sea power threatening the umbilical cord of Spain's overseas empire. The first really world wide Anglo-French confrontation was that of the Seven Years War. The glaring weakness of Spanish American defense was laid open when the British easily seized Havana in 1762. This eloquently showed the need for greater military resources, that is greater state revenues, by turn obtainable only by means of improved administration and a broader economic basis. This is one aspect from which Bourbon reformism has to be seen. On the other hand, the close links with France provided this reformism with its main source of inspiration. The refined mercantilism and centralized administrative machinery of Colbert's France became the models of Spanish reformism. The old-fashioned Spanish intellectual world was little by little lit up with French "enlightened ideas." But not the latest, most radical ones. Essentially it was a question of the long-overdue impact of Cartesian rationalism, Newtonian natural science and Lockean empiricism. Utilitarianism spread.

a. Reforms imposed

Under Charles III (1759–88), government policy with respect also to the overseas possessions were guided by new reformist values. Inspired by Gallicanism, the French insistence on the subordination of the Church to the State, Charles III and his advisors decided to crush the most efficient branch of the Catholic Church. After top-secret preparations, all members of the powerful Jesuit Order were suddenly expelled from Spain and its possessions in 1767. In the Peruvian Viceroyalty, the secret orders were efficiently carried out by Viceroy Manuel Amat y Junient (more famous for his liaison with a famous actress, "La Perricholi"). The numerous properties of the Jesuits were confiscated and retained under state administration (as *Temporalidades*) until gradually auctioned off.

As university teachers and missionaries the Jesuits left a great void. Some had themselves been early exponents of cautiously "enlightened" ideas. After their expulsion, however, scholasticism was routed and the new sciences imposed in the academic environment, as exemplified by the reform of the San Marcos University of Lima in 1771. But the recognition of unrestricted royal power was the price to be paid for more advanced thinking in the scientific, social, and economic realms.

The old convoy system had ceased to exist by the 1730s. Regional monopolistic trade companies were one of the solutions attempted to recover trade from foreign smugglers; also, registered ships were sent out now and then. From 1740 onwards, some went to the Pacific via Cape Horn. The restrictions on intercolonial trade were largely lifted in 1765. But the trade reform that would affect the Peruvian Viceroyalty most deeply grew out of strategic considerations.

In the course of the eighteenth century Buenos Aires became the main South American bulwark against the perceived Anglo-Portuguese military threat. In 1776, while the English were tied up in North America, Charles III decided to make a preemptive strike against the Portuguese to force them to give up Colonia do Sacramento, their fortress on the River Plate. The commander chosen was made a Viceroy. To provide him with an enlarged financial base, the Audiencia of Charcas, with its mines, was made part of his jurisdiction. After his success (the Portuguese were forced to conclude a treaty of "friendship" in 1778), the new Viceroyalty quickly consolidated itself. Henceforth, all bullion and other trans-Atlantic trade would be conducted directly with Spain via Buenos Aires.

In a way, the creation of the new Viceroyalty and the inclusion of Upper Peru was the logical conclusion of a development already under way for almost two centuries, by means of contraband trade. But the links and common interests of Southern Peru and the Audiencia of Charcas had remained strong. Thus, from the Peruvian Viceroyalty's point of view, a virtual amputation of its economy had been carried out. At the same time, the preparations for a new war against Britain (as revenge for the defeat of 1763) required a forceful mobilization of the financial resources of the Peruvian Viceroyalty as well. Colonial Secretary José de Gálvez in Madrid sent Antonio de Areche as an Inspector General (*Visitador general*) to Peru in 1776 to repeat the success Gálvez had achieved in New Spain during the 1760s. His main task was to improve fiscal and other administration. He soon clashed with Viceroy Manuel Guirior, however. His efforts to augment state income by raising the sales tax (*alcabala*) from 4 to 6 percent led to riots in Arequipa, La Paz, and Cochabamba. Similarly, another Visitador sent to the Audiencia of Quito caused widespread riots there when he announced his intention to increase taxation. The violent opposition against reformism among the urban lower and middle strata was probably backed up by upper strata Criollo elements. At the same time, however unintentionally, the reformist endeavor also helped to provoke the great rural Indian rebellion of 1780.

b. Rebellion

Any repressive society has an inherent potential of rebellion. In colonial society, Negro slaves, Indians, and many poor Mestizos suffered from severe repression. For reasons that are not quite clear, the eighteenth century witnessed their most defiant reactions.

On the Peruvian coast, Negro slavery had functioned relatively smoothly on the huge Jesuit plantations. Slaves were provided with subsistence plots of their own and had fixed schedules of work. After

1767, in order to economize, state administrators of the estates curtailed these benefits. Some uprisings are known to have taken place.

In the Indian sector, local riots were endemic. Mostly they were directed against abuses committed by the corregidores, priests, or curacas. By the mid-eighteenth century they tended to increase in frequency and seriousness. In 1742, Juan Santos Atahuallpa, a cuzqueño Mestizo who claimed royal Inca descent and Jesuit education, made himself the leader of a rebellion among the Campa Indians of the Ceja de Montaña on the other side of the Sierra east of Lima. This was a time when many lowland tribes were striking back against the Spaniards, who had been trying to pacify them through missionary activities. This rising had clearly millenarian aims. It was never suppressed. Geographical isolation helped to bring about a stalemate that lasted for 14 years.

In the late 1770s another leader and spokesman for Indian grievances emerged. José Gabriel Condorcanqui — curaca of Surimana and Tungasuca in Southern Cuzco, who called himself Tupac Amaru — was like Santos Atahuallpa a Mestizo proud of his Inca origins. But the circumstances that shaped the rebellion and the medium where it took place differed widely. In a letter to Areche in 1781, Tupac Amaru gives a concise presentation of the social conditions responsible for the outbreak. Among the abuses of the corregidores he stresses the forced sale of merchandise (*reparto*). He also mentions their collusion with the large landowners at the disposal of whom they put Indians to work on the obrajes, on the sugar fields, to gather coca in the montaña. Tupac also files the usual grievance about the mita minera. It appears to him to be less justified in Cuzco than previously because sufficient labor could now be found closer to Potosí. Areche, in his reply, admitted that the Indian spokesman was right. To become a rebel was his error. The reparto had been canceled shortly after the rebellion broke out. The abolition of the corregimiento and the establishment of a new Audiencia in Cuzco (1787) to protect Indian interests more efficiently followed after pacification.

Even so, the relation between exploitation and upheaval is usually complex. Maximum exploitation does not automatically trigger rebellion. The reparto had been legalized in 1756. Maximum amounts were fixed for each corregimiento. As time went on, though, the burden per

Indian tended to drop with demographic recovery. In Cuzco, in 1780, paradoxically, the reparto per capita in the province of Tinta, where the rebellion broke out, happened to be particularly low. This does not make Tupac's claim absurd, though. The corregidores must have been especially tempted to exceed the legal limits imposed on reparto precisely in such areas. When solemnly executing the corregidor of Tinta, Tupac's irreversible challenge to Spanish authority, he accused him of having extracted almost three times his legal share.

As far as the mita was concerned, it certainly constituted much less of a hardship for Cuzco Indians than it used to do. Widespread commutation made it at the most an added economic obligation. Anyway, it is clear that we also have to look at other circumstances than those alleged by the rebel leadership itself to explain the spread and aggressive potential of the rebellion. It characteristically spread along the Cuzco–Potosí route, where countless mule tracks brought merchandise back and forth. Tupac Amaru himself was a curaca – businessman (a common combination at this time) who kept some 350 mules for his arriería enterprise. The arrieros were directly affected by the increase in sales tax and might also suffer from competition with the reparto trade. Mestizo arrieros were conspicuous among Tupac's early followers. The obrajes were the prime employers or customers of the arrieros. There were cases when the rebels destroyed obrajes and freed their captive workers, but on the whole they were spared by Tupac Amaru, despite their horrible labor conditions. This was hardly a coincidence. To what extent did rebels come from the communities and from the haciendas? We do not know, but it is obvious that, in Cuzco at least, the curacas and Indian allegiance to them played a key role. Particularly around the City of Cuzco the curacas remained loyal to the cause of Spain. In fact, one of them, Matheo Pumacahua of Chincheros, proved himself to be the most efficient royal commander. Others, such as the curaca Tomasa Tito Condemayta, a large landholder, opted for Tupac Amaru. She was eventually executed with him.

It would seem that, in the eighteenth century, the more wealthy curacas, while becoming more acculturated also took greater pride in the Inca past. This was parallel to the attitude of wealthy criollos, increasingly aware that their birth in the New World set them apart from Peninsular Spaniards. Thus, the relationship between the two

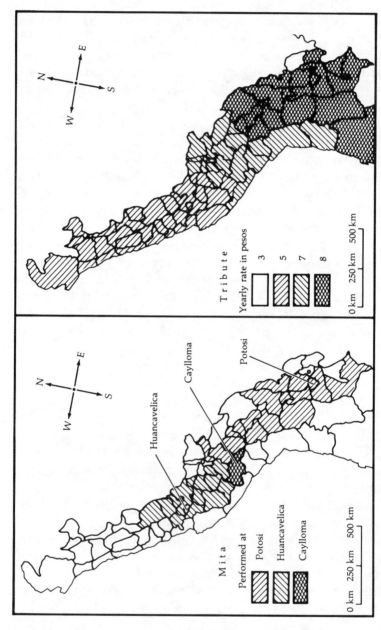

Figure 5.1. Indian Tribute and Mita in the Late Eighteenth Century. (From Golte 1980: maps 12-13. Location of mines added.)

groups was complex and hard to analyze. The Bishop of Cuzco, who was a criollo, was deeply involved in intrigues against Tupac's enemy, the Spanish Corregidor of Tinta. But once the revolt had broken out, Tupac had to wait in vain for support from the urban criollo elite of Cuzco. Accumulated Indian hatred against the oppressors made no distinction between Peninsulars and others. As a consequence most of Tupac's non-Indian sympathizers probably abandoned him. Yet most

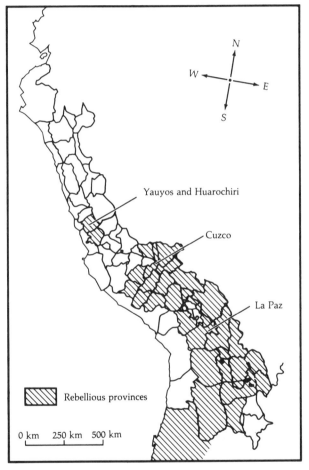

Figure 5.2. The extent of Indian Rebellion at the Time of Tupac Amaru. (From Golte 1980: map 27. Names of provinces added. We believe, however, that he draws the border of rebellion a little too far west of Cuzco.)

of the commanding officers of his army were middle-strata criollos and mestizos. The rebels defeated local militia at the battle of Sangarará, but they were never able to occupy Cuzco. Tupac's wife, Micaela Basti-das, acted as a competent chief-of-staff but when Spanish reinforce-ments arrived, rebel resistance collapsed. With some of his relatives and collaborators, Tupac Amaru "II" was cruelly put to death at the main plaza of Cuzco in 1781.[1] A few years later, his cousin Diego Cristóbal, under suspicion of preparing a new rebellion, was also killed.

The Aimara Indians of Upper Peru had, under the Catari brothers, risen in arms somewhat earlier than Tupac Amaru. The relationship between them and the Cuzco leader remained ambivalent. Instead of following their curacas/mallkus, the Indian masses at times tried to kill them as well. The city of Puno on Lake Titicaca fell into the rebels' hands but La Paz, like Cuzco, resisted their onslaught.

The Indian revolts in Upper and Lower Peru were no doubt costly in human lives as well as material destruction. Even so, the study of demographic records from the 1780s suggests that population losses were in the order of tens of thousands of people rather than 100,000 as has usually been claimed. Wars during this era simply were much less formidable killers than disease. The suppression of the rebellion cost much in terms of fiscal expense, and many haciendas were sacked by the rebels. At the same time, though, the campaigns must have pro-vided a certain stimulus for the producers of food, clothes, and trans-portation supplies.

In recent times, Tupac Amaru has been raised to the rank of a Peruvian national hero. He is conceived of as a precursor of National Independence. His real intentions remain somewhat obscure, though — if, indeed, they were ever clear even to him. Toward the Spanish authorities he never gave up his attitude of basic loyalty to the King while eagerly punishing those committing crimes in his august name. When facing the Indian masses, on the other hand, Tupac Amaru, a charismatic leader, naturally stressed the sovereign rights inherent in his descent from Inca monarchs. The rebel leadership did not want to destroy Spanish institutions but occupy them. Once suppressed, the rebellion helped to bring about the very measures demanded by the rebels, as we have seen. Abuses against the Indians certainly continued after pacification as well but, thanks to improved administration, possibly on a somewhat smaller scale.

On the other hand, the Crown tried to eradicate the roots of "Inca" nationalism. In 1782, the King declared that supposed descent from the "primitive, pagan kings" gave no right to nobility or the use of the Inca title. Also, all copies circulating of History of Inca Garcilaso "from which the natives learned many harmful notions," were to be gathered up discreetly by the authorities.[2] Temporarily at least, the fear of another indigenous explosion helped to unite non-Indians, rich and poor, in a basically anti-Indian stance. The Criollos learned how to combine love for their native land and its glorious past with a strict demand for continued, unlimited subjugation of the natives of the land.

c. Imperial Reorganization

After the outbreak of the rebellion, Areche was replaced as a *Visitador general* by Jorge Escobedo. This efficient bureaucrat carried out administrative reform in the Viceroyalty in the form of the *Intendencia* system (see fig. 5.3), on the French model. The corregidores, the provincial officials of the Treasury, and other functionaries were now replaced by new, qualified, decently salaried *Intendentes,* each responsible for a group of provinces. They corresponded directly with Madrid, thus serving to increase imperial control and centralization. Because of the authority they wielded on the regional level, the administrative influence of the Audiencia was sharply reduced. Even though the quality of the Viceroys rose, the prestige of their office probably dropped. Judges on the Audiencias had in the past often been Criollos. But from the 1770s onward, as a consequence of Madrid's insistence that they have no personal ties to the local community, the Criollo proportion of these high judges fell. Furthermore, the Intendentes were almost always recruited among Peninsular Spaniards. Thus, the increasing number of Criollo lawyers produced by the reorganized universities keenly felt subjected to discrimination. That lower administrative positions were usually filled by them was scant consolation. Such was the position of the *Subdelegado,* representative of the Intendente on the provincial level, the low salary of which did not attract candidates of quality. In turn, this made the subdelegados the weak link in the Bourbon effort to streamline and improve territorial administration. The division of the Viceroyalty in 1776 was upheld, but minor adjustments were made. In 1796 the Puno region was restored to Peru; in 1802–4, in the North, the montaña province of Mainas and, much more important, that of Guayaquil, were transferred from New Granada to Peru. In New Granada, the Intendencia system had never been introduced.

However difficult it proved to eradicate the old abuses and administrative weaknesses, the Peruvian Intendentes did succeed in their primary task of raising Crown revenues as is illustrated by figure 5.4.

Figure 5.3. The Intendancy of Lower Peru at the End of the Colonial Period. Based on Fisher 1970:273.

This, among other things, meant improved defense. The militia units, to judge from their performance during the rebellion, were of inferior quality. Instead, regular troops, many of whom were sent out from Spain, henceforth formed the bulk of viceregal defense against internal as well as external threats.

As long as historians relied mainly on the gloomy reports of the Lima Guild of Merchants and other biased testimonies, the economic decline

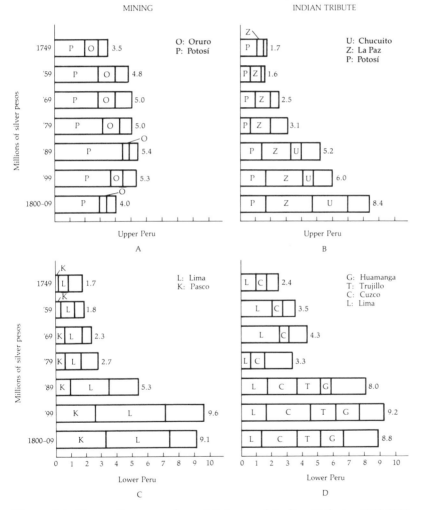

Figure 5.4. Crown Revenues from Mining and Indian Tribute, 1749-1809. (Source: J. Tord 1977.) **A.** Mining, Upper Peru **B.** Indian Tribute, Upper Peru **C.** Mining, Lower Peru **D.** Indian Tribute, Lower Peru

of the Peruvian Viceroyalty after the "amputation" of 1776 was taken for granted. In fact, as shown by figure 3.4, silver production in Lower Peru experienced a notable rise from the late 1770s onward. The mine of Cerro de Pasco, at an altitude of 4350 meters, east of Lima was mainly responsible for this development. The mercury output at Huancavelica, where efforts of modernizing production largely failed, could no longer supply all the needs of Andean mining. Mercury imports from Spain were at times interrupted by war. This helps to explain the ups and downs of the production curve. Remarkably, though, the installation of three steam engine pumps from Cornwall contributed to a rise in production of silver at Cerro de Pasco to a final peak in 1820. In Upper Peru, silver output doubled between the 1740s and 1790s. Even so, the efforts of a group of German mining experts to modernize mining technology at Potosí had little success. While Cerro de Pasco and other Lower Peruvian mines relied exclusively on free labor, mita continued to keep wage costs down at Potosí until production reached another low after 1800. (See fig. 3.4.)

For a long time, the Upper Peruvian mining districts still constituted an important market for the producers of textiles and foodstuffs of Southern Peru. But from the 1790s onward, the market drastically shrank for Cuzco sugar, textiles, and coca leaves, and for Arequipa liquors. Also the imports via Buenos Aires of European textiles had a negative impact on domestic producers, as in the Valley of Cochabamba. But in Central Peru, Cerro de Pasco managed to play a role similar to that of Potosí two centuries earlier in stimulating regional producers of cloth, coca, sugar, and rum. Lima merchants also sold great quantities of European goods there at a profit. In the North, economic performance was more dismal. The City of Trujillo, for instance, lost a great part of its population from the 1760s onward, and the deteriorating city administration could not even maintain an adequate supply of water. In the Audiencia of Quito, three small highland towns have been found to exhibit similar malaise from 1778 onward. Even though an earthquake in 1797 was partly responsible, economic depression provided the backdrop. As the Viceroy of New Granada observed in the 1790s, production of textiles in Quito, which used to reach the value of 1.5 million pesos, now only attained 600,000. Direct imports of Spanish textiles to the Pacific had this effect, the Viceroy noted with colonialist satisfaction. The city and province of Guayaquil offered a brighter picture. Cocoa exports, largely to Peru, rose considerably from 1790 onward, population as well.

By now, population growth was well under way. The early introduction of smallpox vaccination in Spanish America by Balmis in 1804 also included a branch expedition to the Peruvian Viceroyalty. Thanks to a number of population censuses beginning in the 1770s, we have a pretty good idea about the size, spatial distribution, and ethnic composition of population. In the early 1790s, present-day Peru had 1.1 million inhabitants, some 60 percent still being classified as Indians. There were about 40,000 Negro slaves, but by this time further imports had virtually ceased. Present-day Ecuador had about half a million people, Bolivia approximately a million. Lima, with some 50,000 inhabitants, was followed at a distance by Cuzco, Quito, and Potosí (see fig. 5.5).

Administration during the late colonial period, for all its weaknesses, was not only better than before but also superior to what would follow in the course of the nineteenth century. Therefore it did produce a remarkable wealth of good data on economic as well as social conditions. Historians have only started to explore these wonderful resources, though. In the case of one Cuzco province we have found that production per rural inhabitant of maize, and possibly potatoes as well, was notably higher in the 1780s than in the mid-twentieth century. It was only slightly lower in the case of wheat. The patterns of different types of production were apparently interrelated with varying living conditions. In Cuzco, both the sugar plantation areas and those of the obrajes exhibited unfavorable conditions for population growth. While women commonly outnumbered men in highland Indian areas, both the Cuzco and an Upper Peruvian sample show that the coca-gathering districts of the montaña had an excess of men. This is only to be expected in an in-migration zone.

In parts of Upper Peru, many Indians moved out of their communities to settle down in estancias outside the villages. A case study of the district of Tiahuanaco (with its famous ruins), shows that all of these Indian estancias were eventually taken over by Hacendados between

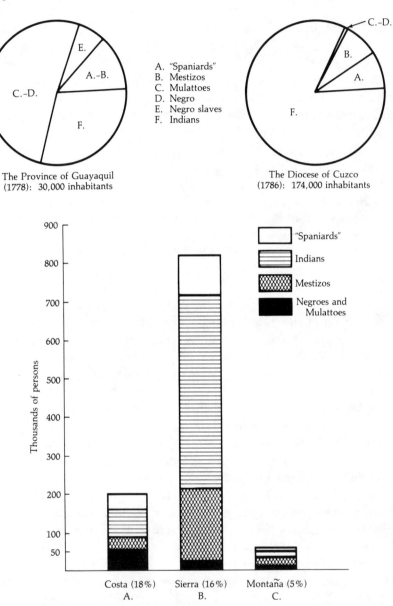

Figure 5.5. Population Composition and Distribution. (Sources: Vollmer 1973:279; Hamerly 1973:89.) The percentage figures for Costa, Sierra, and Montaña are based on Peru's total population of 1,076,122 in 1792.

1773 and 1817. But the motives of that appropriation are not clear and it would be risky to generalize about this phenomenon. (See figures 5.6 –5.8.)

Toward the end of the colonial period, the socio-racial classification of the *Régimen de Castas* proved increasingly difficult to apply due to the continuation of the process of race mixture. The very fact of discrimination encouraged the phenomenon of "passing." By virtue of wealth and/or education, greater numbers of individuals of humble origins and dark skin were able to improve their social status. In this way the "Spanish" (or "Criollo") group swelled when marriage became more normal within an expanding middle-stratum of mixed blood. On a lower level, Indians becoming "cholos" made even more rapid the relative increase of the non-Indian group. As an eighteenth century traveler who knew the Andes well explained, a master might teach an Indian "to wash his face, to comb his hair, to cut his nails. When this is done, and he is clad in a clean shirt, the Indian though otherwise maintaining his own dress, passes as Cholo; that is, as somebody who has some Mestizo admixture. If his service is of use to the Spaniard, he gets a [Spanish] dress and shoes are put on his feet. Within a couple of months he is a mestizo by name."[3]

The colonial authorities tried to maintain legal discrimination against all those of African descent and with the stigma of slavery. Logically, also, the exclusiveness of the whites tended to increase under the menace of well-off, racially mixed elements challenging the traditional white monopoly of wealth and power. The Negroes and Mulattoes, euphemistically termed *Morenos* and *Pardos*, were recognized as good soldiers. They could therefore expect some improvement in their depressed situation if they joined the military. But we know that in Peru, their status remained clearly inferior to that of white soldiers. They were constantly harassed by bureaucrats who were resentful of the exemption from tribute granted Negroes and Mulattoes in military service. Others were subject to tribute just like the Indians.

Despite the great geographical distance, in a sense Pacific Spanish South America drew closer to Western Europe under the Bourbons. In the 1730s, a French scientific expedition under La Condamine was allowed to visit the Audiencia of Quito, where they measured a meridian under the equator. Toward the end of the century and early years of

A

B

Figure 5.6. Tropical Grace and Pleasures.

A Quito girl (A), "Yapanga...in the dress used by this class of women who want to please," and an Indian noble (B) in gala attire. Both are surrounded with plants and good-tasting fruits from the Ecuadorean coast. Eighteenth-century paintings by Vicente Albán in the Museo Antropológico, Madrid. (Reproductions from Vicens Vives 1961, 4:405, 435. Courtesy of Libros Vicens-Vives, s.a.)

A

B

C

Figure 5.7. The World of the Hacienda.
A. The owner on his horse. **B.** His
wife, in graceful rustic rococo dress.
C. The Cholo peon with his hat in
hand. (From the drawings of Bishop
Baltasar Martínez Compañón at the
Biblioteca de Palacio, Madrid. Reproductions from Vicens Vives 1961,
4:360-61, 391. Courtesy of Libros Vicens-Vives, s.a.)

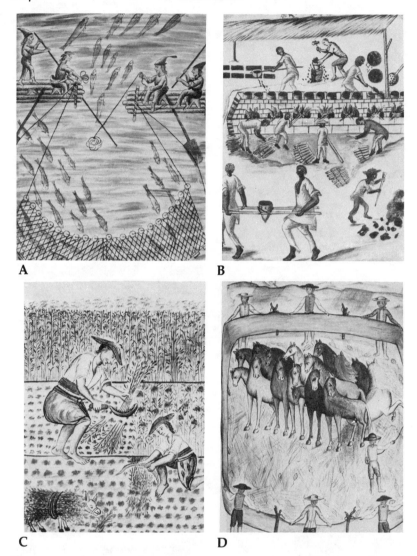

Figure 5.8. Life and Work in Late-Eighteenth-Century Trujillo. **A.** Fishermen at work. **B.** Slaves. They are working with and carrying pitch. **C.** The wheat is harvested with the help of a sickle. **D.** For the threshing, horses were used, a method you can also witness today in the Sierra. (From the drawings of Bishop Baltasar Martínez Compañón at the Biblioteca de Palacio, Madrid. Reproductions from Vicens Vives, 1961, 4:444, 448-49, 456. Courtesy of Libros Vicens-Vives, s.a.)

the nineteenth, a host of scholars and scientists visited the lands of the Incas, among them the Germans Alexander von Humboldt and the mineralogist Nordenflycht, the Spanish botanists Ruiz and Pavón, and the Czech natural scientist Haenke.

As in other parts of the Western world, professionals and aristocrats with cultural interests gathered together in learned societies. They sponsored journals such as the *Mercurio Peruano*, edited by José Hipólito Unánue, a diligent Lima scientist, surgeon, and savant. In exile, Jesuit Juan de Velasco wrote his History of the Kingdom of Quito. In Trujillo, Bishop Martínez Compañón carried out a thorough study of his diocese, which included pictures of popular life and archeological remains as well as musical notation of secular songs. Of a brilliant, sharply satirical mind, the journalist-physician Francisco Javier Eugenio Espejo y Santa Cruz of Quito, a zambo born out of wedlock, dared to challenge the extreme inequality that pervaded the entire society. From jail Espejo wrote to the President of the Audiencia: "... I have produced writings for the happiness of this country as yet a barbarian one... My sins have been the frankness with which I brought forth the truth, my energy in presenting it."

While Espejo was a brilliant, native representative of radical enlightened ideas, Juan Wallparrimachi Sawaraura, a passionate young Indian (or Mestizo) poet from Upper Peru, who wrote in Quechua, was a deeply romantic figure in life as well as poetry. He fell in battle against the royalists in 1814, when he was only 21.[4]

Small newspapers, such as *Diario de Lima* (in 1790) began to appear. But all the intellectual activities were undertaken under the constant threat of censorship. Also, the literate group in society was very small. Qualified university instructors were available for a tiny elite, whereas school teachers, being poorly paid and of low social standing, were hard to recruit. There were members of the elite who realized that the material prosperity that bureaucrats as well as intellectuals aspired to could hardly be obtained without basic education for the masses. But, on the whole, the hierarchical values of society would be better served if the masses were kept in ignorance. In architecture and the arts, the Rococo period yielded in turn to Classicism. The rustic little palace of Quinta de Presa on the outskirts of Lima, where the Viceroy is said to have been seduced by La Perricholi, and the refined religious sculp-

tures of the Quito master Caspicara both reflected the elegant grace of
Rococo. With naïvist imagination, the muralists of Cuzco parish
churches (for instance Andahuaylillas), also produced a more intimate
and graceful art congenial with Rococo. The advent of classic architecture is less noticeable in the Andes than in hitherto marginal areas like
Chile and Argentina where public buildings were constructed precisely
at the end of the colonial era.

d. The Bulwark of Spain

Several factors were in the long run pushing Spanish America toward
separation from the mother country. They had to do with the achievements rather than the failures of late colonial administration. Commercial expansion, especially in Venezuela and the River Plate, had caused
the growth of a bourgeoisie eager for increased influence. Also, in both
demographic and economic terms the Spanish American possessions
were bypassing the mother country. Spanish America had 15 to 16
million inhabitants as compared to 10 to 11 million in Spain. Furthermore, enlightened ideas underlying Bourbon centralizing reformism,
as in Europe itself, were proving to have a revolutionary potential.
Finally, the traditional antipathy between Peninsular Spaniards and
Criollos was becoming increasingly bitter. Administrative reform led
to an *increasing* share of Spanish-born functionaries while Criollos,
aware of their improved education, wanted monopoly over bureaucratic positions. Even so, nobody would have been able to predict the
timing of independence, had not the mother country been subjected to
a violent upheaval.

In March 1808, Charles IV of Spain abdicated in favor of his son
Ferdinand. Both surrendered themselves to Napoleon and meekly gave
up their rights to the Spanish crown. Spain was occupied by Napoleon's brother Joseph, backed up by French troops. A violent popular
revolt against the invaders broke out in Madrid on May 2. Resistance
was led by provincial Juntas which in September established a *Junta
Suprema Central* as a coordinating agency. The enlightened reformist
Spanish elites were split by these events. Some joined the French-
supported government, others joined the resistance. The liberal ideas

of the early French revolution guided both. Grass-roots resistance, on the other hand, was fanatically clerical and royalist in spirit. The British, naturally, helped the patriots against the French. But the advance of the latter could not be halted. On January 29, 1810, the Junta Central, which had resided in Seville, dissolved when the French occupied that city. But it had named a Council of Regency and convoked the parliament (Cortes) to Cádiz, a last refuge. Despite the really desperate military situation, the Cortes proceeded to issue a series of liberal measures, above all the Constitution of March 19, 1812. Napoleon's Russian defeat soon helped to defeat him in Spain as well. In March 1814, Ferdinand VII, a singularly unworthy object of popular rejoicing, was back in Spain. Far from approving the constitution, he immediately restored absolutism to persecute the leaders of national resistance in his name. On New Year's Day 1820, however, liberal officers waiting in Cádiz for embarkation to fight rebels in Spanish America proclaimed the restoration of the Constitution of 1812. Ferdinand now grudgingly accepted his role as a constitutional monarch. But not for long. With the mandate of the conservative European powers, the King of France sent his army across the Pyrenees in 1823; jubilant masses greeted the restoration of Ferdinand to absolutist power. It is this long series of events that determined the timing of Spanish American Independence. The paradoxes of Spain would also be reflected overseas where the rivalries between different areas and ethnic groups made developments even more complex (see fig. 5.9).

The British controlled the seas and the Spanish American possessions were regularly informed about the shocking events taking place in the mother country. The efforts of agents sent to Spanish America by Napoleon to gain acceptance were ill-founded and without success. In political theory, however, the monarch was the only link between Spain and Spanish America. There were many young criollo lawyers who were well versed in this theory. Therefore, the recognition of the authority of those leading Spain in the King's name became a crucial issue on which local authorities had to take a stand. But their decisions were influenced by the internal rivalries of these authorities and by the ever-present tension between criollos and Peninsular Spaniards.

It should be noted, then, that the authority of the Junta Central was recognized everywhere except Chuquisaca and Quito. In the former

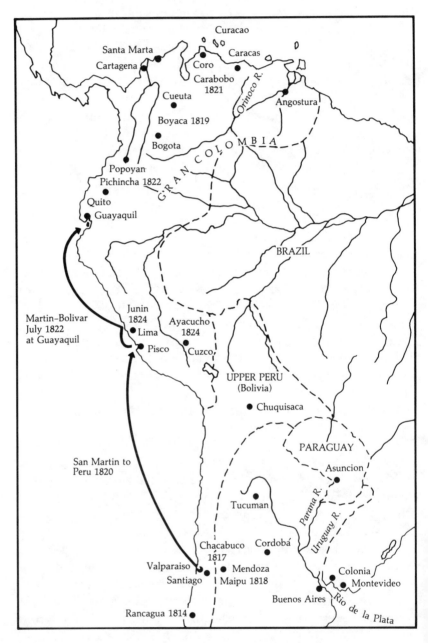

Figure 5.9. The Wars of Independence. (Source: Shafer 1978:317.)

city, the Intendent, also President of the Audiencia, and the Archbishop were both at loggerheads with the judges of the Audiencia. When in May 1809 the President made clear his intention to recognize the Junta Central, the judges imprisoned him in order to form, instead, a regional interim government in Ferdinand VII's name. There was a quarrel among Spaniards and Criollos of an equally conservative outlook. In nearby La Paz, a much more subversive movement, led by a Mestizo soldier, erupted, boldly proclaiming that the time had come "to raise the standard of liberty in these unfortunate colonies."[5] But forces quickly sent from the two viceregal capitals of Buenos Aires and Lima easily put out the two fires in October 1809.

In Quito, the repressive measures taken by the President of the Audiencia against criollo critics of his administration to ensure stability after the bad news from Spain proved counterproductive. He was overthrown by a number of wealthy criollo aristocrats in August 1809. They claimed allegiance to, and probably also intended to rule in the name of, Ferdinand VII but without any odious participation of *gachupines* (as Peninsular Spaniards were derisively known). But by October, troops sent from Lima put down this undertaking as well. Reprisals were so harsh that a second, more widespread rebellion broke out two years later. The Quiteños now even produced a constitution for an independent state in 1812. They failed in spreading their rebellion outside their own province, however. Thus, it was easily put down late in the year.

The news coming from Spain about the dissolution of the Junta Central in 1810 had very serious consequences for the Empire. The establishment of governing *Juntas* in Caracas, Bogotá, Buenos Aires, and Santiago de Chile, soon after the message arrived, was a direct challenge to the whole colonial system. Set up with spontaneous popular backing in these important administrative and economic centers, the Juntas quickly tried to extend their control within the respective captaincy-general or viceroyalty. Thus, in late 1810, the troops of Buenos Aires, led by a Robbespierre-like lawyer by the name of Castelli, attempted the incorporation of Upper Peru. Castelli's mass excutions of prisoners proved counterproductive, however, and he was soundly defeated.

The Lima Viceroy now saw fit to restore Upper Peru to his Viceroyalty. Two more Argentine campaigns to conquer Upper Peru, in 1813 and 1815, were also routed by a Spanish general, Pezuela. In Chile,

Junta government, as in Buenos Aires, acted independently, even though some lip-service was still paid to the captive king. In October 1814, however, a military expedition sent from Lima succeeded in defeating the Chileans and restoring royal administration.

As we have just seen, the viceregal government in Lima displayed impressive counterrevolutionary force also in territories normally outside its jurisdiction, as Upper Peru, Chile, and Quito. The exceptionally vigorous Viceroy José Fernando de Abascal, who occupied this position between 1806 and 1816, undeniably helped to shape events. At the outset, the regular troops at his disposal were very scarce, but he used them and his militia units well. In Lima, as in Mexico, the viceregal bureaucracy was firmly entrenched. Together with the merchant elite it formed a complex of power which, for all the tension between gachupines and criollos, was much more tied to status quo than the administrative-commercial elites of the more marginal territories of the Empire.

But on local levels, unrest increased almost everywhere, even though outright revolts were rather few. One such place was Huánuco in the Central Sierra, where Indians and non-Indians were both involved, but for largely different motives. In Upper Peru, Castelli had tried to raise the Indians to revolt by using all kinds of demagoguery, including quechua versions of his proclamations. This apparently had a long-distance effect on the Indians of Huánuco, naturally fed up with the oppression that the administrative reforms had not removed. In their minds, Castelli's imaged fused with that of an Inca redeemer. At first, they invaded lands of the hacendados, unable or unwilling to distinguish between those of criollos and those of gachupines. Then, they also fought among themselves, poor against better-off, village against village. The grievances of local criollo traders, on the other hand, included restrictions on their hoarding for speculation agricultural produce obtained from the Indians.

Conspiracies and risings of this kind were no problem for Abascal. What really threatened his control was the well-meaning liberal policy of the Cádiz Cortes, which he tried to apply even though he loathed it. The Cortes, including Spanish American deputies, abolished the Indian tribute in 1811, mita in 1812, the Inquisition (at this time used as an instrument of political rather than religious repression) in 1813.

According to the Constitution of 1812, the cabildos were to be recruited by annual elections and were also to help in electing the deputies to be sent to the Cortes. In this way, the authority of the hitherto rather tame municipalities was greatly enhanced.

In Cuzco, in 1814, the "constitutionalist" criollo group, which in this way had obtained control over the cabildo, challenged the authority of the Audiencia. Led by the three Angulo brothers, the criollo and mestizo militants persuaded the old Indian Brigadier Pumacahua to become the nominal leader of the revolution. He was the same curaca who in 1780 had helped to crush the Tupac Amaru rebellion and had suppressed revolutionary riots as late as 1811. He had been greatly honored by the authorities (serving as an interim Intendent shortly before), but at the same time he was popular among the Indian masses. Thus, Indian support for the revolution was now secured; indeed, its very extent made the non-Indian revolutionaries scared. For a moment, Cuzco forces controlled Puno, Arequipa, and the Central Sierra. But Abascal and his generals handled the situation with skill. By mid-1815, the patriots had been defeated and all the leaders, including the old curaca-brigadier, put to death. When Abascal handed over his exacting job to Pezuela in 1816, all Spanish America, apart from the River Plate, appeared to be solidly under the now absolute Spanish monarch's control once more.

But great ambitions had been raised among the criollos, much blood had been shed — not least by the King's judges and firing squads — much property had been destroyed, people's attitudes had been greatly changed. All this could not be undone. Under the surface, the bitterness of the various socioracial and economic groups increasingly directed itself against colonial rule as such. In Upper Peru, guerrilla warfare was also alive even if most of the foci (*republiquetas*) had already been extinguished by 1816. A diary of one of the participants has come to light. It shows that, despite their struggle for survival, the *guerrilleros* were concerned with feuds among themselves. Brutal, senseless killings, innumerable acts of treason are faithfully, naïvely recorded. At the same time, these ruffians used the same rhetorical language as the intellectual leaders of the revolution. They make abundant use of concepts like "patria" and "freedom"[6]

e. Independence Imposed

After Napoleon's defeat in 1814, the British loyalty toward the wartime Spanish ally gradually eroded because of the attraction that independent Spanish American nations offered for English trade. Not without a sense of premonition, Abascal observed in 1816 that in case the revolutionaries ever obtained their goal of Independence from Spain,

that very moment would mean enslavement to the English because the immature state of America coincides with the despotic rule of this Nation over the seas which the transports of colonial produce to the places of consumption have to cross.[7]

English financial aid and volunteers helped Simón Bolívar to wage his final liberation of Venezuela and New Granada, beginning in 1817. Under the Cúcuta Constitution of 1821, he became President of the strongly centralized Republic of Colombia, successor of the Viceroyalty of New Granada. Guayaquil, in October 1820, ousted local authorities and established a revolutionary Junta. Bolívar sent his most trusted lieutenant, José Antonio de Sucre, there to ensure Guayaquil's security and incorporation with Colombia. In May 1822, Sucre also succeeded in crushing loyalist troops in the highlands at the battle of Pichincha near Quito.

Meanwhile, Buenos Aires had given up its efforts to defeat the loyalists in Upper Peru. Instead, General José de San Martín showed his superiority as a strategist by choosing another route for breaking loyalist power. In 1817 his army crossed the Andes near the city of Mendoza. After a couple of battles, the freedom of Chile was secured. But, like Bolívar, San Martín was perfectly aware that Independence of any territory in Spanish America would be precarious as long as the Peruvian bulwark had not been conquered. To attack Peru from the Pacific, the invaluable aid of a British naval veteran, Lord Cochrane, was enlisted; he helped create the Chilean navy. The navy transported 4500 troops from Valparaiso to Pisco on the Peruvian coast (a three to five day march from Lima) in August 1820. From the plantations, several hundred slaves joined San Martín's army to achieve their personal freedom. But San Martín did not attack the viceregal capital. He obviously wanted the Peruvians themselves to rise in revolt. In the

Central Sierra, several bands of guerrilleros were, indeed, active, but their number was small. Though mostly Mestizo, there was also an Indian curaca, Ignacio Quispe Ninavilca, among them.

At any rate, San Martín cut off Lima from the north as well. Now a number of north Peruvian cabildos were induced to declare for independence. Accused of inaction, Viceroy Pezuela was deposed in 1821 by younger military commanders. The new Viceroy, La Serna, was more to the taste of the new liberal regime in Spain, but from now on loyalist ranks were unavoidably split between the partisans of absolutism and constitutionalists.

In July 1821, La Serna abandoned Lima, withdrawing into the southern Sierra. The Lima elites now declared for Independence (July 28) and San Martín was given the powers of Protector. With his conservative, even monarchist, leanings he seemed to be a guarantee against social upheaval. Yet San Martín, an excellent, honorable man, wanted Independence to mean something for the oppressed as well. He declared free the child of any slave born on or after Independence Day. He also abolished Indian tribute and mita (as the Spanish Cortes also had). This action had little effect, as most lived in loyalist territories. Under the influence of his Argentine collaborator Monteagudo, San Martín also had the gachupines expelled, a step necessarily involving a considerable flight of capital and a loss of knowhow.[8] San Martín's position in Lima was also weakened by the severe problems involved in supplying some 65,000 inhabitants. His bold issuance of paper money to overcome the lack of specie proved to be an utter failure. Opposition to his rule, foreign-dominated as it was, increased. Liberals such as the cunning cleric Luna Pizarro and the ideological Sánchez Carrión detested his monarchical stance.

Therefore, San Martín's bargaining position was very weak when he had his famous encounter with Bolívar in Guayaquil in July 1822. He reluctantly had to accept Guayaquil's incorporation with Colombia; he was unable to make Bolívar accept monarchy as a solution to Peruvian woes, and he could not secure the military assistance he needed to defeat La Serna. As a result, San Martín returned to Lima to lay down his powers and went into European exile. His was a dramatic decision but not as enigmatic as often presented by historians.

The Junta replacing San Martín was itself replaced by a criollo aristocrat, José de la Riva Agüero, as President. He was aided by criollo officers who had recently deserted loyalist ranks, such as Andrés Santa

Cruz and Agustín Gamarra. Apart from trying to maintain the privileges of the elites these new masters of Peru began struggling for
personal power. Treason became the order of the day. Soon, two patriot
factions were fighting each other — that of "Presidents" Riva Agüero

Figure 5.10. San Martín (l) and Bolívar (r) as seen by a contemporary Peruvian painter, José Gil de Castro. (Bolívar reproduction courtesy of the Venezuelan consulate, New York City.)

and Torre Tagle. Fortunately for them, the issue of liberalism was dividing loyalist ranks as well. The absolutist General Olañeta established a fiefdom of his own in Upper Peru.

From Ecuador Bolívar somberly watched events, when not enjoying the passionate affair with the beautiful criolla Manuela Sáenz, wife of an English physician. Reluctantly, he finally decided to intervene. Once a fiery Jacobin, Bolívar had already taken on a rather disillusioned, conservative stance when entering the Andean scene. In Peru, his desperation often reached extremes. "There is not one good man in the place, except if he be good for nothing. Those who are capable behave like a legion of demons," he exasperatedly wrote to Vice President Santander in Bogotá in 1824.[9] Yet, one Peruvian, Sánchez Carrión, served him loyally and well. His own organizational genius also prevailed against all problems. From the northern highlands, his troops, mainly Colombian, pushed southward. A brief cavalry clash at Junín, fought with swords, not guns, was a loyalist defeat. While Bolívar now liberated Lima, Sucre on December 7, 1824, won the decisive battle of the Wars of Independence at Ayacucho, followed by the surrender of La Serna's entire army. La Serna's resistance had been undermined by Olañeta's absolutist regime in Upper Peru, supported by the local criollo aristocracy which had threatened the loyalists in their back. But in 1825 he, too, fell in a battle with the forces of Sucre. After heroic resistance, the loyalist garrison at Callao surrendered the following year. The Wars of Independence were over.

Triggered by European rather than New World events, Independence had been *imposed from outside* rather than achieved from within in countries like Peru, Ecuador, and Bolivia. The wars had largely been fought by Argentine, Chilean, and Colombian troops. But they should also be seen as civil wars. Out of 9000 loyalists in the battle of Ayacucho, only 500 had been born in Spain. On both sides, poor mestizos and Indians were the bulk of the fighting force, together with Negro slaves who obtained their freedom this way, if they survived. Also, spontaneous actions by patriot Indian guerrillas should not be forgotten.

But the real winners were the criollo aristocrats and the gaudily uniformed generals. They really knew how to turn the new situation to their advantage. The gachupín rivals had now been removed. While paying lip service to the wonderful ideals of liberalism and nationalism, the old/new elite soon proved that the unequal colonial social structure could be maintained, even strengthened within the new republican, national framework.

The reactionary attitudes were deeply entrenched. When, as early as 1809, a Peruvian representative was sent to the Junta Central, the Lima cabildo instructed him to work for the abolition of the Intendancies, the reduction of the sales tax, and the renewed legalization of the repartos, so favorable to Lima merchant interests. Their ambivalent attitude toward the Indians and mixed-bloods also expressed itself on many occasions. When, in the Cortes of Cádiz, Peninsular liberals wanted to exclude the non-white population as a basis for parliamentary representation, the Spanish American deputies demanded that the total population be included. In this way they would of course be able to outvote the Spaniards. But the Peruvian deputies did not want the Indians to exercise the franchise, even less be eligible because of, as one of them put it, "the grave disadvantages which equality of this sort would have, notably in Peru."[10]

Against this background, the concepts of "patria" and "freedom," so abundantly used, deserve keen critical scrutiny. The cultural dimension of patria may have been more determined than its geographical limits. It expressed "Americanism" as opposed to things Spanish but the Indians were probably excluded or tacitly ignored. Their situation probably worsened despite the efforts of both San Martín and Bolívar to help them. Bolívar, in 1825, writes from Cuzco: "I intend to help them all I can: first as a matter of humanity, second, because it is their right, and finally, becuase doing good costs nothing and is worth much."[11] Like San Martín and the Cortes he proclaimed their freedom from mita and personal service, to no avail. On the other hand, when, in a liberal move, he made the Indians of the communities individual owners of their parcels of land, clever hacendados would soon use this as a device to cheat the Indians of them. In Upper Peru, the tribute, after being abolished by the Cortes, was reintroduced by Ferdinand VII under the euphemistic name of *contribución* in 1815. Its suppression in 1825 would last for only two years. After all, it contributed 30 to 40 percent of regular government revenues. The abolition of Negro slavery, initiated by San Martín in Peru and Bolívar in Ecuador through laws of free birth, would also prove a very lengthy process. In general terms, post-Independence social legislation would not just perpetuate the traditional gap between social theory and social reality but actually widen it.

The wars obviously implied prolonged sufferings for people of all social strata, but especially those already poor. Though pitched battles were small-size, irregular warfare and executions probably killed more. In a small Ecuadorean town, the male population fell by 45 percent between 1780 and 1825, the female population by only 29 percent. This does suggest the role of war casualties. For longer or shorter periods, people from the cities sought refuge in the countryside, considered less unsafe. In the highland province of Conchucos and elsewhere north of Lima, which had Mestizo majorities in the 1790s, a reversion to "Indian" majority had taken place in the later 1820s. This was probably related to economic decay and the destruction of war. Cholos and mestizos who had become exceedingly poor may have been classified as "Indians" by the authorities.

The wars were, indeed, destructive from an economic point of view. The mining industry was virtually destroyed, in Upper Peru as well as around Cerro de Pasco, which had been the site of almost constant fighting from 1820 through 1824. At Potosí, the dwindling fortunes of the azogueros were tapped through one forced loan after another. The plantations suffered from acute lack of labor when slaves were drafted or deserted. Textile production, already on the wane, suffered severely from the competition with imported English cloth. As early as 1808 – 1811, when Britain admittedly was excluded from the markets of continental Europe, a third of English exports were destined for Spanish America, more often than not as contraband. Because of patriot corsairs and other problems of supply, even the strict Viceroys of Lima had to tolerate or give licenses of trade to many English and other foreign merchant vessels. In 1821, the patriot government naturally opened the port of Callao to all trade with friendly nations. The value of imports from Britain boomed. On the other hand, according to the British consul in Lima, "commercial capital" there totaled some 15 million pesos in 1800 while in 1826 it had dwindled to less than 1 million. The flight of capital had taken on major proportions. Between 1819 and 1825 an estimated total of 27 million pesos were shipped abroad from Lima on British ships, only part of which were payments for imports actually received. Also, enormous, high-interest debts for the purchase of war materials had been contracted abroad. All these were the realities the new States had to cope with, as they were built up from the ruins.

VI.

The Hope of Liberalism; Realities of Caudillism

Since the 1960s, we have been witnessing the independence of one country after another in Africa and Asia. At times, this independence has come as the result of protracted, destructive struggle. Although these new nations were constructed on the model of Western political democracy, in most cases, they have become more or less crude one-party states or have experienced the emergence of military dictatorship. These latter systems have the inherent weakness of recurrent succession crises resolved by force of arms. Why should one colonel feel less qualified to rule the nation for the benefit of his relatives, friends, or tribe than another? From this new perspective, we should be far less puzzled by the same phenomenon occurring in Latin America than earlier observers were.

a. The External Impact

In our three Andean countries, the destructive impact of war, in material as well as spiritual terms, was probably no less than in Zaïre or Angola. In both cases, educated, professional people formed small minorities, mentally distant from the conditions and outlook of the masses. The gap between the export economy inherited from colonial times and village subsistence activities was similarly wide. Dictatorship was an almost inevitable way of filling the power void left by colonialism.

Yet the process of early national development in Peru, Bolivia, and Ecuador must above all be considered within the broader political and economic context of that time. In the political sphere, France had just completed its extraordinary revolutionary-imperial cycle (1789–1815), providing a variety of constitutional models, apart from that already given by the United States. Meanwhile, Britain, through the Industrial Revolution, had established the basis for a long-lasting economic hegemony overseas. In its long struggle with France, the British navy proved second to none. Both liberal and conservative ideas, of mixed Anglo-French origin, would find immediate response among the elites of the new countries; meanwhile, British trade, followed at a distance by that of the United States and continental European countries, less economically advanced, began a transformation of the Andean relationship to the outer world and the ways of life of the upper and middle strata.

At the outset, the British were extremely optimistic about the economic potential of the new republics they had cautiously helped to create. Toward the mid-1820s a great number of mining companies were set up to exploit the supposedly inexhaustible mineral resources of countries like Bolivia (the former Upper Peru) and Peru itself. The largely speculative boom did not take into account high production costs as a result of war-time destruction and, in the case of silver, the rapidly rising cost of mercury which had to be imported because Huancavelica's output had been reduced to a trifle. Instead, the agents sent out from London dreamt about the application of new machinery difficult even to transport to the mines and brought, at great expense, "model miners" from Germany and Cornwall only to find that Indian miners, in this harsh environment, did a better job. In 1825, speculations led to a collapse at the London stock exchange and the mining agents returned home, some of them to write travel books which remain the only lasting results of the first British venture into production in the Andean countries (tables 6.1, 6.2).

However, until mid-century, the Andean countries remained economically interesting to the British, mainly as markets for industrial goods — especially textiles — rather than for what they produced. We have to keep in mind, also, that the period between 1815 and 1850 was one of a relatively depressed business climate in the North Atlantic

economic sphere. As soon as independence threw open the Pacific
ports to external trade, the British, with their oversupplied warehouses, almost immediately glutted the new but in reality narrow

Table 6.1
British Exports to Peru in Pound Sterling, 1818–1825

1818	3.149
1819	30
1820	39.322
1821	127.498
1822	112.489
1823	551.771
1824	430.950
1825	602.770

SOURCE: Estimate by R.A. Humphreys. Notice that in 1821–23 52.6 percent of the exports went to
the port of Arica instead of Callao/Lima.

Table 6.2
Development of the Export Economies During the Second Quarter of Nineteenth Century

Cocoa Exports yearly from Guayaquil in "Cargas" (muleloads)[a]		Bolivian Silver Production. Five-year-periods. Thousands of ounces.[b]		Peruvian Exports to France and Britain in constant pounds sterling[c]	
1820	130.000	1825-1829	10.254	1827	114.263
1825	89.000	1830-1834	11.745	1828	98.384
1833	83.000	1835-1839	9.564	1829	101.174
1834	136.000	1840-1845	9.188	1830	112.332
1835	170.000	1845-1849	7.424	1831	65.729
1836	105.000			1832	74.943
1838	89.000			1833	50.943
1839	150.000			1834	134.656
1840	141.000			1835	155.470
1842	83.000			1836	153.522
				1837	296.900
				1838	218.478
				1839	274.056
				1840	340.204
				1841	363.360
				1842	407.950
				1843	444.835
				1844	459.626
				1845	620.014

[a]Hamerly 1973: 122 [b]Estimates by Mitre 1977: 278 [c]Bonilla 1980: 22.

markets. "On entering a house in Lima," an English traveler reports, "almost every object reminded me of England; the windows were glazed with English glass. . . . the brass furniture and ornaments on the commodes, tables, chairs, etc. were English. . . .the linen and cotton dresses of the females, and the cloth coats, cloaks, etc. of the men were all English. . . . even the kitchen utensils, if of iron, were English."[1] Thus, the British introduced completely new patterns of consumption into the urban upper and middle strata. The impact on domestic artisans is easy to guess. The British merchants also learned henceforth to proceed more cautiously in order not to hurt themselves.

As a consequence of independence, the commercial link with the Iberian Peninsula had been cut off; Spanish-born merchants were forced out of business and even expelled. One of the English in Lima at the time says that on May 2, 1822, some 600 Spaniards in Lima, "of all ranks. . . were dragged out of their beds at a moment's warning, without being allowed to take even a change of linen with them" and forced to leave their Peruvian families behind. "The old and infirm, each strapped behind a soldier, were carried on horse back; the remainder. . . were marched on foot to Callao, to be embarked."[2] The places of the Spaniards were, on the whole, taken by the foreigners. By 1824 there were twenty British merchant houses established in Lima and no less than sixteen British trade agencies at Arequipa. In 1836, a Swedish commercial agent reported that the major merchants of Lima included four British firms (led by "Gibbs, Crawley and Son"), two North American ones, two French, and one Spanish enterprise. "Of native merchants, not a single one is engaged in foreign trade." In Guayaquil, as in Valparaiso, the Gibbs house also played a leading role; but the North American "Switser et Co." was at least connected with two native merchants.[3] Needless to say, overseas navigation, and also that between the various ports along the South American Pacific coast, was carried out mostly by foreign ships.

British and other foreign merchants began to function within a traditional commercial system which had been built up on the basis of a long series of credits linking the regional center/harbor with smaller merchants and producers far up in the interior. With their preference for cash transactions, the British caused considerable damage to that system. As touched upon already, even though customs dues on for example foreign textiles were quite high, the marketing of English cloth and other merchandise combined quality with a reasonable price. Thus it proved extremely harmful to native production. For the crude products of the obrajes, already in trouble at the end of the colonial period, this competition sounded the knell of death. More seriously, from a social point of view, the income and numbers of urban artisans dropped. To take one example, even in a faraway tiny provincial town of the Cuzco region, the number of artisans fell from 42 in 1824 to 25 in 1830. In Bolivia, in 1846 their number has been estimated at less than 1 percent of those economically active. The harbor and area of Guayaquil also offers a different economic environment during this period because cocoa exports expanded. Yet, even there, the artisans were those most adversely affected by rising living costs as they were not able to raise the prices on their products.

During the Wars of Independence, Britain, in particular, had granted extensive loans to the governments of the South American republics. These were used mainly for defense and administrative expenses. Because the interest rates were also quite high and government efficiency at a low, it is not at all surprising that the republics (including those of Peru and Ecuador but remarkably enough not that of Bolivia) found it hard to meet their debt obligations. These problems and the political feuds and civil wars added to the growing disenchantment of Britain and other foreign countries with those on the faraway Pacific coast, however desperately their elites tried to emulate European patterns in their modes of consumption and their cultural and political ideas.

b. Political Models and Realities

As Argentine historian Halperín Donghi points out, it always proved "hard to adapt European doctrines to an entirely different context"; in the case of the new Spanish American republics, "the intellectual disarray of postrevolutionary Europe after the defeat of the revolutionary movement of 1789 compounded the problem." Even more striking than the ideological clashes along liberal-conservative lines was the ambivalence of the new elites, simultaneously accepting and rejecting the outcome of their own revolution. The principles of popular sovereignty and of equality were accepted but, in fact, slavery as well as Indian tribute and submission was allowed to persist in only slightly modified external forms.[4]

The situation of the Church suffered significant change, but not so much because of the influence of French and Spanish anti-clerical liberalism. The main factor behind the weakening of the Church was its own political split during the struggle for independence and the stubborn refusal of the Papacy to recognize the *fait accompli.* Thus, the hierarchy was weakened at the very moment when new political masters, from Bolívar onward, were continuing the Bourbon policy of reducing the nonreligious influence of the Church, especially that of the Orders. At the same time, liberal-minded priests, like the Peruvian Luna Pizarro, were conspicuous among the new parliamentarians.

In the spheres of social and economic thought, the collision of liberal free trade with traditional mercantilism and protectionism usually produced compromises. The belief in superiority of individual ownership to that of corporations was, however, beyond doubt also for figures otherwise in most regards quite conservative, such as Bolívar and San Martín. In 1824, the former, at Trujillo in northern Peru, issued his famous decree, ordering the sale of state lands at a 33 percent discount. As far as the Indian communities were concerned, their general right to the land should be respected but individualized. Soon, however, Bolívar saw himself obliged to forbid the new Indian proprietors from selling their parcels before 1850, as a safeguard against the loss of their lands. Entails (*mayorazgo*) were suppressed in Peru in 1829.

In the case of Church property, Bolívar and his successors found it necessary to proceed more cautiously, but beginning in 1826 convents with fewer than eight monks had their lands confiscated and their yield reallotted to support educational or charitable institutions (*Sociedades de Beneficiencia*). In the new republic of Bolivia, its first President, General Sucre, was in fact quite active and successful in reducing ecclesiastical wealth without major problems. The full impact of *desamortización* (as the privatizing of property was called), on Indian communities in particular, would not be felt until considerably later. The well-intentioned decrees of San Martín, Bolívar, and others designed to eliminate forced labor and services had little, if any, impact. They either confirmed a process already well under way (as in the case of (*mita*) or the abuses they were supposed to prohibit would continue unabated throughout the nineteenth and even into part of the twentieth century.

In 1821, San Martín decreed that, from the day of Independence, July 28 of that year, no Peruvian children would be born slaves. Faced with the violent opposition of coastal landowners, however, he soon had to let the young "libertos" be placed at the disposal of their respective landlords until they reached the age of 24. In practice, this simply meant a continuation of slavery; in 1839, this "tutelage" was extended until they reached 50. Even the slave trade (mainly with Colombia) was legalized once more in 1835. In Bolivia, Negro slaves were always very few so the issue was not an important one. On the other hand, in coastal Ecuador, there were already fewer than 2000 slaves by 1825. They were little by little replaced with free laborers, some of whom were Indians from the highlands. Only in coastal Peru did slavery remain an important economic reality; thus, abolition failed.

An experienced English traveler paid a visit to a profitable sugar plantation on the northern coast in the early twenties; he found the slaves well fed and rather well treated, much better off, he exclaims, than the "half-starved and hard-worked state of a day-labourer" of Britain. On the other hand, another European visitor, Flora Tristan, a famous Paris intellectual of her day, was told by a compatriot who ran a sugar plantation near Lima that the whip was a necessary stimulus for his 900 slaves and saw for herself the slave women imprisoned for having let their babies die.[5] Even with such methods, slaves did not reproduce, however, and in the end, slavery was doomed.

Against the backdrop of what happened to the great political issues of the time, constitutional and political developments can be briefly summarized. The Peruvian constitution of 1823 was a pathetically unrealistic exercise in liberal parliamentarism, almost immediately put aside by Bolívar's stern, authoritarian rule. In 1825, his trusted lieutenant, José Antonio Sucre, sent with his army to Upper Peru, gave in to the demands of the regional elites that they determine the political destiny of what so far had been the jurisdiction of the Audiencia of Charcas. On receiving the news in Lima, Bolívar was outraged because, as he reminded Sucre, he firmly believed that the basis of the new nations should, on principle, be the Spanish Viceroyalties as of 1810. Upper Peru should therefore naturally form part of the nation succeeding the Viceroyalty of the River Plate. Yet on this crucial issue, the will of Sucre and the Upper Perivians, who had fought their first struggles against colonial rule as early as 1809, prevailed.

To soothe Bolívar, they named the new republic after him and asked him to write a draft for the new Bolivian constitution. He did so in a way which reflected his growing disillusion with the revolutions for which nobody was more responsible than himself, and his increasingly reactionary ideas. According to the constitution of 1826, virtually all power would be placed in the hands of a lifetime president, on the model of the constitution which Napoleon had imposed on France in 1799. Bolívar imposed the same type of constitution on Peru, and he started to play with the idea of an all-encompassing Andean federation. Yet, dangerous events in Gran Colombia, his power base, forced him to return there in 1826.

By now, the Peruvian elites, and soon those of Bolivia, as well, had had enough of their liberators and their Colombian or Venezuelan armies. A new Peruvian constitution was enacted in 1828, based this time on that of the United States, with universal suffrage, restricted however to those able to read and write and not of dependent status. This meant, of course, a rather small segment of the total population. Sucre had made admirable efforts to establish some kind of new order in Bolivia, and keen British observers at that time found it to be more promising than the neighboring republics. Yet, he first had to face a mutiny in which he was wounded, then a Peruvian attack under a native general, Augustín Gamarra, and finally growing internal opposition. Disgusted, Sucre withdrew in 1829; back in Gran Colombia he had to use his great military talent to prevent, instead, the Peruvians from wrestling the earlier Audiencia of Quito or part of it from that Republic, now under Bolívar's dictatorial rule. Sucre was soon to be assassinated, however, and Bolívar, stricken with consumption, gave up his control of the government and died on his way into exile in 1830.

At that moment, Gran Colombia was already falling apart. In Quito, the Venezuelan-born military commander, General Juan José Flores, easily set up another republic of his own, like his colleague Juan Antonio Páes had done in Venezuela. As in the case of Bolivia, the

Republic of Ecuador was thus based on an Audiencia of colonial times, with borders ill defined and national consciousness, apart from misgivings about strangers, as yet to be created.

At this time, it became clear that the eloquent and sometimes learned lawyers and priests of the Constituent Assemblies and National Congresses held no real power, if they ever did. Also, the prelates, the senior bureaucracy, and the leading merchants tied to the trade with Spain had been seriously weakened in the process of political change. Instead, the regular armies and to some extent militia units held a monopoly on armed force, which spelled political power. Generals who managed to control their own troops were destined to become the political leaders on national or regional levels. Their rivalries, intrigues, and occasionally open fights made for a political history as full of names and events as it is ultimately tedious. In Peru and Bolivia, these leaders were now native-born, at times of rather humble birth and darkish skin, and thus, as such, not eligible for elite status in society. They usually started their military career on the royalist side but were wise enough to switch sides before the battle of Ayacucho.

Of all those *caudillos*, Andrés de Santa Cruz, of Upper Peruvian mestizo origin, was clearly more capable and far-sighted than the rest. He came to power in Bolivia in 1829 where, with considerable success, he continued Sucre's work of national organization. In 1836, he felt strong enough to pursue an ambitious scheme, forcing Peru to accept confederation with its Southern neighbor in a way that would allow for the supremacy of the Southern highlands, knit together traditionally by close links of trade. For this purpose Peru was divided into a Northern State, with Lima as its capital, and a Southern one, the capital of which was Cuzco, the old capital of the Incas from whom Santa Cruz claimed to descend. In Arequipa, with its strong involvement in trade with the Altiplano, the Confederation received enthusiastic support. At the same time, undoubtedly, this new political creation seriously threatened the power balance that at that time had come into being in South America. This is best shown by the adverse reaction of the neighbors to the South. The Chileans feared that the impressive growth of Valparaiso as a main trade center on the Pacific would now be eclipsed by the Confederation's main port, Callao. They went to war, joining Gamarra and other military rivals of Santa Cruz; the Argentines, too, started war. In 1839, Santa Cruz was defeated and forced to leave Bolivia. In 1841, the irrepressible Gamarra once again attacked Bolivia but his forces were soundly routed, and he was killed in action. Since then, Bolivia's nationhood, though sometimes questioned, has been a reality.

Yet, the handicaps and vulnerability of the new nation became increasingly evident. The territory of the new country was about twice as large as that of the present Republic but consisted largely of desert or jungles. Navigable waterways were lacking to the Amazon as well as to the River Plate basin. The jurisdiction of Charcas did extend to the Pacific but only through long stretches of desert where the only port, little Cobija, suffered from an extreme lack of fresh water. A much more natural Pacific outlet was Arica, on the Peruvian side. From the City of La Paz, the journey to Arica took seven or eight days, as compared with more than three weeks to Cobija. However, all efforts of Sucre and others to make the Peruvians yield on the Arica issue proved in vain.

Silver production, which had once made Potosí the "richest Crown jewel" of the monarchy of Spain and had experienced somewhat of a revival in the eighteenth century, had shrunk drastically after the war and continued to drop more slowly until the late 1840's. Destroyed machinery and lack of capital made the output very small indeed. Almost half of the silver came from the scavenging of slag piles left from the glorious past. Agriculture was almost entirely of the subsistence variety and did not yield enough produce for export. Only in the *Yungas*, the forested Northern mountain slopes, did the collection of chinchona bark (for the preparation of quinine) and coca provide items for outside markets. The meager income of government rested heavily on the *contribución* exacted from the communities which held most of the Indian population (half of the total in 1846) and also on a colonial device for draining off the incomes of mining entrepreneurs (forced sale of the produce at a sub-market price to the so-called *Bancos de rescate*). Contraband was the logical answer.

In Peru, silver mining had hit a low in 1823, in the midst of the war. In 1832 production was 10 times higher but still 20 percent less than in 1820. To begin with, chinchona bark and hides helped maintain exports. In the late 1830s, the trade volume began a steady climb based on cotton and nitrate from the coast, wool and copper from the Sierra.

In the 1840s, these products would themselves be eclipsed, however, by *guano*, an incomparable fertilizer since pre-Hispanic times for which modernizing Western European agriculture was now providing a rapidly expanding market. After decades of relative stagnation this would revolutionize Peruvian economy and politics, with important social consequences as well.

In Ecuador, Flores was able to establish a firmer control than in the republics to the south. Military rivals were crushed. Yet the age-old rivalry between Quito and its harbor, Guayaquil, increased with the growth of the latter under the impact of high-level cocoa exports and trade in general. While the people of Guayaquil believed that their great contribution to the nation's income was not wisely spent by Quito bureaucrats, highlanders saw Guayaquil as a monopolistic bottleneck. This economic-geographical contrast also reflected itself in political attitudes. While liberalism had its center in Guayaquil, Quito formed the bulwark of the conservatives. Thanks to his continued control of the army, Flores, however, could afford the luxury of letting a civilian, a liberal political rival, Vicente Rocafuerte, be the President in the later 1830s. This competent politician was kept quite busy during his term to improve education and communications, both sorely needed. Afterward, Flores returned for another term, but he was finally ousted by a liberal revolt in 1845. The country then lapsed into an utterly unstable but mostly liberal-dominated period that would last until another strongman, of a different stripe, seized power in 1859.

From the days of the Wars of Independence, political rhetoric had flowered in all the Spanish-American republics with "fatherland" (*Patria*) and "Liberty" as the main ingredients. The caudillos made lavish use of this vocabulary and required homage from legislators and local functionaries. This did not hide, their usually pragmatic political approach and sheer lust for power. "Where nobody is able to *govern*," a European agent exclaims when talking about the Andean countries in the 1830s, "the throne is occupied by he who, at the least, knows how to *command*."[6]

The partisans of the caudillos were held together more by links of personal loyalty than by political programs or positions held. Patron – client relationships traditionally played an important role in Spanish American society, often reinforced by ritual kinship (*compadrazgo*). Nor should the informal power system of the caudillos be regarded in isolation. On the parish level, as well, effective control was exercised by local strongmen, known in the Andean countries as *gamonales*. They were usually resident landowners with personal retinues or militia units to back up their local economic power. Even though the national caudillo was forceful enough, the weakening of the bureaucracy on all levels after Independence was a fact. Against this background, what occurred during the first decades of national government was probably a certain fragmentation of power benefiting the rural *gamonales*. Provincial cities tended to lose population as a consequence of diminished trade, by turn the result of the decay of mining, new national boundaries, customs barriers, or other factors. Paradoxically, while the harbors and capitals became increasingly cosmopolitan in outlook and appearance, the isolation of inland areas apparently increased. This is why, as already touched upon, many poor mestizos now, from the point of view of tax collectors at the least, reverted to "Indian" status.

Rural society might appear self-sufficient and "feudal"; yet our own research on land sales in the Cuzco region between 1826 and 1869 shows that they were very frequent indeed. They were facilitated by extensive ads in local newspapers, of which there were surprisingly many. But hacienda sales, because of the indebtedness to mainly religious institutions, as in colonial times, also meant that no more than about 60 percent of land prices were paid in cash. At the time, a bad harvest might be enough to make a new owner unable to meet the heavy interest obligations that he had assumed, thus leading once again to a sale.

Living conditions varied from area to area, even valley to valley, in the vast Andean space. As yet, however, we can only catch a few glimpses of this. The Peruvian province of Azángaro in Puno, bordering on Lake Titicaca, has been minutely described, during the second half of the 1820s by one of its native sons, José Domingo Choquehuanca. A population of some 50,000 souls, dependent on a declining pastoral economy, encompassed a total of 70 privately owned haciendas. They had an average yield of only 137 pesos. The 40 properties of the Church were almost twice as profitable. In this environment the person who gained between 1500 and 2000 pesos annually was "rich." Two priests and one layman did. On the whole, only priests were able to save money. Most mestizos and Indians were poor but *indios forasteros* "regarded merely as cattle, were destined to obey." Even so, Indian peasants held more than half of all the cattle and sheep. In the district of Paucartambo, Cuzco—with less than 400 non-Indian inhabitants—only one person earned more than 1000 pesos in 1830; but 50 haciendas yielded an average of 172 pesos. More than half of total income above 50 pesos came from the possession of land. Tenancy, commerce, and mule-bearing (arriería) counted for most of the rest. Even though some of these non-Indians were clearly very poor, there were no servants among them. This was an obligation to be performed by the Indians in turn (*pongo*).

In Bolivia, in 1846, according to an extraordinary "social scientist" for his time, José María Dalence, there were some 5000 haciendas and no less than 106,000 communities. These held three different categories of Indians, *comuneros* with land, (48,000 families), *agregados* with lesser parcels (58,000), and landless *forasteros* (32,000). On the haciendas, there were service tenants (*colonos:* 80,000 families). Their usufruct rights were hereditary; seldom would they be dismissed or leave voluntarily.

In tropical, export oriented Guayaquil, with its mobile, heterogeneous working population, basic conditions in the 1830s clearly differed widely. Out of a total of 1735 taxpayers in the city, as many as 20 earned more than 2000 pesos, another 22 more than 1000. More than 80 percent of the taxpayers earned less than 200 pesos, though. The total population of the city at this time may have reached some 12,000. Even in such a city, of easy access and considerable economic means, the cultivated, politically active elite was surely exceedingly small.[7]

Before mid-century, due mostly to the weakness of the bureaucracy, life in the Indian communities, for good and bad, was probably little affected by the "liberal reforms" intended to turn the *comunitarios* into independent small-size landowners on the liberal model. Recent research suggests, also, that in the Southern Andean highlands, where most of these communities were situated, the landowners did not expand their holdings at their expense to any considerable extent. There was simply no incentive for such expansionism during a time of economic stagnation. Peasants, especially those of Indian status, were exploited and controlled efficiently in so many other ways. If public works were needed, for instance the maintenance of roads and bridges, the Indians, if available, were those who had to perform them. Whenever soldiers had to be recruited, and that was often enough, young Indians were forced or tricked into service. In their own village, they were at the disposal of the priest and the gamonal. The parish priest was usually the wealthiest individual of his district, with an income based on a variety of fees with which he burdened the baptisms, marriages, and funerals of his parishioners, and during religious feasts. A traveler tells us that in a poor place called Andamarca on the Bolivian Altiplano, he saw the priest drawing much money from the Indians on the day of a Saint. "One of his principal emoluments was derived from the highest bidder for carrying the flag in the procession.... For a marriage among these poor people, this extortioner took ten dollars and a half; a christening was four reals; and a funeral was paid according to what could be extracted from the property of the deceased." It so happens that we have this very priest's statement to the authorities about his income (see table 6.3). It shows an annual total of 2103 pesos, only 400 pesos less than the salary of the Minister of the Interior.[8]

The other powerful person, at times backed up also by the spiritual authority of the priest, was the gamonal. The travelers of the time often and rightly praise the hospitality and cultured manners of many hacendados. But a curious and conscientious diarist accompanying a President/Caudillo on a triumphant journey through the South of Peru in

Table 6.3
Parish Income in Andamarca, Bolivia, 1826

Source	Amount	
	Pesos	*Reales*
21 fiestas at $26 each	340.0	
10 fiestas at $16 each	160.0	
12 fiestas at $12 each	144.0	
Marriages at $4	165.5	
Masses at $4 and $8	72.0	
20 funerals at $12	240.0	
10 funerals at $6	60.0	
Infant funerals at $3 and $4	140.0	
"Cabos de año" at $6 and $8	210.0	
14 "Renovaciones" at $2 each	126.0	
12 "Aguinaldos" at $4 each	24.0	
3 "Aguinaldos" at $4 each	12.0	
"Honrras" at $6 and $8	100.0	
Miscellaneous income	304.4	
TOTAL	2.103.1	

SOURCE: Lofstrom 1972: 122: "Cabos de año," "Renovaciones," "Aguinaldos" and "Honrras" represent various kinds of customary donations.

1834 gives us a revealing glimpse of what was probably a frequent phenomenon:

[The Village of Curahuasi] lacks water because though it possesses some, the Hacendado of Mollemolle [a sugar plantation], Don Cayetano Ocampo, has appropriated himself of the source of supply. When he finds fit, he lets the villagers suffer from thirst so they have to ask for water at the Hacienda, often to be rudely rebuffed.[9]

In Spanish America, as in Europe and North America, the second quarter of the nineteenth century was the heyday of literary and artistic romanticism. Perhaps, on the whole, brutality of men against men in the West tended to be somewhat less crude than during earlier and later eras. Even so, the danger of idealizing conditions during this period is close at hand, if you rely too much on contemporary witnesses. Yet, in countries like Peru, Bolivia, and Ecuador, economic stagnation may have made for somewhat lesser degrees of exploitation from above than would otherwise have been the case. Stagnation made paternalism easier both to afford and to accept.

VII.

Export Boom, War, and Defeat

In the course of the third quarter of the nineteenth century, the Andean countries, like the rest of Latin America, were integrated within a North Atlantic – dominated world economy which imposed a global division of labor. It became the clearly defined function of countries like Peru, Bolivia, and Ecuador to export certain staples for the expanding West European market. This crucial development was a consequence of the process of industrialization spreading out from Britain and Belgium, of the increased mobility of capital and population, greater technical knowledge, and improved transportation. The integration of overseas countries with the world market was facilitated by the rising European demand during this period, which corresponds to the ascending phase of the so-called second Kondratieff cycle, abruptly ended by the crisis of 1873. World trade increased by leaps and bounds. After 1873, during the descending phase of the cycle (until 1896), the economic expansion in Western Europe and the United States slowed down, while, on the other hand, in Latin America it generally picked up speed, under the impact of foreign investments. In the case of Peru and Bolivia, however, their defeat, at the hands of Chile in the Nitrate War of 1879 – 1883/4 temporarily halted their economic advance.

a. Export Boom

For decades, Peruvian guano enjoyed rising European demand until the point of exhaustion was reached and another fertilizer of Andean origin, nitrate, took over its role. As we shall see, apart from railroads, guano wealth produced no major economic changes. Both Ecuador and Peru were exporters of tropical agricultural commodities while Peru, like Bolivia, also depended on the export of mineral products. In neither case did trade expansion automatically spell development. In tropical agriculture, if not based on slave labor, low wages prevailed within the framework of traditional plantation society. In the mineral economies, the expansion triggered by the interplay of investments and exports merely led to the formation of enclaves, linked rather to their external markets than to the surrounding national society.

In 1840, German chemists analyzed samples of guano and discovered its extraordinary value as a fertilizer. In the current effort to raise the productivity of European agriculture, guano had a given place. It was far from easy, however to launch and operate guano exports from the main deposit on the Chincha islands off Pisco on the Central coast. In Peru, capital and entrepreneurship were scarce and labor hard to attract. Francisco Quiroz, a Peruvian entrepreneur, allied himself with British merchants, and paid the Peruvian government an advance to obtain temporary exclusive rights for the marketing of the product in Europe. Prices proved so advantageous that the government soon withdrew Quiroz's privilege and declared guano state property.

Foreign merchant houses such as Anthony Gibbs and Sons of London now took over the guano sales abroad with exclusive rights in their respective country. Under a system of consignment they paid cash advances to the Peruvian government, which retained the title to the product until the final sale. Guano receipts made it possible to reach an agreement with the foreign holders of Peruvian bonds, in default since 1825. Even more important, in 1850 the government was able to carry out the consolidation and conversion of the domestic national debt. In this way, Peruvian supply of capital increased and, favored by government policy, native contractors took over an increasing share of guano export and marketing from the foreign ones. Britain was by far the greatest customer, but North American sailing ships were the main carriers of the foul-smelling merchandise. Extraction was facilitated when in 1849 the government started to grant subsidies for the introduction of Chinese contract labor. Until suspended in 1875, this new slave trade brought some 90,000 coolies to Peru. Even though most were destined to work in coastal plantation agriculture, the labor force of some thousands on the Chincha islands filled a crucial need. Simultaneously, guano revenues were used by the government to finance the abolition of Negro slavery through the award of generous compensation to the former owners. Thus, the freeing of 25,500 slaves cost a total of 7.6 million pesos. Also, the *contribución de indígenas*, which so far had formed one of the main revenues of the treasury, was abolished in 1854. Both measures gave President Ramón Castilla the liberal aura that he needed. The old tax structure was, in fact, almost wholly replaced by a dependence on guano revenues, paid in advance, and customs dues. Thus in 1868, a sharp financial crisis set in. A young politician, Nicolás Piérola, then Minister of Finance, boldly ended the consignment system. Instead, he concluded a sales contract for 2 million tons of guano with the Paris finance house of Dreyfus, which ensured steady income for several years.

The Dreyfus contract permitted the government to engage in large-scale national railroad construction, led by the dynamic American promoter Henry Meiggs. With American machinery, 6000 Chinese, and thousands of Chilean and Bolivian workers, Meiggs built several railroads from the coast inland, with bridges and tunnels which crossed the Andes at altitudes of as much as 16,000 feet. No wonder they proved exceedingly costly.

To finance rising costs the government had to contract a great external debt. In 1872, the new government of Manuel Pardo faced another severe financial crisis. He was backed up by the domestic guano capitalists who had been bypassed by the Dreyfus contract, the core of his so-called Civilista Party. Pardo tried fiscal reform, but the world-wide crisis of 1873 and the diminishing guano supply forced him to suspend service on the Peruvian foreign debt in 1876. State bankruptcy was a fact. From now on, the Peruvian government began to rely instead on income generated by the rapidly increasing exports of nitrate from the Southern desert. The deposits were nationalized in 1875. (Table 7.1 and fig. 7.1 show Peruvian exports to Britain and France during this period.)

Twelve million tons of guano were exported from 1840 to 1880. No less than 60 percent of the income accrued to the Peruvian state (1847–73). More than half of that impressive revenue was used to inflate the armed forces and bureaucracy. Railroads absorbed a fifth. They would not pay off until later on. Most of the profits made by individual

Peruvians probably went into conspicuous consumption and urban housing. Yet some found its way into the modernization of plantation agriculture on the coast where, among other things, steam engines were introduced. Taking the long view, guano wealth was on the whole a development opportunity missed. However, the infrastructural and attitudinal problems faced would be easily recognized in any of the oil-rich Arab desert countries of today. (Table 7.1 shows the expenditures made by the Peruvian state during this period.)

In contrast to the dramatic story of guano, the evolution of wool trade in the south progressed steadily from the 1830s until the Pacific War. It was handled by foreign merchant firms residing in Arequipa. They bought a great deal of the wool at large fairs, such as that of Vilque in the highland of Puno. For a couple of weeks each year, this sleepy village was transformed into a busy center of trade, with some 10,000 to 12,000 people gathered there from Cuzco and Bolivia, and even Argentina. The demand covered the sheep wool provided by local *estancieros* as well as the finer alpaca wool put up for sale by the Indian communities. The sales agents of the firms (*rescatistas*) also went to the Indian dwellings to get hold of the wool, using all kinds of threats and deceits to get it at a bargain. Mule-track drivers brought it down to Arequipa and the small ports. In 1876, however, the railroad from the coast had reached Juliaca on Lake Titicaca, which would soon eclipse

Table 7.1
Peruvian Exports to Great Britain and France, 1845–1894[a]

	Guano	%	Nitrate	%	Wool	%	Sugar	%	Cotton	%
1845/49	475	46.1	265	25.7	122	11.8				
1850/54	1.818	73.1	433	17.4	222	8.9				
1855/59	2.479	66.6	590	15.9	328	8.8				
1860/64	1.815	47.8	1.104	27.5	373	9.8				
1865/69	2.670	62.'	1.587	37.4	430	10.1				
1870/74	2.328	35.7	2.583	39.5	489	7.5	299	4.6		
1875/79	1.957	23.3	3.624	43.2	475	5.7	1.524	18.2		
1880/84	583	11.4	2.738	53.5	371	7.2	879	17.2		
1885/89	128	2.2	3.423	59.9	501	8.8	765	13.4	171	3.0
1890/94	106	3.8	689	24.7	512	18.4	845	30.3	266	9.5

[a]Constant pounds sterling. Five-year-averages. Absolute values in thousands of pounds and percentages of totals.
Based on yearly figures in Bonilla, 1980, pp. 33, 39, 43.
Exports to Britain and France constituted about 70-80 percent of Peru's foreign trade. Bonilla 1980: 20.

the Vilque fairs as a center of the wool trade, a commerce which fatefully forged strong links between the textile factories of Lancashire on the one hand and Puno estancieros and Indian communities on the other. At the same time, north of Puno, the first Peruvian textile mill was set up in 1859 at the Hacienda of Lucre, the place of an old *obraje*

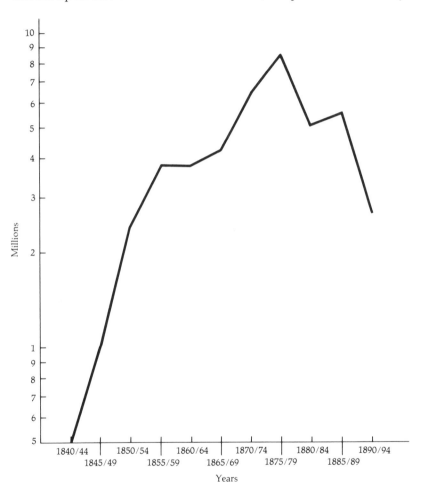

Figure 7.1. Peruvian Exports to Great Britain and France.

(Constant pounds sterling, five-year averages. Based on figures in Bonilla 1980: 22.)

near the City of Cuzco. The French machinery was brought there on muleback from Arequipa. In 1872, a German hacendado also established a brewery in Cuzco. But these were exceptions in those backward areas during a period of free trade.

Compared with the wool trade, the exports of silver and copper were of less import before the Pacific War. Plantation agriculture also remained on the traditionally rather low level of production, apart from an upward surge in cotton during the American Civil War and the rise of sugar exports in the 1870s. In any case, the rather diversified export pattern of modern Peru could already be discerned at the end of the guano era.

In Bolivia, silver mining slowly ascended again after having reached a low in the late 1840s (see fig. 7.2). A small group of miners (Aniceto Arce and others), in alliance with merchants, finally succeeded in dismantling the colonial type state monopoly over the commercialization cf silver in 1873. Together with the inflow of foreign capital, new methods of amalgamation, and transportation of the ore, this helped to increase production greatly. At the same time, though, expanding world production (especially in the United States and Mexico) caused world market prices to drop.

In the Bolivian parts of the Atacama desert, from 1866 onward, nitrate production rose dramatically. Yet, by virtue of an unwise treaty with Chile in 1866, customs revenues from the territories of both nations in the desert (between latitudes 23° and 25° South) should be shared equally (see fig. 7.3). British capital and Chilean entrepreneurship and labor were, in fact, responsible for the dynamic economic activities in the combined zone.

According to a convention of 1872, latitude 24° South was confirmed as the Chilean – Bolivian border. Bolivia promised not to increase the

Table 7.2
Expenditures by the Peruvian State, 1846-1877 (in percent)

Military and administrative; public works, education	Railroads	Payments to bondholders (internal debt)	Foreign Debt	Costs replacing the contribución	Compensation to former slave owners
53.5	20.0	9.5	8.0	7.0	2.0

Based on figures given by Klaren, 1978

tax on Chilean enterprises in its territory for 25 years, but this clause was not ratified by the Bolivian Congress. Since 1874, the port of Mollendo had been connected with Puno, in turn linked to the Bolivian shore of Lake Titicaca by steamship service; from the shore, a wagon road led to La Paz. This helped to focus Bolivian attention on the neglected seaboard. In 1878, the imposition of a Bolivian tax of 10 centavos per quintal (100 kgs) of nitrate exported aroused strong opposition among the Chilean entrepreneurs. Within a year this led to the fateful war with Chile which made Bolivia a landlocked country.

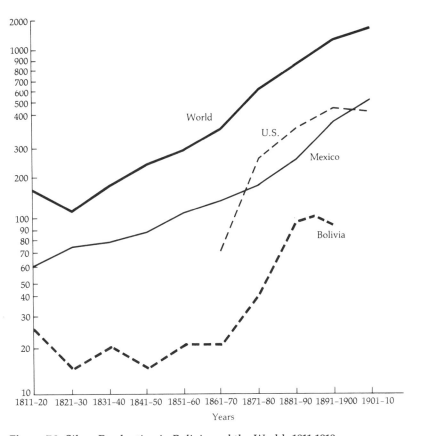

Figure 7.2. Silver Production in Bolivia and the World, 1811-1910.

(Millions of ounces, 10-year averages, semilog scale. Approximation in the case of Bolivia; from Mitre 1981: 29.)

Meanwhile, rural society of the Bolivian *altiplano* seems to have undergone no structural change. Until recently, a continuous expansion of the haciendas at the cost of Indian communities was taken for granted. Recent research, though, shows that between 1838 and 1877 the proportion between Indian taxpayers on hacienda and community lands respectively remained practically the same.[1] The *contribución de indígenas* long remained responsible for some 40 percent of total state revenues (see table 7.3). Yet the year 1866 witnessed a formidable assault on the Indian communities by the government of an utterly inept caudillo, Mariano Melgarejo. His decree, paradoxically, first declared the Indians full owners of their parcels, but added the fateful

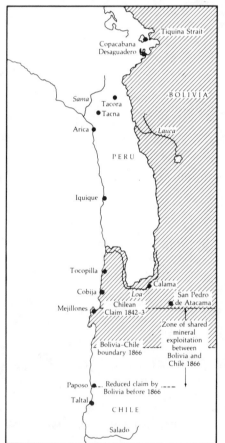

Figure 7.3. Boundary Problems in the Atacama Desert. (From Fifer 1972: 97.)

Table 7.3
The Share of the Indian "Contribución" of the Bolivian State Revenues

	Percentages
1832	46.3
1845/46	36.5
1851/52	43.8
1860	36.9
1865	40.7

Based on figures in L. Peñaloza, 1953: 288

provision that within merely 60 days they were required to pay the state a considerable fee; if they did not, their lands were immediately auctioned out. Large tracts of lands now passed to non-Indian landowners, but Indian revolt soon helped to overthrow Melgarejo in 1871. The lands appear to have been restored to the Indians. In 1874, however, a law was passed dividing the communities into Indian smallholdings. It paved the way for whites and Mestizos to purchase Indian lands. They did so, on a massive scale, from the 1880s onward. In 1872, the government, relying increasingly on the revenues from mining exports, made the Indian *contribución* a departmental rather than a national source of revenue. The Bolivian state wanted to acquire a more modern-looking economic basis for its activities. At the same time, though, the increasingly powerful group of miners and merchants were interested, as well, in the acquisition of Indian lands, be it as a means of securing labor for their mines or to offer as security for loans.

As in Peru, gathering activities in the *ceja de montaña* were of considerable importance, especially that of chinchona bark for the preparation of quinine. But this preparation took place in Europe. As an American visitor in the 1850s observes, a Bolivian "woodsman pays for one ounce of quinine the same price" for which he once sold 100 kgs. of the bark to the middleman.[2] After Brazil opened the Amazon for navigation in 1866, the immense lowlands attracted more attention and an American promoter initiated a bold scheme of building a railroad around the cataracts of the Madeira and Mamoré rivers, but failed. In the 1880s, Bolivia was drawn into the Amazonian rubber boom, triggered by the vulcanization process, discovered some forty years earlier. Notwithstanding its unfavorable location, immensely far away from the highlands and cut off from the route to Manaos, the main depot, by the cataracts, Bolivian rubber production boomed in the 1890s, in connection with the new demand for bicycle and motor car tires (see table 7.4). The Suárez brothers from Santa Cruz were the main entrepreneurs involved; unfortunate forest Indians formed a forced labor pool of tappers.

In Ecuador, the national economy continued to center around the cocoa exports of Guayaquil. Cocoa production rose from an average of 15,300 tons annually in 1854–59 to 31,480 in 1885–89 (table 7.5). The large plantations of colonial times were joined by new ones, along the many rivers of the zone, but the controlling group of large landowners remained small. The abolition of Negro slavery in the 1850s caused no major problems for the landowners. They received compensation from the government, and their former slaves often asked to be kept on as "conciertos." They were paid a very low wage, combined with the usufruct of a parcel of land for subsistence.

Straw hats were another substantial export item. The centers of production were on the Central coast, from Manta to Santa Elena. Demand was especially strong in the West Indies where these fine hats were called "Panama" hats, because they reached the market from the Isthmus.[3] From 1859 to 1875, Guayaquil landowners (Colombian immigrants were conspicuous among them) founded three commercial banks, which provided much-needed credit and even issued notes. In

Table 7.4
Bolivian Rubber Production

	In tons
1890	289
1891	339
1892	357
1893	388
1894	622
1895	806
1896	1.121
1897	1.644
1898	3.100
1899	2.102

SOURCE: Fifer, 1972: 138

Table 7.5
Ecuador: Total Export Values and Cocoa Production
(Five-year-averages. Values in U.S. dollars. Export in tons.)

a. Exports		b. Cocoa prodution
1854/59	3.131.600	15.313
1860/64	3.043.420	15.864
1865/69	5.267.520	17.017
1870/74	3.817.920	21.925
1875/79	4.401.280	20.538
1880/84	5.902.200	22.453
1885/89	7.947.680	31.479
1890/94	8.183.740	36.340
1895/99	6.442.260	43.044

Based on figures given by Carbo, 1953: 447, 449

the words of the United States Minister to Ecuador in the 1860s, "Guayaquil monopolizes at present the business of importation, because its roads to the interior are mule paths. . . . It is a common saying in Ecuador that 'Our roads are roads for the birds, but not for men.' "

During the six summer months Babahoyo, north of Guayaquil on the Guayas River, served as the depot of all goods to be introduced from Guayaquil and vice versa; merchant activities were lively there. During the rainy winter season, though, the place was partly under water and the roads to the highlands simply impassable. Thus, President García Moreno's construction of a wagon road between Quito and Guayaquil beginning in 1862 was a pioneering undertaking. But our American Minister underscores the primitive way in which the work was carried out, with the help of forced Indian labor. "He works unwillingly, and is kept to his task by the whip of the overseer."[4]

In the highlands, apparently, economic life was almost stagnant. Yet, in Quito, too, a small-size commercial bank was founded in 1867. The urban elites were simultaneously landowners who lived off the backs of their submissive Indian tenant labor. As another American observer put it in 1881, "The energies of the upper class are feeble. There is no spirit of enterprise, nor faith enough in each other's honesty to combine and carry out public works. . . . Half the population oppress the other half."[5] Clearly, the isolation of the Ecuadorean highlands from the outer world was in glaring contrast to the penetration of international commercial interests in the wool districts of the Southern Peruvian Sierra.

In general terms, the impact of the world market on the Andean countries between the mid-nineteenth century and the 1880s can be summarized as having increased the disparity between different regions and groups of producers, by tying some to the fluctuations of international prices while other regions and groups remained even more strictly constrained within the limits of a near subsistence economy than they used to be.

b. The Growing Ambitions of Government

Logically, the impact of increasing state revenues was felt first and foremost in Peru during the guano boom. Among all the generals who won their laurels in the battle of Ayacucho, only Ramón Castilla played

A

B

C

Figure 7.4. Pancho Fierro Looks at the Elite of Lima.

This most original self-taught artist (d. 1879) here shows us a Lima lady (A) as she was dressed for the street (*tapada*), (B) Lawyer Castro, and (C) Marshal Ramon Castilla and a fellow politician named Morales. (From Cisneros Sanchez 1975: 190, 125, 141. Used by permission of Mrs. Cisneros Sanchez.)

A

B

C

Figure 7.5. Workers as Seen by Fierro. **A.** The guild of water carriers in Lima had the obligation to kill stray dogs. They did this on Wednesdays. **B.** A *chola* fishmonger on horseback. **C.** A muleteer *(arriero)* with a load of brandy *(pisco)*. (From Cisneros Sanchez 1975: 85, 96.)

A

B

Figure 7.6. On the Trail. **A.** The soldiers were often accompanied by women (*rabanas*), who took care of the various needs during the campaigns. This soldier apparently played guitar for her in the evenings. **B.** A woman with her llama loaded with copper. The white hat suggests a *chola* rather than an Indian woman. (From Cisneros Sanchez 1975: 136, 210.)

no major role in politics until the 1840s. This vigorous, clever soldier from Tarapacá served as President for two terms (1845 – 51, 1855 – 62). Systematically using guano revenues to strengthen the authority of the state, Castilla imposed order by means of a sizable civil administration as well as a standing army. He also built a navy, promoted public education, finally ended the system of entails, and had the first railroad in the whole of South America built (in 1850), a strip connecting Lima and Callao. When in 1846 Ecuadorean ex-Caudillo Flores threatened to use British and Spanish support to regain power in his country, Castilla also took a remarkable initiative in foreign affairs. Convoked by him, a

Figure 7.7. A Chinese fishmonger as seen by Fierro. (From Cisneros Sanchez 1975: 148.)

"Continental Congress" in Lima took up questions of Latin American common defense against external aggression. (A second Continental Congress would also take place in Lima 18 years later.) Economic prosperity provided international prestige as well. After an interlude under a less capable President, Castilla raised the banner of rebellion in the liberal stronghold of Arequipa in 1854. The abolition of slavery and of Indian contribución should be seen in this context, as should Lincoln's Emancipation Proclamation. At the same time Castilla, by initiating the coolie trade, saw to it that coastal plantation owners got the cheap and servile labor they wanted. Once in power, pragmatic Castilla soon disassociated himself from the liberals; his constitution of 1860 imposed a clearcut presidential system once again. Also, the public exercise of religions other than Catholicism was prohibited. Through the introduction of a civil code of French model in 1852, private property had been strengthened.

In 1864, the Quixotic behavior of a Spanish naval expedition to the Pacific suddenly exposed the vulnerability of Peruvian power. After a quarrel over the conditions of a group of Basque immigrants in Central Peru, the Spaniards quickly occupied the Chincha islands. By bombarding both Callao and Valparaiso, before withdrawing in 1866, they succeeded in bringing about an alliance between all the republics along the Pacific, however short-lived. Another President-General, Mariano Ignacio Prado, in 1867 enacted a liberal constitution. Old Castilla took up arms against him but died of natural causes; Prado was overthrown anyway, giving place to a Colonel, José Balta, who restored Castilla's conservative constitution (which would remain in force until 1919).

Under Balta, Piérola carried out his Dreyfus deal while Meiggs was let loose building railroads. In 1872 elections were won by Manuel Pardo and his plutocratic, reformist Civilista Party. When a military faction tried to stop Pardo's ascent to power, sanguinary riots, probably instigated by the Civilistas, broke out in Lima; finally, the corpses of the military insurgent leaders, three brothers, were hung from the towers of the Cathedral. Its financial and political problems notwithstanding (Piérola rebelled), Pardo's government was quite active. It promoted education (a school of engineering was founded at last) and administrative decentralization. At the same time, however, Pardo's secret alliance with Bolivia in 1873 and his reduction of military costs would soon prove fateful. After leaving office to General Prado, Pardo was assassinated a couple of years later, for which his rival Piérola was blamed. While Chile attacked Bolivia over the "ten centavo tax" in 1879, Prado, by honoring Pardo's agreement, threw Peru into a disastrous war.

Bolivia, meanwhile, went through another sequence of caudillo rule. Manuel Isidoro Belzú (1850–55) is of interest for his protectionist policy and demagogical appeals to the poor artisans and workers of La Paz. As he told them, "an unfeeling bunch of aristocrats ... exploit you ceaselessly but you don't see it; ... they accumulate vast fortunes from your toil but you aren't aware of it.... Wake up now; it is time to question the titles of the aristocracy and the basis of private property."

To some extent, Belzú anticipated twentieth century "Populism." He is recorded as having suppressed 42 revolutionary attempts before leaving office — voluntarily.[6] The first civilian President, José Linares, a patrician from Potosí, tried to remedy the financial chaos and reduced the size of the army. Not surprisingly he soon lost his office. In 1865, Bolivia was ripe for its worst caudillo, Mariano Melgarejo, a brutal drunkard, especially disastrous in his foreign policy. Through the treaty with Chile of 1866, Bolivia's position on the seaboard was irretrievably weakened; a year later, Melgarejo lightheartedly ceded an immense tract of frontier territory to Brazil. After his overthrow in 1869 and the rule of another caudillo of the same stripe, two short terms of well-intentioned, civilized presidents followed. In 1876, however, another inept military caudillo, Hilarion Daza, seized power. His efforts to secure revenues from Atacama were understandable, but they were carried out in disregard of previous arrangements and above all without any understanding of the consequences.

Ecuador went through a period of extreme political liability from the overthrow of its Venezuelan-born nation-founder Flores in 1845 until the revolution of 1859, once again led by the irrepressible old caudillo. During this period, General José María Urbina was the most conspicuous among a number of self-proclaimed liberal politicians. The abolition of slavery in the 1850s was a rare redeeming feature. By 1859 the situation had become extremely chaotic. A Peruvian invasion and Colombian threats made the partition of the country seem a likely possibility. The victory of Flores, however, paved the way for Ecuador's most statesmanlike ruler until the present. Interestingly, Gabriel García Moreno emerged as the fourth of a group of almost contemporary, constructive national leaders on the Pacific: Manuel Montt in Chile, Castilla in Peru, and Linares in Bolivia. The Ecuadorean was born in Guayaquil and started in politics as a liberal. Yet, both travel in Europe after the revolutions of 1848 and the chaos in his own country made him conclude that his immature nation needed some unifying set of values. Only the Church, with its hierarchical organization and rigid institutional structure, could serve as the backbone of society, preventing it from disintegration. In Ecuador, the church itself, was in sore need of reform. This explains why Garcia Moreno, in a Concordat of 1862–63 willingly conceded more control to the Vatican than it had ever before enjoyed in Spanish America: he wanted its help to speed up national Church reform. In ten years, foreign priests and friars helped to double the number and to improve the quality of the Ecuadorean clergy. In 1869 García Moreno imposed a constitution which required one to be a practicing Catholic in order to preserve citizenship. It should be kept in mind that Catholicism had become more exacting than before; in 1870 Pius IX even demanded of believers that they accept the dogma of papal infallibility.

From the liberal point of view, Garcia Moreno's ecclesiastical policy was a most abhorrent form of theocracy. They never ceased to loathe him. Thus, historiography on this fascinating period of Ecuadorean history is either sharply defamatory or exceedingly apologetic about its leading figure. Yet it cannot be denied that García Moreno's public work (wisely cautious when compared with a Balta) and generous support of education were praiseworthy achievements. A Polytechnic school was founded in 1870. Primary school enrollment more than doubled, to 32,000, between 1865 and 1875. The Indian communities enjoyed certain protection during this era when they were endangered everywhere else. At the same time, there is no doubt that the chilly dictator submitted his opponents to a very severe and ruthless suppression. Many were executed, others sent into long years of exile. In 1875, the President was cut down by assassins on the steps of the government palace at Quito. From exile, a famous liberal intellectual, Juan Montalvo, proudly wrote: "My pen has killed him."

The liberals did not yet manage to come back to power, however. An opportunistic Caudillo, General Ignacio Veintemilla, controlled the political situation between 1876 and 1883. During these very years,

Ecuadorean foreign trade derived considerable benefit from the war which raged among its Southern neighbors. Subsequently, moderate elements from liberal as well as conservative ranks, for some years, miraculously held together a middle-of-the road government headed by a son of Juan José Flores by the name of Antonio (1888–92). Led by General Eloy Alfaro, the more dogmatic liberals would finally come to power through the revolution of 1895 successfully launched from Guayaquil against Quito. This was a delayed victory of the dynamic export-import lowland economy over the landed oligarchy of the Sierra.

c. The War and its Aftermath

The question of nitrate deposits in the Atacama Desert and the boundary problems leading up to the war have already been mentioned. Essentially, the outcome was a given from the outset. Chile's naval power was clearly superior and thus gave it greater mobility of military forces and flexibility of attack. Also, even if Chile's financial situation was shaky, partly a result of the worldwide depression, the national consciousness of its people and the firmness of purpose of its leaders made it much stronger than its two adversaries. The Chileans appear to have enjoyed a stronger backing from European capitalists, but Britain's reputed diplomatic support for Chile has not been substantiated.

To begin with, a tiny Bolivian force in the seaboard area was easily routed by the Chilean troops who seized Antofagasta in February 1879. As the Chileans did not bother to proceed inland, Bolivia, for all practical purposes, was now out of the struggle. But from April onward, Peru was also at war. For some time, a Peruvian ironclad cruiser, Admiral Miguel Grau's *Huáscar*, challenged the Chilean navy. In October, however, it was destroyed and Grau killed in the Battle of Angamos off Antofagasta. After the news reached Lima, a British diplomat stationed there wrote: "Peru appears to be struck as with paralysis; the people themselves seem as indifferent to the future as the governing classes who are thinking more of their personal ambitions than the welfare of their country."[7] By the end of 1879, the inept President Prado, under the pretext of seeking financial aid, fled the country. Following Gambetta's example during the French–German War ten years earlier, Nicolás Piérola now seized power to improvise the defense of Lima.

Despite some courageous fighting, however, the city was occupied by the Chileans in January 1881.

What followed was a period of disintegration, revealing, as a "revisionist" Peruvian historian, Heraclio Bonilla, has emphasized, the deep rifts within the ruling class itself as well as between the various social classes and ethnic groups.[8] Operating with the consent of the Chilean forces of occcupation on the coast, three consecutive Peruvian provisional governments were set up. Their partisans quarreled and even fought each other, but all the officials told the Chileans they were willing to make peace. Yet, for long, none appears to have had the authority or moral courage to do so.

Under these circumstances, landowners and merchants sometimes found themselves no longer able to control their subordinates. Acts of pillage and rioting took place. The rich people often blamed Piérola for having unleashed "anarchy" among the lower classes during his short tenure. The Chilean army, in 1881, marched northward along the coast to control economic resources and to extort money from landowners. It was enthusiastically greeted and joined by Chinese indentured laborers, who took the opportunity of sacking the estates of their patrons. Yet, in time, other Chinese, who after completing service had managed to become the owners of numerous shops, became themselves the victims of pogroms at the hands of Indians and Mestizos from the defeated army. To take another example, in the coastal town of Cañete, a thousand or more whites and Chinese were killed by Negroes. The mutal destruction of humble and despised elements reflected the lack of cohesion and social awareness prevailing in Peruvian coastal society.

In the Central Sierra, on the other hand, recent research shows the situation to have been quite different. Here, General Andrés A. Cáceres began in 1881 to organize a vigorous resistance in the form of guerrilla bands (*montoneras*) which harassed the Chileans and allied Peruvian forces. Among the guerrillas, the Indians of the communities appear to be much more numerous than hacienda peons. Outraged by Chilean abuses and influenced by Cáceres's fiery speeches, the Indians became fervent defenders of their lands against the invaders. Whether they eventually attacked collaborationist landowners primarily for being traitors or just because they were whites is still the subject of scholarly dispute. What is clear, anyway, is that Cáceres himself, in

1884, turned against some of his earlier Indian montoneros and had some of them shot.[9]

In 1883, another Peruvian provisional President with Chilean blessing, General Miguel Iglesias, did at last conclude peace. According to the Treaty of Ancón, Chile obtained Tarapacá with its important nitrate center of Iquique. Chileans would also continue to occupy Tacna and Arica for ten years, after which a plebiscite would be held to determine the final fate of the two areas. It would not be held, though, and a solution was not reached until 1929. Cáceres opposed the severe terms of the treaty and Iglesias lost the support he needed when the Chilean forces now withdrew. During the civil war between the two caudillos, Indian uprisings became more frequent than ever before; either they were the result of manipulations by the two parties or the Indians themselves understood how to use the chaotic situation for taking revenge. The most famous of these episodes was the Atushparia uprising in Huánuco in 1885.

Oral tradition gathered in the 1950s probably gives a fair view of the events, even though "Chileans" were in this tradition substituted for what, in fact, were Peruvian military forces:

There was a very brave man... called Uchcu Pedro. He was a leader and he formed a group of a thousand men. They had guns and attacked the Chileans.... Uchcu Pedro had a *compadre* who deceived him, telling him: "You have won this war." Believing this, Uchcu Pedro went off, contented, to get drunk with his people.... The Chileans killed him [and] began to look for all the Indians.... they raped all the women they could find, young and old.... They burned everything, houses and clothing. All the people that they found they took as prisoners to the town of Carhuaz.[10]

In the Yanamarca Valley, Cáceres, during the war, raised a large peasant guerrilla force, the fighting qualities of which made local landowners tremble. Disappointed at their treatment after the war, peasants from several villages joined to form a "Federation" in 1888. Its de facto autonomy was not crushed until 1902.

In 1886, Cáceres had won the bitter civil war but he took over a largely devastated, demoralized country. Among the most pressing problems were the demands of foreign bondholders for the resumption of service on Peru's sharply increased external debt. Through the mediation of an American businessman, W.R. Grace, a solution to the tricky problem was found. Peru turned over to the bondholders who, in 1890 formed the so-called "Peruvian Corporation, Ltd.," the exclusive right to sell 2 million tons of guano annually, and all the 769 miles of the state railroad system for a prolonged period plus other benefits in return for the servicing of the external debt. This was, no doubt, a surrender comparable to that of Ancón, but in neither case, probably, did Peru have much choice.

In Bolivia, meanwhile, the defeat had a sobering effect on politics. After Daza vanished from the scene, a civilian group of politicians, calling itself liberal, opposed any settlement with Chile. Like the Peruvians, they vainly hoped for American intervention. The truce with Chile in 1884 confirmed the loss of the seaboard. Between that year and 1899, Bolivia enjoyed relative political calm. Civilian conservative presidents followed each other by virtue of elections, however staged. Both the conservatives and their liberal opponents (who attempted occasional coups) were interested mainly in material progress. They encouraged foreign investments and railroad construction. As a result the vital railroad connecting the mining district of Oruro with the new Chilean port of Antofagasta was opened for traffic in 1892. With easier transportation, the export of refined silver declined in favor of the export of ore. Even before the Nitrate War some of the European and Chilean capital, firmly entrenched on the seaboard, began to enter Bolivian highland mining. In 1886, only a third of the shares of the most important silver mining company, that of Huanchaca, remained in Bolivian hands. In the mid-nineties, however, silver production suddenly dropped, a victim of accelerated price fall and still deficient technology.

To finance, instead, the promotion of manufacturing, the conservative President and silver mine owner Aniceto Arce raised the export tax on tin, an export article of growing importance. This helped to make the owners of tin mines throw their support to the laissez-faire oriented liberal party. Also, liberals, centered in La Paz, espoused the cause of federalism versus the centralism of the Sucre-based conservative government. In order to defeat the conservatives, the liberal leader, Colonel José Manuel Pando, succeeded in enlisting the support of a famous Indian chief, Pablo Zárate Willca. As in the case of Cáceres' guerrillas, however, Willca's Indians correctly sensed that their real enemies were white landowners, whatever their political allegiance, and spontaneously took revenge wherever possible. After his victory, in 1899, Pando saw to it that his former Indian ally was disposed of, as Cáceres had also done. The revolution of 1899 plays a comparable role in Bolivia's history to that of Piérola in Peru and that of Alfaro in Ecuador four years earlier: they inaugurated a new era.

d. Society During a Period of Economic Change

Population growth was strikingly slow in the three Andean countries between the middle and end of the nineteenth century. Peru's population had grown from about 2 million to 2.7 million at the time of the census of 1876. No further censuses were taken until 1940, but the population should have reached somewhat more than 3 million in 1900. Lima's population had grown rapidly during the 1840s and 1850s to about 100,000. It was transformed into a "modern" city with wide streets, opulent buildings, monuments, and gas lights. Then stagnation set in, caused by crisis and by a high incidence of disease. The population of Bolivia was about 1.4 million in 1845, 1.7 million in 1900. Yet a census in 1854 gives a total of no less than 2.3 million. This figure is surely inflated but an epidemic, probably typhoid, in 1856–58 was very devastating both here and in the south of Peru. Twenty years later, another demographic disaster hit Bolivia, combining drought, famine, and plague. In normal times, too, child mortality appears to have been extremely high. Ecuador's population was about 1 million, that of Quito may have been as much as 80,000, Guayaquil's 20,000 in the 1850s (see table 7.6). In 1900 national population had grown to about 1.4 million; Quito had 50,000, while Guayaquil, despite the havoc caused by yellow fever, now had considerably more. In Ecuador as much as 12 percent of the population lived in cities of more than 10,000 people in 1900, whereas in the other two countries urban population did not exceed 8 percent.

Out of these totals, the elites, national and regional, formed only a tiny portion. In the case of Bolivia it has been estimated that about 500 people were politically active, a group composed of large landowners, journalists, merchants and mine owners, even though as many as 32,000 people were legally entitled to vote. To be able to read and write, to hold certain property or receive certain income were normal constraints on political rights in most Western countries at the time. In Peru, because of the guano boom, the upper class was reinforced by new elements at an earlier stage and to a greater extent than in the other countries. As the great Peruvian historian, Jorge Basadre, emphasizes, the richest families in 1879 were a very different group from the one twenty years earlier. After the war, another group of *nouveaux riches* pushed their way to social prestige and power. Among them, foreigners like the Larco brothers from Italy, Gildemeister from Germany, and the American Grace were conspicuous. In Bolivia, on the other hand, the

Table 7.6
Some Social and Economic Data About Ecuador in 1856

Population
Total: About 1. 108.000
     42 percent Indians
     0.7 percent Negroes
     In addition: possibly 200.000 forest Indians
     Population of Quito: About 80.000 Guayaquil: 20.000
Exports
Total value of exports via Guayaquil and Manta: 2.265.600 pesos
                                44 percent cocoa
                                33 percent straw hats
Total quantities: 166.000 *cargas* of cocoa
                    463.130 straw hats
Government budget
Total income: 1.372.800 pesos
                36 percent customs dues
                11 percent *contribución de indígenas*
                10 percent salt sales (state monopoly)
Total expenses: 1.358.500 pesos
                  24 percent military expenses
                  9 percent service on foreign debt
Defense
Regular army: 1.200 troops (1 colonel; 131 other officers)
Irregular forces: totals unknown (11 generals, 32 colonels, 253 other officers)
Education
Higher education: 53 chairs, 1.299 students
Primary education: 13.411 school children

Based on data in:
Villavicencio 1858.

great entrepreneurs, such as Gregorio Pacheco and Aniceto Arce, were native even though closely linked to foreign capital. In Ecuador, Colombians were conspicuous among the cocoa oligarchy of Guayaquil. Everywhere, old and new rich, through marriage alliances and imitation, in Basadre's words, helped aristocracy survive "as a way of life and myth of social style."[11] Thus, a great deal of upward social mobility long went unnoticed. Highland landowning elites seem to have undergone less change in their composition. Yet, as the Bolivian case makes clear, the great hacendados were closely linked to, at times even identical with, leading mine owners and merchants. They were all behind the first commercial banks.

Members of the urban middle class, such as those in the professions, were also often landholders. Professionals were also especially avid readers of the books and newspapers which brought news about the outer world. In Bolivia, 32 papers were issued regularly in 1878, as much as 74 in 1900. In the merchant sector of Lima, the presence of foreigners was especially striking. Out of 500 Italian-born people in the city in the 1870s, almost 300 were the owners of retail stores—especially groceries. As much as 15 percent of Lima's population was born abroad, a third in China. Later, the foreign share declined. In the cities and towns, artisans were desperately struggling to maintain themselves in face of the competition with imported goods. They enthusiastically cheered Belzú in La Paz around 1850 and were numerous among the crowds rioting in Lima in 1872. Domestics (in the highlands including hacienda Indians) were obliged to serve their masters as "pongos" by turn. They were always numerous in the urban environment, perhaps forming a third of the active urban population.

The coolies had been imported to Peru to fill the labor needs of both the guano extraction and plantation agriculture. They were exclusively male and kept isolated, practically as prisioners, from other people during the time of their contract, which was for at least eight years. This naturally led to homosexuality which, in turn, strengthened prejudice against the poor Asiatics. They were despised and bullied also by the former Negro slaves. Also, before the Nitrate War, they sometimes rioted against their oppressors. If they survived their contracts, many settled in the cities, intermarrying with Peruvian women to form the rather prosperous group of *injertos*. Ruthless traders in order to get labor for the odious guano extraction started a traffic in Polynesian slaves. Fortunately, French and Hawaian authorities soon put an end to this. The Coolie traffic was also suspended owing to the international scandal it provoked and the protests of the Chinese government in 1874. The hopes of the Pardo administration to replace the coolies on the plantations with European immigrants were doomed to fail. Those who arrived settled down in Lima and Callao; only a scattering went to Bolivia and Ecuador. A couple of immigrant agricultural colonies were formed in the interior of Central Peru. On the coast, a variety of labor systems took shape to replace the coolie system. Apart from the labor given by tenants (yanaconas), sharecroppers, and day laborers, migrant seasonal labor (*enganche*) became increasingly important. These were mostly Indian peasants hired in the highlands by special contractors (*enganchadores*), well remunerated by plantation owners. Whether this labor system was mainly abusive or largely benefited both parties is today the subject of debate among social historians.[12]

Highland society continued to be characterized by the dichotomy between haciendas and Indian communities. Yet in some areas Mestizo smallholders were also numerous as, for instance, in the Cochabamba basin. In Bolivia, the greatest pressure on the Indian communities apparently set in from 1881 onward. In the province of La Paz, some 7 to 9 percent of the Indian communities, legally dissolved, were induced to sell their land to the whites in the course of only 16 months. Most probably became service tenants (*colonos*) on the haciendas. Some joined the labor force of the mines which, in 1900, had doubled to about 12,000 from their number in 1880. Women were employed, in the sorting and classifying of ores. Conditions were harsh, no less because of the barren location of the mines. Yet, from 1873 onward, they improved somewhat. Often paternalistically minded mine owners set up simple health facilities and schools and a nine-hour working day was adhered to. Workers were paid in depreciating silver coins, though, which helped reduce the owner's own losses because of the drop in silver prices.

In Peru, almost a third of the rural population lived on 4400 haciendas in 1876. The density of haciendas and the ethnic composition of highland population differed widely from region to region, even from province to province. During the third quarter of the nineteenth century, Mestizo colonization eastward in the Northern Sierra can be discerned. Compared with the situation in the 1850s, Mestizos had also increased in the Southern Sierra. From a longer perspective, though, "Indian Peru" was probably still more extensive in 1876 than in late colonial times, a situation due largely to greater poverty and isolation in the countryside. In 1866, the Indian contribución was temporarily reintroduced. In combination with the activities of the *rescatistas*, this began to make Puno on Lake Titicaca a "trouble spot." Juan Busta-mante, a liberal deputy from Puno, was well known for his travels around the world. He had just been one of the founders of a pro-Indian society in Lima, and went to Huancané in Puno to head the Indian rebellion, but in 1868 he was caught and killed by the military who also let some seventy Indian prisioners die from suffocation in an over-crowded hut. Even though always put down, Indian uprisings helped to focus some attention among the intellectuals on their sufferings. The first "Indianist" novel was published in 1889 by the daughter of a Cuzco hacendado. Logically, her "villains" are the priest, the wool merchants, and the Sub-Prefecto, not the large landowners and local bosses, deri-sively known as *gamonales*.[13] Yet, among the immense non-Indian majority the general image of the Indian as a lazy, lying, inferior brute continued to prevail, as a convenient pretext for cruelty and oppression.

Indian peasant conditions were probably especially bad in Ecuador. The Ecuadorean variety of service tenants, "conciertos," provided with tiny parcels (*Huasipongos*) for their own subsistence, were normally heavily indebted to their landlords. Even written records state that, in fact, they "belonged" to them. They could also be sold to another landowner to whom they would then be in debt. If they fled only to be recaptured, the owner's outlay was simply added to their debt. A foreign visitor to Quito in the 1880s noticed that whips to be used on Indian backs were sold in the stores, "according to the size demanded for girls, women, boys, and men."[14] The Indians of the remaining communities in Ecuador were also often very badly treated by the authorities, who used them for any kind of public works without compen-sation, and bullied by whoever passed through their villages. Yet uprisings appear to have been considerably less frequent than in Bolivia and Peru.

In all the three countries, the period stretching from the mid-nineteenth century through the early nineties witnessed remarkable efforts of strengthening the authority of the State, and the furthering of the exploitation of national resources by means of ambitious public works. In the case of Peru, in particular, the proud program of political and economic expansion suffered a severe debacle on account of the financial crisis of the 1870s, followed by a devastating war. In Peru as well as Bolivia, recovery was notably fast in the 1880s and 1890s. It spelled increased dependence, however, on the sources of foreign capital (see table 7.7). "Progress" also meant that, in particular, the condition of the Indian masses in the three countries, notwithstanding the legal abolition of the Indian contribución, would become even worse than before.

Table 7.7
British Investments in 1880 and 1890
(Public issues, nominal values in thousands of pounds sterling)

	1880		1890	
BOLIVIA	1.654	0.9[a]	.503	0.1[a]
PERU	36.177	20.2	19.101	4.5
ECUADOR	1.959	1.1	2.190	0.5

[a]Percentage of total British investments in Latin America
SOURCE: Platt 1972: 289.

VIII.

World Market Domination Reinforced

From the mid-1890s until World War I, the international economy was characterized on the whole by rising prices. That was the upward phase of the so-called third Kondratieff Cycle (fig. 8.1), abnormally extended throughout World War I. The increased European and American demand for the products of other parts of the world included "new" raw materials such as tin, copper, petroleum, and rubber, of vital importance for what has been termed the "Second Industrial Revolution." Also, the numbers of consumers of earlier "luxury" items such as cocoa had swelled considerably in Europe and the United States toward the end of the nineteenth century. Thus, the patterns of export specialization and dependence in Africa, Asia, and Latin America were reinforced. The rising curves of the foreign trade of these countries would benefit, mainly, foreign interests and tiny domestic elites.

In the case of our three Andean countries, this well-known worldwide pattern would be valid to a great extent. Yet even a short look at each of them will reveal interesting variations.

a. Economic Dynamics

A common characteristic was the increasing influence of the United States, both in trade and investments, at the cost of, mainly, the British. This trend was strongly reinforced during World War I. The effects of the opening of the Panama Canal in 1914 were not revolutionary, perhaps, but they helped to bring about the change. For example, the United States in 1913 absorbed 33 percent of Peru's exports as compared with 47 in 1919. The U.S. purchased 30 percent of Peru's imports in 1913, 62 percent in 1919. With respect to Ecuador the rise of the export share was even more abrupt, from 25 to 78 percent. United States investments in Peru practically trebled between 1914 and 1919 (table 8.1). Short-term depressions like the one of 1907 (of mainly American origin) and the initial shock produced by World War I reflected the increased vulnerability of the Andean countries to world-wide business fluctuations. Yet, during most of World War I, demand for Andean staples and export values reached new heights. Economic expansion through exports remained the unquestioned model in order to achieve not only wealth but also political power and national "progress." The gold standard had been adopted in Ecuador and Peru in the late nineties, in Bolivia in 1906.

In Bolivia, external demand for tin abruptly increased as a result of changes in industrial technology. At the same time, prices on Bolivia's other staple, silver, continued to drop (see fig. 8.2). Thus, Bolivian yearly tin output grew from about 1000 tons in the early 1890s to 9000

Figure 8.1. British Wholesale Prices (From Lewis 1978: 25. Used by permission of Allen and Unwin.) Because of the fall in shipping freights during this period, the author has also included the "ex freights" curve.

in 1900 and 15,000 in 1905. By this time, it already constituted some 60 percent of the country's value (fig. 8.3). Bolivia now held almost a fourth of world production. Part of the Bolivian tin production would for long remain in native hands. Simón Patiño, a former clerk from Cochabamba with exceptional entrepreneurial skills was the most conspicuous among the "tin barons." On the other hand, it is seldom noticed that Chilean capital also played a most important role for the development of Bolivian mining. By 1920 it controlled what remained of silver production, a third of that of copper and, sometimes in alliance with English or French interersts, a very large part of the production of tin. The United States was a main market but no major investor.

Meanwhile, Bolivia also took an active part in a more short-lived export boom — that of Amazonian rubber (fig. 8.4). The output experienced a tenfold increase during the nineties. More important, prices

Table 8.1
Foreign Investements in the Andean Countries, 1900–19

a. British investments in 1913 in pounds sterling

BOLIVIA	419.720[a]
ECUADOR	2.780.974
PERU	25.658.298

SOURCE: Platt (1972), p. 289

b. Foreign investments in Peru in millions of US dollars

	United States	Britain	Both
1900	3	27	30
1905	15	51	66
1910	30	54	84
1914	38	58	96
1919	111	50	161

SOURCE: Bonilla (1980), p. 100 based on estimate by Geoff Bertram

c. Exports and foreign investments in 1913

	Exports in millions of US dollars	British investments in millions of US dollars	US investments in millions of US dollars	Percentage held by main export item of total export value
BOLIVIA	36.5	2	10	79[b]
ECUADOR	15.8	13	10	64
PERU	43.6	123[c]	35	29[d]

SOURCE: Cardozo & Pérez Brignoli (1979), II, pp. 136-7

[a] Platt's comment: "…particularly unreliable. £100 million…may be nearer the truth."
[b] Only Chile, Guatemala and El Salvador show even higher shares in Latin America according to this source.
[c] Notice discrepancy with b) for 1914. The latter seems to be the better figure. See Thorp & Bertram (1978), p. 338.
[d] In Latin America, only Paraguay has a lower percentage in 1913.

continued to rise even more steeply until 1910. The exploitation spread out from the faraway shores of the Beni–Madeira Rivers, where a native entrepreneur, Nicolás Suárez, and his brothers soon controlled most of the output and trade in rubber and supplies. Rubber was exported via the Amazon, especially to England where the Suárez companies had their London headquarters. North of Beni, the even more faraway territory around the Acre River was known, by 1900, to be the richest rubber region in the world. It is not surprising that it attracted the attention of both the rubber gatherers (*seringueiros*) and the government of Brazil. By virtue of *seringueiro* penetration and armed uprising against the Bolivian authorities, followed by heavyhanded diplomacy, Brazil, in 1903, succeeded in seizing the more than 70,000 square miles of Acre (see fig. 8.5). Yet, Brazilians who, of course, controlled the only feasible export route, faithfully fulfilled their promise of 1903 to construct the so-called Madeira – Mamoré railroad around cumbersome

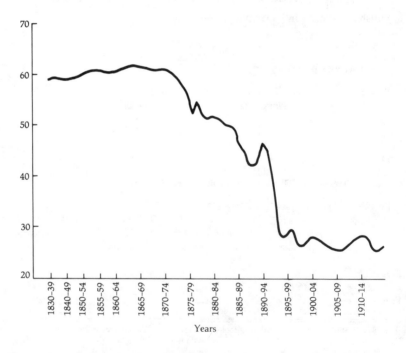

Figure 8.2. International Prices on Silver.
(Per ounce in pence; from Mitre 1981: 26.)

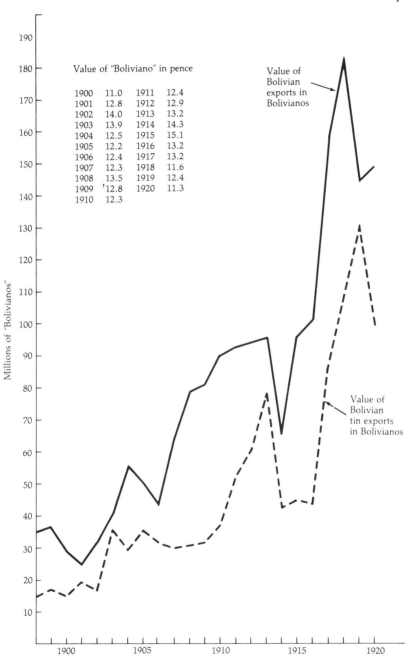

Value of "Boliviano" in pence

1900	11.0	1911	12.4
1901	12.8	1912	12.9
1902	14.0	1913	13.2
1903	13.9	1914	14.3
1904	12.5	1915	15.1
1905	12.2	1916	13.2
1906	12.4	1917	13.2
1907	12.3	1918	11.6
1908	13.5	1919	12.4
1909	'12.8	1920	11.3
1910	12.3		

Value of Bolivian exports in Bolivianos

Value of Bolivian tin exports in Bolivianos

Figure 8.3. Bolivia's Export Economy. (After López Rivas 1955: 12, 24, 35, 49. Figures for value of "Boliviano" are from *ibid.*, pp. 16, 27, 39.)

cataracts to facilitate the export from remaining Bolivian rubber territories. Like production itself and river transportation, the construction
of this railroad in the middle of the jungle took a dreadful toll in human
lives.[1] In 1912, a violent drop in the price of rubber, caused by the
sudden flooding of the world market by the cheaper Far Eastern plantation rubber, hit Bolivian, Brazilian, and also Peruvian rubber producers alike. When inaugurated that very year, the Madeira – Mamoré
railroad served no real function.

Tin production, would also face Asian competition, from Malaya,
but would for a long time withstand it better. The railroads connecting
the Bolivian altiplano with the Chilean ports of Arica (1913) and Antofagasta (1910), built with the help of Chilean compensation money,
greatly facilitated the exports of tin ore. Even though tariffs on this
export remained low, they helped the state to expand public works.

In Peru, too, the 1890s witnessed an impressive economic expansion,
both in mining and coastal plantation agriculture. The entrepreneurial
sector was mostly Peruvian or resident immigrants. The high returns

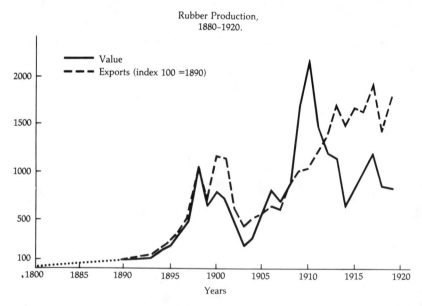

Figure 8.4. Bolivia and the Rubber Boom, 1881–1920. (Source: Demelas 1980:
79.)

from sugar, cotton, and mining exports were partly plowed back into industrialization. These light industries were concentrated (though not exclusively) to Lima. By 1900, there were a total of 6500 factory workers in the capital, but they were still far fewer than the number of artisans. Domestic textile supply from the factories satisfied a third of the national market. The surpluses derived from export earnings were allocated with the help of the national stock exchange and commercial banks. In the early 1900s for various reasons, the trend toward integrated growth would, unfortunately, peter out. The pure export economy model once again prevailed.

Yet, the Peruvian export pattern remained far more differentiated than in the other two Andean countries. Besides sugar and cotton on the coast, copper and other minerals in the Central Sierra, it comprised rubber in the northeastern corner of Loreto, wool in the Southern Sierra, and oil in desert areas on the Northern coast. The export expansion reached a higher level from 1908 onward. A further acceleration

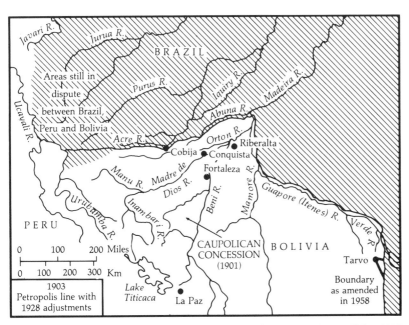

Figure 8.5. Boundary Problems in Bolivia's Rubber Zone. (From Fifer 1972: 97. Used by permission of Cambridge University Press.)

took place during World War I (fig. 8.6). A process of denationalization of ownership started after 1900 in the mining sector whereas sugar plantations, on the whole, remained in Peruvian hands (even though the Larco and Gildemeister families were both of immigrant origin). The Cerro de Pasco Mining Co., formed in New York in 1901, controlled the bulk of copper production; vanadium production also came into American possession. The oil deposits at Lobitos were exploited by a British company from 1901 onward; in 1913, Standard Oil of New Jersey started to acquire Peruvian oil fields. Its Canadian subsidiary, International Petroleum Company (IPC), was put in charge. This sector remained a pure "enclave" from which Peruvian state and society would draw no real benefits. Otherwise, even foreign-owned enterprises "returned" some value to the host country in the form of local expenditures and taxation. The quick growth of Cerro de Pasco mining, for example, provided important stimulus to the agriculture of the fertile Mantaro Valley. According to an early 1900s estimate, the costs of a unit of Cerro de Pasco copper for sale abroad were broken down as follows: no less than 35 percent corresponded to animal transportation between the mine and the nearest railroad station, 100 miles away, at La Oroya. Freight by railroad from there to Callao (137 miles) took 11 percent while extraction costs totaled no more than 6 percent. To extend the railroad to the mine itself, as soon occurred, was, indeed, good business.

The function of the railroads, considerably extended thanks to the Peruvian Corporation, was to connect centers of production with the harbors on the coast. Meanwhile the inland areas of Peru remained more or less isolated from each other. In the south, the railroad from the port of Mollendo to Arequipa and Puno finally reached the City of Cuzco in 1908. It opened up the plantation production of the *ceja de montaña* to the North. More importantly, though, this railroad served the interest of mostly foreign-owned merchant houses of Arequipa, exporting wool from the highlands around Lake Titicaca of both the sheep and alpaca varieties. As different from the rapidly modernizing plantation and mining sectors, the process of wool production remained primitive and extensive, with little input of capital.

The production of wild rubber was, by nature, even more primitive and also regionally restricted. As in Bolivia, both exports and supplies

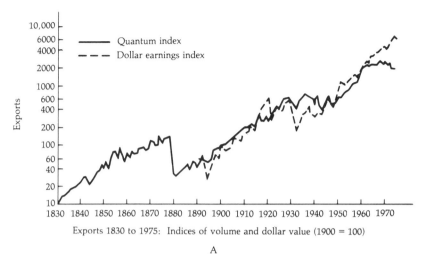

A

Exports 1830 to 1975: Indices of volume and dollar value (1900 = 100)

B

Figure 8.6. Peru's Export Economy. **A.** Exports, 1830–1975. Indices of volume and dollar value (1900 = 100) (From Thorp and Bertram 1978: 5.) **B.** Exports and government expenditure, 1899–1929 (millions of $ US). "Returned" value refers to export surplus benefiting Peru in the form of local expenditures or profits. (From Thorp and Bertram 1978: 113.)

were necessarily shipped on the Amazonian waterways. In 1910, rubber formed no less than a third of Peruvian exports. Exploitation of Indian labor was even more dreadful than in the Bolivian rubber districts and caused international scandal at the very time (1912) when the boom collapsed.

Among the great world trade items that, by exception, suffered adverse price trends throughout our period was sugar. The process of concentration in sugar production then taking place on the Peruvian coast should be seen against this backdrop. To lower the costs of production, land as well as milling facilities were amassed by a few producers. Using their monopoly on milling and transportation, the aggressive sugar companies forced one after another of the traditional planting families to sell their holdings.

In Ecuador, cocoa production and exports reached their culmination during the period surveyed here (fig. 8.7). In 1917, cocoa constituted no less than 75 percent of the total value of Ecuadorean exports. Between 1894 and 1905, the country was the foremost world producer. Then it was bypassed by Brazil, and soon West African producers were also playing a major role. World consumption of cocoa experienced an eightfold increase from 1894 to 1924. Even so, the accelerated increase of Ecuadorean cocoa exports during World War I raised the spectre of oversupply. Production methods suffered little change, but new varieties of the plant were introduced from Trinidad and Venezuela. They were of lower quality but could be grown in marginal soils. Even though small planters were responsible for about a fifth of cocoa production, latifundistas family landowning clearly dominated the picture. The Aspiazu family, for example, possessed 59 plantations comprising 4.7 million trees, that is 5 to 8 percent of the total Ecuadorean output of the crop. Production expanded continuously in the lowland area. Large landowners usually invited enterprising peasants (called *sembradores*, seedsmen) to clear the land and plant the trees while using the land also for their own subsistence crops. After five to seven years, the trees were ripe for their first crop. The *sembrador* then received his cash reward and, perhaps, moved on to some other periphery of the property. Peons might be used by him as well as by the planter.

Because of the length of the production cycle, adaptation to international business trends was not so easy. However, large producers had a well-developed credit system to rely upon. The banks of Guayaquil became increasingly important. To be sure, a few large plantations became denationalized company properties. By and large, however, both the large plantations and their leading bank, *Banco Agrícola y*

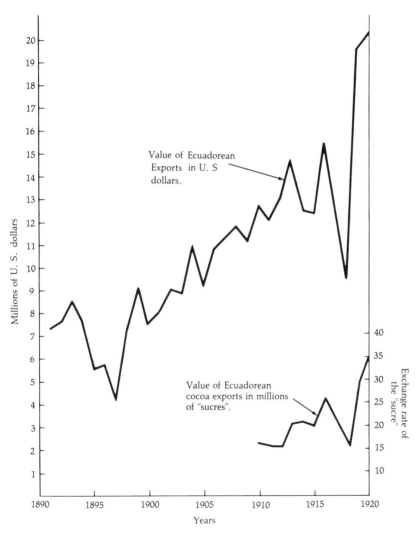

Figure 8.7. Ecuador's Export Economy, 1891–1920. (Source: Carbo 1953: 447.)

Comercial de Guayaquil, remained in Ecuadorean hands. Yet, outside
their control were the companies engaged in transoceanic transportation, such as the Pacific Steam Navigation Company. Between 1905 and
1913, costs of transportation increased by 25 percent. Also, the coast
depended on large-scale imports of food and other supplies from
abroad for its very survival. Imports formed the basis for another
powerful economic pressure group with a bank of its own.

The completion of the railroad from Quito down to the Gulf of
Guayaquil in 1908 was a tremendous engineering and political-finan-
cial achievement for which Alfaro and an American promoter could
share credit. Shipping costs remained too high, however, to resolve the
food supply problem. Even so, the railroad did help to promote local
production and economic activity along the route. Recent research

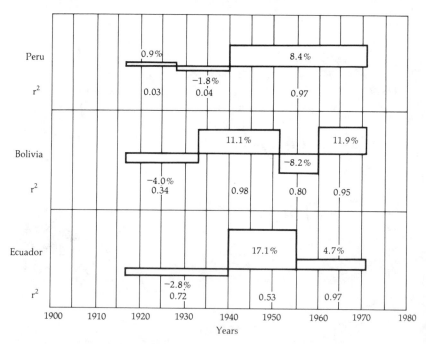

Figure 8.8. Andean Exports: Growth Rates in Value, 1900–1970. (Source: Cardoso and Perez Brignoli 1979: 182.)

(r^2 is a measure of variance. The closer to the coefficient of 1, the lesser the
fluctuations with respect to the average.)

suggests that, even in the 1890s, the traditional economic structures of the Ecuadorean highlands had begun to suffer some limited change. Flour mills were established here and there. The last textile sweat shops (*obrajes*) finally vanished while in the cities some manufacturing plants appeared.

According to a recent effort to measure the degree of integration of the Latin American countries into the world market as of 1913, Peru belonged to the second highest category, together with Chile, Uruguay, and Venezuela. Bolivia and Ecuador both belonged to the following middle category. On a per capita basis, however, they all ranked lower. Only Bolivia defended a place in the middle category whereas Peru and Ecuador both belonged to an inferior group. The breakdown on a per capita basis is found to reflect the fact that the three Andean countries comprised huge populations living virtually outside the money economy. Yet Bolivia's tin exports were so overwhelmingly important in relative terms that on a per capita basis it obtained a higher rank.[2] In other respects it was clearly the most backward one. In relation to both population and export values, government receipts, for instance, were considerably higher in Ecuador and Peru than in Bolivia (fig. 8.8). In terms of growth rate, Ecuador's export expansion during 1883 – 1913 (5.1 percent yearly) was particularly impressive.

b. Politics

The liberal victory under Eloy Alfaro in Ecuador, José Pando in Bolivia, and Nicolás Piérola and his Democratic Party in Peru all appeared to inaugurate a new and more progressive era. These revolutionary movements had a broader popular basis and more ambitious policy goals than had been the case so far. Yet their programs of political and social reforms would have little impact outside the urban sector. In fact, the vast resources offered by the easy expansion of the export economy during the first two decades of the twentieth century forced the "modernizing" regimes to opt for a rather peaceful accommodation with the outmoded traditional social order still prevailing in most parts of the countryside. Thus, the relatively high degree of political stability was the result of compromises. Whatever the formal political system, large landowners retained de facto control over the rural population. Even though all literate males — and in Ecuador since 1883 women — had the franchise and political debate went on rather freely, the system would not allow any radical change. Deeply imbued with traditional elitism as well as by the Social Darwinism (Spencerism) *en vogue*, the upper class, regardless of its political affiliation, believed in firm social control and leadership of the masses. It is true that a radical "heretic" such as the Peruvian Manuel González Prada had already made his appearance. His message was for the future, however; it met with little response in his own time.

If these basic limitations are kept in mind, Piérola's administration in Peru, 1895 – 99, can be characterized as innovative and remarkably successful. It brought about monetary and fiscal stabilization as well as real economic planning and extensive public works. Suffrage was extended to all literate male adults.

The more conservative stripe of *civilismo* soon came back, with José Pardo, a son of Manuel's as leader between 1904 and 1919. His contribution to the growth of public education was especially noteworthy. Until 1912 political calm prevailed. Then, Guillermo Billinghurst, a Democratic politician started a stormy administration cut short by a military coup in 1914. The President had picked up a fight with Congress on account of his plans for constitutional reform. He even challenged gamonales by threatening to introduce minimum-wages. Soon, World War I also made politics more difficult. Inflation increased social tensions considerably.

In Bolivia, Pando's liberals, once victory was theirs, soon abandoned the notion of federalism that had been on their program. They also clamped down hard on their former Indian allies. While conservative party leaders had been silver miners themselves, tin miners supporting "liberalism" decided to leave the political roles to others. In all important matters, though, the views of the "tin barons" were clearly crucial. In Bolivian terms, the period from 1899 to 1920 was exceptionally stable with no single revolutionary attempt. The dominant figure was Ismael Montes, lawyer and general, twice President of the Republic. He was strong enough to conclude, in 1904, the long-awaited formal peace treaty with Chile which, of course, confirmed the loss of the seaboard. He also modified the relation between State and church, authorizing civil marriage. Practical politics differed considerably from the constitution, though. An expert on the period speaks about "a system of electoral violence" which, obviously, made political defeats harder to swallow. A new political party, the Republican, emerged in 1914. There was hardly any news on its program but the leaders resented Montes. They finally seized power in 1920.

In Ecuador, the Church – State issue, because of the extreme stance García Moreno had taken, remained much hotter in ideological terms than in the other two countries. After his military victory in 1896, liberal chieftain Alfaro therefore, at first, showed himself quite cautious. The constitution of 1906, however, carried out the separation between Church and State. Civil marriage, lay education, and religious freedom were introduced. The landed properties of the Church were nationalized to fund public hospitals. These reforms were, of course, deeply resented by the conservatives. Yet they proved less of a menace to political stability than the feuds among the liberal leaders themselves. Both Alfaro and his rival General Leonidas Plaza were themselves caudillos of the old type. Yet a basis for military professionalism was laid when the military college was founded in 1899. Alfaro was attempting a comeback when imprisoned by his opponents and assassinated in a Quito jail by a mob in 1912. In the northern lowland province of Esmeralda, Alfaro's partisans bitterly fought the new regime for years. In their traditional opposition, Guayaquil and Quito sometimes vied for the support of Cuenca, the center of the southern highlands, economically linked to the former but similar to Quito in social structure. The Presidents increasingly depended on loans awarded to the state by the Banco Agrícola y Comercial of Guayaquil. The unrestricted bank note issues of this powerful bank made inflation and popular discontent steadily worse in the course of World War I.

All three Andean countries suffered a great deal from boundary conflicts during our period. The Peru – Chilean border issue after the Pacific War lingered on without solution whereas, as just noted, Chileans and Bolivians agreed on a settlement in 1904. On the other hand, Bolivia succumbed to Brazilian pressure in the north in 1903. At first, the mostly Brazilian settlers in Acre set up a "Republic" of their own, which Bolivia tried to suppress. Then Bolivia was required to give up the whole territory of Acre by the Petrópolis treaty of 1903. Finally, the

Argentine arbitration of their lowland dispute with Peru in 1909 also turned to their disadvantage.

For Ecuador, squeezed in between three larger neighbors, the border problems were especially traumatic. This republic, too, had to make a huge territorial concession to Brazil in 1904 (about 10 percent of the national territory, although merely jungles). In 1910, adverse Ecuadorean reaction against Spanish arbitration of the long-standing border issue with Peru almost led to war. In 1916, finally, a border settlement with Colombia cost Ecuador a fourth of its remaining territory. It was now cut off from any common frontier with Brazil in the Oriente. Border issues could be used to strengthen national unity momentarily, as Alfaro tried to do in 1910 (fig. 8.9). However, during the rubber boom particularly they took on much greater economic significance than before and concessions bred widespread frustration.

From the long view, politics on the national level in the Andean countries during the early 1900s were less destructive than either before or after. Political behavior had become more "civilized." Expectations were widely held that the formation of professional armies, trained by European instructors, would in the future both guarantee order and prevent violence in politics. Already, many presidents, constitutionally elected, managed to serve their full four-year terms, and then yield office because of constitutional bars to their succeeding themselves. Yet, politics, in reality, remained a play reserved for small elites; in the countryside, whatever the letter of the constitutions, the will of the gamonales remained paramount. Even so, granted that the economic expansion of the period had been channeled into integrated development, it might have been possible later to extend democratization little by little on the basis laid during the early 1900s. An "if" makes no history, however.

c. Elite Pleasures and Popular Misery

"A country in itself," stated Bolivia's Ismael Montes, " has nothing. Its wealth is nothing more than the sum of private wealth. Therefore it is scientifically necessary to stimulate the growth of the latter so that it will contribute with the greatest effectiveness to the national prosper-

Andean countries in 1910

PERU

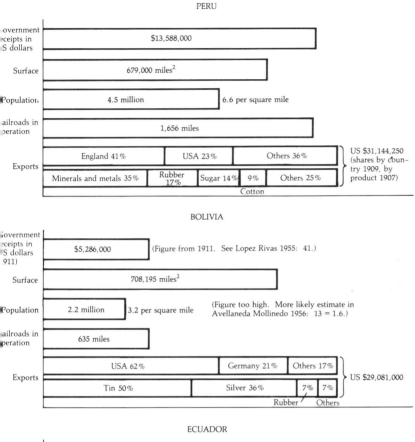

BOLIVIA

ECUADOR

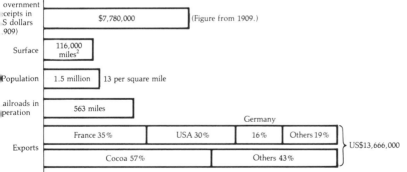

Figure 8.9. Andean Countries in 1910. (Based on PAU 1911.)

ity."[3] Economic expansion in the Andean countries in the early 1900s certainly promoted individual fortunes. Whether this also increased "national prosperity" is another matter.

First, in line with traditional values, an out-of-proportion share of individual revenues was absorbed by conspicuous consumption. Near Sucre, Bolivia, there is, for example, a huge castle constructed in a strange mixture of architectural styles by a tin millionaire who bought a title of nobility from the Pope. According to official figures, jewelry, perfumes, and wines constituted "only" 7 percent of Ecuador's total imports during 1900–11, but it is obvious that very much more came in as contraband.

Second, there was the great outflow of money that enabled the rich and their families to travel or live abroad, preferably in Paris, at least part of the year. According to one estimate from Ecuador in 1900–13, the drain of money for such purposes equaled the service on the foreign debt. For most absentees, perhaps, travel or stays abroad served the purpose of acquiring an education or promoting family economic interests from there. Even quite a few of the children of such absentees, born abroad, eventually settled down in the native country of their families. Other absentees, however, ended up selling their family estates to foreign interests and usually remained abroad.

Third, and most importantly, export-based individual wealth no doubt contributed toward making the whole socio-economic structure even more skewed than it had been before, to the long-term detriment of "national prosperity." That the distance between rich and poor grew was in itself hardly the worst aspect of the matter. A remedy could have been found later on. More serious was its relationship with growing urban–rural and regional disparities. "Modernization" made the large cities even more attractive for and less representative of their countries. Sewage and drinking-water facilities, hospitals, telephone and telegraph, restaurants and hotels, English-type clubs, private and public education were only to be found in cities. Even in Guayaquil, plagued by fires and yellow fever, life became more comfortable and safe. The elites easily engaged in escapism under the impact of the impressive urban façade. Here incredibly numerous papers, cultural and political journals saw the light of day. Great poets of the current Modernist trend used their fertile imagination to evoke in the case of Bolivia's

Jaimes Freire, Walhalla, and the Graal, or in the case of Peru's Santos Chocano the elegance and gallantry of eighteenth-century France. Among the "thinkers" (*pensadores*), "Krausism," an obscure body of ideas derived from a minor European philosopher, gained many adherents because it attempted a synthesis of modernization and traditionalism. The concern for material progress, already established during positivism, joined with respect for hierarchical and vaguely idealistic values. The pseudo-scientific racism of the time also found partisans. As a Peruvian intellectual of great reputation, Alejandro Deustua, put it, "the Indian is not now, nor can he ever be, anything but a machine."[4] In Bolivia, Alcides Arguedas somberly concluded that race mixture was the main cause why his people were "sick." It should be added, though, that a compatriot of his, Franz Tamayo, found Indian strength and endurance to be a basis of national optimism, granted that mass education and intelligent Mestizo leadership could be provided. In the large cities, the first trade unions and anarchist or socialist organizations also appeared. Thus, the gap between city and countryside became increasingly wide in all aspects of life. The cities grew more quickly than the national population but still harbored only a very small portion of it.

The regional contrasts are, of course, especially well illustrated by the Ecuadorean case. In 1909, there were only five business firms with a capital exceeding 100,000 sucres in Quito as compared to 76 in Guayaquil. The coast attracted people from the highlands and grew more quickly demographically. The Guayas province had 98,000 people in 1890, 194,000 in 1905, and as much as 270,000 in 1925. It was in the interest of the "cocoa oligarchy" to increase the mobility of highland peasants in order to obtain much-needed labor for the plantations. The efforts of the liberal government first to modify, then to abolish (in 1918) the debt peonage of the highlands (*concertaje*) had this backdrop. Yet it seems more likely that the net result may have been to make highland landowners reinforce and strengthen their harsh social control.

In Peru, the process of concentration and modernization within coastal plantation agriculture increased the disequilibrium with the highlands, notwithstanding the fact of mining expansion in parts of the Central Sierra. In the process of concentration the old plantation aristocracy was weakened. By 1918, a single agro-industrial sugar enterprise, Gildemeister's Casa Grande, had absorbed some 25 haciendas. Those who controlled sugar and cotton production preferred to live in Lima. They were linked to banking, real estate, insurance, and mining as well. Three of them, during our period, also served as Presidents of the Republic. On the institutional level they, like Ecuadorean cocoa planters, formed a powerful pressure group, *Sociedad Nacional Agraria*. At the same time, membership in the *Club Nacional* helped to identify the nation's elite in precise yet subtle terms. These people married among themselves. In this rich, aristocratic group, the hacendados from the Sierra and the rough rubber entrepreneurs would hardly be admitted.

In Arequipa, to look at a regional variety, wealth was concentrated in a number of merchant houses, owned by foreign interests or immigrants. Their main business, the wool trade, led to a process of land concentration in the Southernmost Peruvian Sierra. Sales of rural properties in Azángaro Province, mostly by Indians to non-Indians, show the following ascending curve:

Total Sales by Indians to non-Indians

	N	%
1896-1900	347	60.2
1901-5	743	54.9
1906-10	1165	58.3

One of the buyers acquired no less than 70 properties. In the whole of the Department of Puno, 706 haciendas were reported in 1876, 3219 in 1915. The growing hacendado group, however, remained clearly subordinated to the Arequipa merchant community to which it was firmly tied by credit.

In Cuzco, in the early years of the twentieth century, the social pattern, according to Luis E. Valcarcel, a distinguished intellectual who grew up there at the time, was more varied. The politico-economic elite consisted of six different groups; (1) the hacendados producing sugar (rum) and plantation crops (in the Montaña); (2) Hacendados — cattle ranchers; (3) Hacendados producing maize and fruit; (4) Wholesale merchants and managers of the local agencies of the mostly Arequipa-based foreign merchant houses; (5) Industrial entrepreneurs (textiles, beer); (6) High civil and military functionaries and individual professionals. In terms of capital investment, only groups 1, 4 (importers), and 5 could be reckoned with. The middle sectors, in Valcarcel's view, were composed of hacendados owning less than 200 hectares, retail merchants and small businessmen, professionals, and employees in general. Small farmers who owned less than 50 hectares, industrial workers, market vendors, peons and servants, both Indian and Mestizo comprised the lower strata in general. Indians in general were clearly inferior to all the other popular groups as a result of racial prejudice and their very low wages.[5]

In Bolivia, Patiño, thanks to British financial support and mining expertise, had created an up-to-date mining and refinery industry in a backward country. By World War I he had already gone beyond the borders of his country to buy himself into the European smelting industry. Soon he left the management of his many Bolivian enterprises to caretakers. In the absence of Patiño and the other great tin magnates, the national elite was composed, rather, of their lawyers and retainers (the so-called *Rosca*.) While Bolivia's demographic growth was slovenly, La Paz, the capital of the liberals, grew from 70,000 in 1900 to 115,000 in 1920. While those listed as merchants in 1900 totaled 55,000, export – import trade was in the hands of some 50, mostly foreigners. More than half of all land used for cultivation or pastures was the property of about 5000 landowners. The remainder was shared by 15,000 middle- or small-size landowners and by 50,000 Indian peasants forming 2500 communities. Tenant labor or peons (*agregados*) of the haciendas now formed the vast majority of the rural population. By comparison, the urban middle class, artisans and workers, the 12,000 mining workers, and 1500 railroad workers formed no more than minorities. About half the population were Indians with Aymara or Quechua as their mother tongue. Among the population that was at least of school age, only about 16 to 17 percent were literate. About as many lived in towns of 5000 people or more. The share of voters was merely a few percent of the total adult population. Within this small stratum, however, political, social, and cultural activities were intense. The number of journals published in 1900, 72, had more than doubled compared with twenty years earlier.

As in Puno, the process of land concentration gained momentum in Bolivia during the liberal era. In the Province of Pacajes, for example, 25 percent more land (or a total of 45,000 hectares) was acquired by hacendados from 1901 to 1920 than during the period of 1881 – 1900. An Aymara Indian community, Taraco, appropriated by President Montes himself, may serve as an example. First Montes bought some individual parcels, then, with the help of troops he had the Indians brought to La Paz and jailed to force them to sell out cheaply. They were then forbidden to return. Instead, Montes brought peasants in from elsewhere. The reasons for such appropriations are not so easy to discern. On traditional estates, after all, approximately half of the usable land was left for the use of the peasants themselves and the yield to the landowner was low. The value of the haciendas was largely determined by the number of resident colonos. Probably, the main value of the land was to serve as security for credit and, perhaps, as an insurance in case his other activities went bad. To be a hacendado was also a natural thing for a member of Bolivia's elites.

In the course of our period, the conditions of labor in the export sectors, on the whole and at the least until World War I, experienced some limited improvement. In Bolivian mines, wages rose steadily from 1895 to 1908. In the Peruvian sugar fields, real wages are estimated to have increased by 28 percent between 1900 and 1912. On the cocoa plantations of Ecuador, workers received about 1 sucre a day in cash while, by comparison, rural workers in the highlands were credited with some 10 centavos (100 = 1 sucre) daily. Furthermore, they never saw money, as the earnings were normally balanced against the debts to the landowner. At that time, labor organization in the mining and plantation sectors of the Andean countries had hardly begun. In Bolivia and Peru, work in the mines was still mainly undertaken by part-time peasants who now and then left to take care of their own parcels. On Peruvian coastal plantations, the *enganchados*, seasonal labor contracted from the highlands, still constituted a major proportion of the labor force. Both they and recent immigrants such as almost 18,000 Japanese contract workers who arrived in Peru between 1899 and 1924 were difficult to organize and would have had weak bargaining positions. Consequently, it was the sheer scarcity of manpower that helped bring about relatively acceptable wage conditions.

With the advent of World War I and monetary instability, the situation of the workers deteriorated. When food prices on the Peruvian coast doubled during World War I, this also may have had to do with the declining share of the acreage being devoted to subsistence crops during the export boom. For a qualified worker in Peru, with a wife and four children, his nominal income rose by 28 percent while his costs increased by 57 percent. In Guayaquil nominal wages remained almost unchanged between 1914 and 1920 while the prices on key food items rose by 73 percent. Thus, the brewing discontent and radicalization in the relatively "privileged" urban and export sectors of the Andean labor force around 1920 are easy to understand.

In the Andean highlands, human exploitation continued to take place in traditional ways. Yet, remarkably enough, the ingrained disdain for the Indians would be challenged around 1910 by groups of young, dedicated intellectuals, both in the capitals and in provincial centers like Cuzco and Puno. In Cuzco, the students had been encouraged by their American-born university rector to study their surrounding reality. The glories of the Inca past joined with the Indian misery of the present to make these young intellectuals take pro-Indian or *indigenista* stance. In Lima, other intellectuals formed, in 1909, an *Asociación Pro-Indígena* to gather information on the abuses committed against the Indians and to voice their complaints. Yet, González Prada, influenced by anarchism, remained alone in hoping for a revolution to redeem the Indians from oppression. The rest of the friends of the Indians wanted to improve their lot mainly by means of education. In Puno, a tiny group of Seventh Day Adventists from the United States also made a contribution toward this end. Thus, the admonition of a parish priest to Indians of Puno who had set up a couple of schools was quite consistent with the defense of the status quo: "God has ordained that you should dedicate yourselves to pasturing your flocks and not to learning to read, which only grieves your fathers and mothers. This is why you suffer such misfortunes and why, year after year, your harvests are so poor.[6]

The priest and the gamonal formed part of village elites who controlled Indian behavior, as well as irrigation, grist mills, and labor supply. Normally, higher authorities or provincial or regional elites did not bother to intervene on this level. At election times, village or provincial elites were expected readily to deliver the votes, in accordance with decisions taken on higher levels. With regard to labor supply, indebtedness, one way or another, was an indispensable device. The American Hiram Bingham, who in 1911 rediscovered the picturesque Inca settlement of Machu Pichu, describes well how an Indian carrier was recruited by one of his Mestizo followers. When the Indian peasant "came forward to shake hands, in the usual Indian manner, a silver dollar was unsuspectedly slipped into the palm of his right hand and he was informed that he had accepted pay for services which must now be performed."[7]

As always, there were occasional Indian uprisings against oppression, inevitably quelled in blood. For Peru, some 65 have been counted for the period 1901–10, 72 for 1911–20. Participants were mostly the Indians of the communities, less submissive than the *colonos* of the haciendas. The only uprising on a larger scale, the rather enigmatic movement of "Rumi Maqui" in Puno in 1915, was organized by an outsider, a former provincial governor who adopted this Quechua name, later to vanish from sight. On the Bolivian altiplano, a series of outbreaks from 1910 to 1920 mixed millenarian features with conscientious defense of land rights.

By far, the worst forms of human exploitation during this period occurred not in the highlands but in the rubber-producing territories of the *ceja de montaña*. Indians here, unlike the highlands, had no previous experience of forced labor and were also more vulnerable to drunkenness and disease. In the Peruvian Putumayo area, close to the Colombian border, Julio Arana's Peruvian Amazon Rubber Company was found to have engaged in the most horrible and revolting practices of enslavement. According to the one foreign, on-the-spot observer, the 4000 tons of raw rubber extracted here between 1900 and 1911 cost around 30,000 Indian lives. Torture for sadistic pleasure was widespread. Despite the international scandal caused by these revelations, Julio Arana's position as a local boss and the government's need for him in this border zone remained so strong that, incredibly, he was never punished.

On Beni in the Bolivian rubber territories, a British diplomat in 1913 reported that rubber was more abundant there than in Putumayo.

There is apparently a more humane demand for slave labour... than in the Putumayo, and the Beni is a region somewhat less lawless. The Indians are said to have a market value... of about £ 80.... This high value and the relative scarcity of labour make it uneconomical... to treat human life lightly.

One eyewitness added that, unlike Putumayo, "except in very unusual instances, it would not appear that the natives (of Beni) are tortured by their employers."[8] Even so, about 70 percent of the Indian tribes in the Beni zone are estimated to have fallen victims of the rubber boom. Though they were often the very tormentors of the Indians, Mestizo rubber tappers (*seringueiros*) were also victims themselves, tightly bound by indebtedness and one-sided contracts to the company.

As we have seen, the Andean countries during the first decades of our century presented an almost unbelievably wide range between wealth and luxury and extreme human misery on the other, and between the refinement and sophistication of the Paris-obsessed urban elites and the barbarian cruelty displayed by hacendados, entrepreneurs, and foremen in the highlands and jungles. Yet this very polarization was the outcome of a system of narrow export specialization for the world market. The worst expressions of human exploitation were the result of unrestricted capitalist laissez-faire policies and the blending of traditional prejudices with Social Darwinist disregard for the weak and pseudo-scientific racism.

IX.

The Fight for an Andean Revival: Act 1

Compared with the period 1850–1914, when the Andean countries like the rest of the "Third World" were integrated within a seemingly stable and rather smoothly functioning world market with the assigned function of exporting certain commodities, the period from World War I onward was one of abrupt changes. The war boom was followed in 1920 by a sudden price drop in the case of most staples. Yet as in the rest of Latin America and the world for that matter, the reconstruction of the world market from the mid-twenties onwards appeared relatively successful. Under the buoyant leadership of the United States, main exporter of capital, the capitalist world economy allowed supply to outpace demand by far until the speculative boom in 1929 unleashed the Great Depression. Like other export economies, not least those specialized in plantation and mineral products, the Andean countries were more or less severely hit. As elsewhere, the faith in laissez-faire economics suffered a crucial blow. The psychological preconditions were there for the launching of pro-industrialization policy and various forms of state interventionism. World War II reinforced U.S. economic domination but also provided some stimulus for such a new policy. Latin America's exports increased. Yet, by the mid-twentieth century, notwithstanding the great changes that had taken place in the global economy, the Andean countries, as a whole had not undergone any thoroughgoing structural change. Labor productivity remained low. The dependency of the countries on the export of a few commodities continued to be very much the same while worsening terms of trade and greater price fluctuations made their position much more vulnerable and precarious than it used to be. Also, the stagnation of food production for domestic needs began to undermine the foundations of the traditional export economy. The inequality of income distribution seems to have increased. Social and political awareness of poverty and the glaring material inequality between individuals, groups, and countries increased after World War I — in the Andean countries and elsewhere. Under these circumstances, the lack of substantial economic development would have even more ominous implications. This basic discrepancy would set the pattern for the next stage of Andean history from the mid-twentieth century onward. (See tables 9.1–9.3)

a. Economic Vulnerability Revealed

The common experience, in many respects, of the Andean countries within the framework of a more risky, United States–dominated world economy, however, should not overshadow the important differences between them.

In Ecuador, the negative consequences of the post–World War I drop in cocoa prices (from 26 to 14 cents a pound within ten months in 1920) was considerably reinforced by other factors. First, one plant disease (*Monilia*) attacked the Trinidad variety of cocoa in 1918; second; in 1923, the higher quality "national" cocoa trees were in a great part destroyed

Table 9.1
The Percentage Held by the Main Export Item out of Total Exports

	0–29	*30–49*	*50–69*	*70–100 percent*
1913	Peru		Ecuador	Bolivia
1953		Peru	Ecuador	Bolivia
1972	Peru	Ecuador	Bolivia	

SOURCE Cardoso & Perez Brignoli 2:166

Table 9.2
The Development of Latin American Foreign Trade in millions of US dollars (1913)

	Imports	*Change in %*	*Exports*	*Change in %*
1913	1453	–	1588	–
1929	1769	22	2139	35
1938	1320	-25	1601	-25
1948	2529	92	2805	75

SOURCE Cardoso & Pérez Brignoli 2:117

Table 9.3
Latin American and Andean Foreign Trade (Millions of Current U.S. Dollars)

	Latin America	Bolivia	Percentage from Britain	U.S.	Ecuador	Percentage from Britain	U.S.	Peru	Percentage from Britain	U.S.
Imports										
1913	1,452.8	21.3	4.3	1.6	8.9	2.6	2.8	29.0	7.6	8.4
1929	2,415.1	25.9	4.3	8.7	17.0	2.9	6.9	75.9	11.4	31.8
1938	1,485.7	25.0	1.8	6.6	10.5	0.8	3.6	58.3	5.9	20.0
1948	5,981.5	68.7	4.2	33.8	42.1	2.6	30.6	167.7	11.6	90.9
Exports										
1913	1,588.2	36.5	29.5	0.2	15.8	1.6	3.8	43.6	16.2	14.5
1929	2,920.0	50.8	39.2	7.1	17.2	0.5	7.8	134.0	24.6	44.6
1938	1,803.4	34.8	21.7	1.6	12.0	0.6	4.5	76.7	15.3	20.6
1948	6,635.2	112.8	39.7	70.7	48.7	0.3	21.0	162.4	26.2	40.0

SOURCE: PAU 1952

by another fungus known as "witchbroom disease." The labor force was greatly reduced and many unemployed gathered in Guayaquil. Furthermore, the consistent policy pursued by the Banco Argícola y Commercial in fighting the adverse world market trend while allowing domestic prices (including those on imported food) to soar had disastrous social consequences (see fig. 9.1). Reduced real wages coupled with unemployment led to a general strike and riots in the city of Guayaquil in 1922. The disorders were brutally suppressed by government troops at the cost of a thousand lives or more. Even though cocoa prices would soon recover, production volume did not, and the confidence in the cocoa oligarchy of Guayaquil as a force behind the liberal party government had been badly shaken. In 1925, the latter was overthrown and the once all-powerful bank went into liquidation. The process of land concentration on the coast was reversed; many landowners were ruined.

From the point of view of the rural lower classes, however, a partial reversion to subsistence agriculture mitigated the impact. By the late twenties, the volume of cocoa exports had been reduced by half as compared with 1913. Even so, the rise of prices, once again, and the increased output of another crop, coffee, helped to bring about an apparent recovery of the export economy. Soon the Depression would deal another even more definitive blow to the Ecuadorean economy. In the late thirties, exports remained on a considerably lower level than they did in 1913 and the national currency also suffered severe depreciation. Yet, World War II and especially a more diversified pattern of exports for the United States market, once again brought about recovery and expansion of the economy. It should be kept in mind, however, that the exports of oil and gold, about a third of the total from the thirties onwards, brought few benefits to the national economy, as the industries were foreign owned and only lightly taxed. The extreme vulnerability of the Ecuadorean economy had been most eloquently exposed during the 1920–1950 period.

In the Peruvian plantation sector, the post World War I crisis of 1920 also exerted an immediate impact on sugar prices. Cotton prices began to drop five years late. In both cases, domestic producers, large-sized in the case of sugar, smaller in that of cotton, were the victims of the reverse. On the other hand, the United States–controlled mining sector

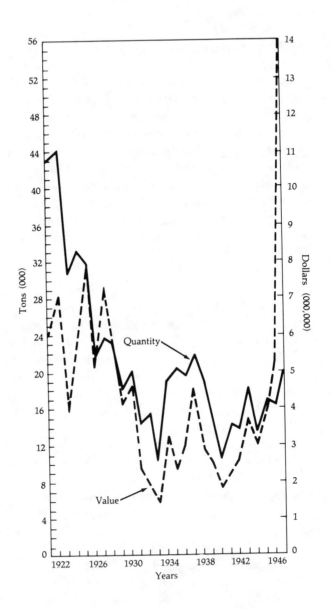

Figure 9.1. Exports of Cacao from Ecuador, 1921–1947. (Source: Erneholm 1948: 97.)

continued to push ahead by virtue of heavy original investments. However, the economic benefits of foreign-owned mining to the local and national economies were rather low, while the remittance of profits and the purchases of the companies abroad totaled almost or about as much (see table 9.4).

Consequently, a recent study draws the conclusion that long-trend Peruvian economic development would have been better off without the United States–owned Cerro de Pasco copper company. The disadvantages of Esso's control (via I.P.C.) over Peruvian oil production, from a national point of view, are even more clearcut. I.P.C. privileges were fixed by an agreement with the government in 1922. Until mid-century shareholders received an average yearly dividend of no less than 40 percent. The Peruvian government under strongman Augusto Leguía (1919 – 30) was offered and accepted large-scale public loans from the United States. On both sides, a naïvely capitalist optimism prevailed.

On the regional level, the rubber production in the Northeastern lowlands suffered its final collapse in 1920. In the Southern Sierra, the wool export boom came to an end at about the same time. This had the positive effect of slowing down hacienda territorial expansion at the cost of the landholding Indian communities. On the other hand, it also undercut the efforts of quite a number of domestic hacendados to modernize wool production by making such efforts too costly. Instead, wool production for sale through Arequipa merchant houses continued

Table 9.4
British and United States
Investments in Peru
(Millions of US Dollars)

	US	*British*	*Both*
1914	38	58	96
1919	111	50	161
1924	145	52	197
1929	162	66	228
1935	–	–	128
1950	145	25	170

SOURCES Bonilla 1980: 100; Thorp & Bertram, 338; Rippy 1949: 85.

in traditional ways. Hacendado producers of sheep wool as well as Indian producers of alpaca wool adjusted to the adverse business trends as well as they could with the use of primitive but inexpensive methods. As a result, however, the economic disparity between southernmost Peru and the rest of the country widened. Using per capita export earnings as a criterion, the gap between those of the south and those of the nation increased by 72 percent between 1915 and 1935.

The Depression naturally had a severe effect on the Peruvian economy, but to a lesser extent than was the case in most other Latin American countries. The crisis (which caused Leguía's overthrow) was for all intents and purposes over by 1933. In fact, foreign owned mining interests had suffered to a greater extent than national ones and the adverse social effects were not so widespread. The relative importance of the plantation sector increased once again and industrialization gained some momentum during the forties. Attempts at increased government involvement in the economy during the latter part of the decade, though, failed miserably as a result of political-administrative ineptitude. This would, by turn, trigger a return to laissez-faire beginning in 1948. Curtailed as a result of the Depression, United States influence in the economic life of Peru was strengthened once again from World War II onward. Ever since the mid-twenties the usual food imports had been reduced but toward mid-century insufficient food supplies were a cause of social tension.

In Bolivia, as elsewhere, 1920 and 1921 were years of crisis which among other things helped to unleash a political coup. Yet, notwithstanding a considerably lower price level than before, tin exports experienced continuous growth during most of the twenties to reach a peak in 1929. In the early years of the decade, Esso, as in Peru, succeeded in obtaining an oil concession on strikingly generous terms. At the same time, the Bolivian government pledged its entire customs receipts in order to secure a $33 million loan from the U.S. for the re-funding of its foreign aid internal debt. Threatened by taxation, tin magnate Simón Patiño also saw fit to grant the government a sizable loan instead. In this connection he opted to incorporate his gigantic Patiño Mines and Enterprises Consolidated in Delaware in 1924. In 1929, to take an example, a 20 percent dividend was paid on its shares. Even though Patiño controlled 50 to 55 percent of the total Bolivian tin production, his assets in his native country gradually became only a minor part of his worldwide mining, smelting, and general business empire. No "dependency relationship" could be more obvious than that of the Republic of Bolivia to this native entrepreneur turned cosmopolitan billionaire.

Depression kept the value of copper exports on a considerably lower level until 1939; World War II helped to raise them once again until 1948. In fact, only the abnormally high war prices helped to offset the steadily declining productivity, due mainly to the lack of new investment and higher-grade ores. Competition on the world market was also hampered by the unavoidably high transportation costs. On the other hand, the Asian and African rivals had Bolivia's "advantage" of low wages, too. Meanwhile, the neglect of agriculture made it increasingly difficult to cope with the provision of however slowly increasing urban populations. In 1925 – 29 food imports absorbed 10 percent of total imports; in 1950 – 52 the share had almost doubled. By mid-century some light industry had been established in Bolivia but otherwise economic prospects were very bleak. Beginning in the 1930s, economic stagnation was accompanied by a steadily worsening inflation.

As we have seen, in all three Andean countries, the economic performance from World War I until mid-century had been very mixed. Agriculture for domestic consumption seems to have been stagnant. In the case of some crops, yields per acreage even appear to have decreased somewhat between the thirties and the late forties, but our knowledge is very spotty. And to what extent did the money economy penetrate the traditional subsistence sector during our period? Little research has been done so far in these areas, which are certainly very hard to explore. In the export sector, on the other hand, we watch periods of expansion and contraction abruptly succeed each other, under the impact of external factors and cycles, without producing long-term development. The greater fragility of the world market itself made the specialized commodity export pattern of the Andean countries increasingly risky and less likely to broaden the economic basis for social development.

b. The Intellectual Awakening

As a consequence of World War I, the existing Western world view was shattered. Trends already in motion, symbolized by the names of Bergson and Freud, Einstein and Picasso, challenged, and won out over, the established, rationalistic tenets of Western civilization. Spengler's *The Decline of the West* (1918–22) expressed a relativistic, pessimistic view of European culture that could not avoid impressing Spanish-American intellectuals, sensitive as they always were to what went on in Europe. Thus, their search for alternative values and sources of strength in the non-European past of their own countries should partly be seen against the backdrop of the new trends in Europe itself. Also, the Russian revolution, leading to the triumph of Leninist Marxism, and the Mexican one, "combining liberal principles with a socialist outlook," offered the intellectuals of our Andean countries of the twenties new stimulating models of social organization. The social awareness of the intellectuals arose. "I care for the naked who are crushed, bowed down, covered in rage," Peruvian poet César Vallejo exclaimed.[1]

Yet, the origins of the Andean reappraisal of the Indian, — essentially Incaic — tradition, *indigenismo*, and its blend with political radicalism lay deeper. As put very well by Manuel González Prada, "there is [in Peru] an unwritten axiom that the Indian has no rights — only obligations. In his case an individual complaint becomes an act of insubordination, a collective petition, an effort at rebellion."[2] Before he died in Lima in 1918, this old "heretic" had already been able to instill some of his anti-oligarchy, anti-clerical, pro-Indian and worker revolutionary ideas, as of late tainted by anarchism, into the minds of a few talented youngsters. Among them were Vallejo, fiery student activist Víctor Raúl Haya de la Torre, and an intense limping typographer-turned-journalist, José Carlos Mariátegui. They would spearhead the most brilliant intellectual generation in the history of the country, that of "1919." As many as ten years before, however, a group of indigenista intellectuals with more genuine roots had emerged in the ancient Inca capital of Cuzco with its hitherto neglected and disdained ruins and Indians. These students, such as Luis E. Valcarcel, later the author of a violent pro-Indian manifesto, *Tempest in the Andes,* and of scholarly works on pre-Spanish civilizations, were guided by an American educator who, steeped in the pragmatism of William James, served as president of the university and made the students carry out studies of regional problems.[3]

In Bolivia, novelist-historian Alcides Argüedas illustrates the ambivalences and contradictions of some of the early *indigenismo*. In two pathbreaking novels (1904, 1919) he condemned, in stark colors, the exploitation of the Indians by their various oppressors, while, as already mentioned in his essay *A Sick People* (1909), Argüedas voiced a fear of race mixture and general pessimism about Bolivia's future that comes close to racist determinism. In a later (1937) edition he would even insert quotes from Hitler's *Mein Kampf* to strengthen his arguments. In Ecuador a pioneering essay on the Indian appeared in 1922. Indigenism would express itself mainly in the form of vehement social protest as in the novel *Huasipungo* (1934) by Jorge Icaza. It is of almost nauseating naturalism.[4]

In all the three countries, indigenista novels, however, were usually written from the outside, inspired by authors such as Dostoyevsky, Gorki, and later, Dos Passos and Hemingway. In 1941, a Peruvian with quechua as his first tongue, José María Argüedas, finally succeeded in producing an indigenista novel written from inside, *Yawar Fiesta*, superior in art as well as substance. It adds to our historial knowledge about obscure encroachments and aggression against the Indians of the Peruvian Sierra, which had taken place some twenty years earlier.

With the spread and superficial acceptance in many quarters of indigenista ideas from the twenties onward, the genuine idealism and concern would increasingly have to coexist with opportunism and hypocrisy; paternalism of either the reformist or the revolutionary brand would downgrade the respect for the Indians' own priorities; bland rhetoric and elaborate laws tried to overshadow the fact that the Indian situation remained very much the same or at times even got worse. In Puno an indigenista organization, the Tahuantinsuyo society, gained many members among the Indians themselves in the early twenties, but it proved short-lived.

President Leguía had come to power in Peru in 1919 with the enthusiastic cheers of indigenista intellectuals. By virtue of the new constitution enacted in 1920, Indian communities became legalized, as they had been shortly before in Mexico as well. Leguía also established protective agencies for the Indians like those existing in colonial times. Policy implementation proved exceedingly slow, however. At the end of his rule (*El Oncenio* — the eleven years), Leguía had extended formal recognition to fewer than 300 out of some five thousand *comunidades* existing in the country. For this smart businessman, Peru's progress depended on the abolition of outmoded land and labor systems and the subsequent incorporation of Sierra Indians into a modern capitalist, cash economy. As he once characteristically declared, "the *gamonal* is retarded in his business sense for his failure to realize that the toil he forcibly exacts from the Indians would multiply a hundred-fold if he worked to keep them well-paid, well-fed and content, instead of squeezing out their very last energies."[5] Integration meant improved communications. To that end Leguía introduced the legal obligation for Peruvian young men to work for certain periods in road construction (*conscripción vial*). As a consequence of existing social relations in the highlands however, conscription was imposed on the Indians only, implying de facto revival of the colonial mita. When Indians rose in rebellion, as in Puno in 1921 and, on a large scale, in 1923, they were put down with great bloodshed by Leguía's troops.

As a matter of fact, the Indians as such were not the prime concern of the young radicals fighting against Leguía either. José Carlos Mariátegui, for all his familiarity with Europe, acquired from 1919 to 1923, never visited the Sierra himself. For his accounts of the Indian problem he relied on information from Cuzco indigenistas and on his own great intuition. In Mariátegui's view, the problem was clearly "rooted in the land tenure system of our economy. Any attempt to solve it with administrative or police measures, through education or by a road building program, is superficial and secondary as long as the feudalism of the *gamonales* continues to exist," as he wrote in his famous book *Seven Interpretive Essays on Peruvian Reality* in 1928.[6] For all Mariátegui's deprecation of Leguía's approach, they share one main priority: the suppression of "feudalism." For Leguía this means the triumph of capitalism, for Mariátegui the ultimate victory of socialism.

For Mariátegui's rival Haya de la Torre, the leader and eclectic philosopher of the radical movement to be known as APRA, the Indian problem had a symbolic importance. The dream of somehow restoring the spirit of an idealized Inca Empire always held a place of honor on APRA's programs. Raised in an impoverished aristocratic environment in the northern coastal city of Trujillo, Haya's eyes for Inca greatness had been opened during a short stay in Cuzco in 1917 – 18. Yet his symbolic and emotional linkage with indigenism grew weaker, the more diverse intellectual elements were added to APRA's doctrine (taken, for instance, from Einstein and Toynbee) and the greater the distance became between this doctrine and APRA's actual political goals.

The indigenistas had in common with many detractors of the Indians a belief that the *comunidades* had basically preserved the collectivistic and egalitarian traits of the pre-Spanish ayllus. More recent social science research has clearly shown that this is not so. Under the increasing pressure of population growth and scarcity of land, communities gradually became, rather, no more than loose groupings of smallholders, kept together only by various traditional kinds of collaboration. Also, the internal organization of the traditional hacienda has been found to have much more in common with that of the comunidad than indigenistas of the early twentieth century could ever have imagined.

Yet for all the weaknessess and contradictions of indigenism as a growing body of cultural, social, and political ideas, and as a source of knowledge, its great importance for succeeding generations of intellectuals in the Andean countries cannot possibly be denied. It helped to provide European-born socialism with a native flavor. It became a main ingredient in a new, more authentic brand of nationalism which, at the least, helped to reduce somewhat the immense gap between the light-skinned descendants of the victors and the dark-skinned descendants of the vanquished. By prolonging the historical perspective and stressing continuity, indigenism helped to promote the self-identity of the Andean peoples. It was very much present in the first struggles for a national revival in Peru in the twenties and thirties and in Bolivia in the forties. Also, when from the 1960s onward, the struggles for an Andean revival entered a second phase, the legacy of elite indigenism finally helped to underpin the widespread mobilization of the rural masses.

c. Revolutionary Challenges and Populist Solutions

Under the impact of revolutionary ideas and economic crisis in the wake of World War I, tremors began to shake the Andean countries' traditional elitist political system. During the twenties, regimes displaying some progressive, modernizing zeal, and backed by United States capital, managed to maintain, for a longer or shorter time, a fair amount of political stability. As in the rest of Latin America, however, they could not resist the onslaught of the Depression. Now, the Marxist and nationalist ideas that had been brewing underground for years came to the surface. Confusing political actions took place, followed eventually by a return to more conservative rule, largely coinciding with economic recovery. Yet this restoration was by no means complete. At the end of World War II the political trends were once again drifting toward the Left.

Yet the Andean countries never witnessed clearcut class struggles. The utterly heterogeneous character of the social structures, which we shall soon analyze, helps to explain why not. While Marxists looked in vain for bourgeois forces strong enough to eliminate "Feudalism," Haya de la Torre, the leader of a new eclectic political ideology, pointing at the weakness of workers, peasants, and the "middle class" asked them to join in the struggle against the "oligarchy" and "imperialism." This was a theoretical endeavor to overcome apparently irreconcilable conflicts of interest. Less ideologically minded politicians found it even more easy to compromise. "Populism" is characterized by a professed faith in representative democracy. It addresses itself in the first place to the urban masses making use of pseudo-socialist, vehemently nationalist, and anti-imperialist rhetorics. In the realm of practical politics, populist leaders are usually quite pragmatic, afraid of hurting seriously powerful interests; they sponsor a greater extent of government economic planning with its concomitant growth of state bureaucracy, with the welfare state as a more or less distant goal.

The success of a populist leader depends above all on his charismatic appeal. It is crucial for the formation of political groupings which cut straight across class borders. Chauvinist nationalism is an excellent political tool, as the twentieth-century history of the Andean republics eloquently demonstrates. Naturally, populist political solutions, of longer or shorter duration, could not bridge all the wide ideological and social cleavages of the Andean societies. Yet, during post-Depression politics, with their shaky economic foundations, different varieties of populism would at times provide surprisingly effective short-term political remedies.

In Ecuador, the liberal party was able to stay in power for a few years after the collapse of the cocoa boom. In 1923, it presented a surprisingly radical program including the request for labor legislation and land reform. It was not adhered to, of course, but probably helped to stir unrest. In 1925, military coups erupted in both Quito and Guayaquil. By far most officers were from the Sierra and the revolution meant that the long Guayaquil hegemony was broken. Yet the leaders proved incompetent for government. A university teacher from Quito, Isidro Ayora, established a smooth dictatorship and carried out a number of well-needed fiscal and administrative reforms. A Central Bank with monopoly over the issue of banknotes was set up in 1927, marking the defeat of Guayaquil banks. Meanwhile, political radicals split into one Socialist and one Communist party. In 1931, the Ayora regime, beset by problems caused by the Depression, was ousted by a military coup. A period of extreme political instability and party fragmentation set in. From 1931 to 1940, there were fourteen Presidents. Among them was a fiery lawyer, José María Velasco Ibarra (1934–35). On the Left, Socialists and Communists helped to bring about some pro-labor and pro-Indian legislation in the late thirties. During World War II, it seemed as if liberal President Arroyo del Río had restored stability with the help of rising export earnings. The longstanding border issue with Peru became fateful, however. In 1941, a Peruvian army invaded a border province. Arroyo del Río failed to oust the enemy and had to sign the so-called Río de Janeiro protocol next year. Thus, 180,000 square miles of jungle territory passed into Peruvian hands. The psychological impact of the defeat was simply devastating. In 1944, a so-called Democratic Alliance of parties ranging from Conservatives to Communists ousted Arroyo del Río. Velasco Ibarra, "the Great Absentee" as he became known during frequent exiles, took power. Velasco was virtually the prototype of a charismatic populist leader. Inept as an administrator, though, he never held the presidency for long. In 1947 he was overthrown and in the course of a month three other Presidents followed suit. The next year, however, a period of political stabilization set in.

In Peru, Augusto Leguía had been elected to the presidency in 1919, but chose to impose dictatorial rule to carry out his ambitious program of "modernization." He had a considerably broader political basis than his predecessors. The "Oncenio" (1919–30) witnessed peace and considerable material progress. Yet, the small group of radical students mentioned in connection with the emergence of indigenism would present him with a crucial challenge. At the San Marcos University a student federation had been formed in 1917. Two years later students led by Haya de la Torre sided with Lima workers in their general strike. Students also helped to push through a radical university reform ensuring them participation in the administration. Haya and his fellow students also set up the so-called Popular Universities, named in honor of González Prada, to give workers a basic education and introduce them to radical thinking. When Leguía staged a provocative religious ceremony, Haya led a protest and in 1923 he was exiled. The next year, in revolutionary Mexico, he launched an incredibly ambitious continent-wide revolutionary movement, APRA (Alianza Popular Revolucionaria Americana). Goals comprised the defeat of Yankee imperialism, the unification of "Indo-America" (Haya's indigenist substitute for Latin America), the nationalization of land and industry, and the internationalization of the Panama canal. Solidarity should be shown with all the oppressed peoples of the world. Within this broad frame, national parties should pursue their own concrete aims. Though influential, Aprismo only produced one national party, that of Peru. Meanwhile Mariátegui had taken charge of the Popular Universities. He also crystalized his own variety of Marxism, intensively nationalist in character:

"Our economy, our political organization, our social architecture, our literature and our art, the forms of our lives must be ours, created by us and for us ... we believe in and feel the creative potential of our race.[7]

Through his efforts to bring into being an indigenist socialist movement of national liberation, Mariátegui appears as a major forerunner of today's third world movement. Haya de la Torre instead set his hopes to a class alliance as a liberating force. On ideological grounds a break between the two was unavoidable. Mariátegui was not accepted by orthodox Marxists until after his death in 1930. The Communist party he founded would above all penetrate labor and intellectual groups in the Southern Sierra. An Indian informant, Gregorio Condori Mamani, for example, when a textile worker in Cuzco, came to admire greatly Communist unionist *compañero* Huamantica.

In 1929, Leguía was able to settle the longstanding border dispute with Chile. The clause of the Ancón Treaty providing for a plebiscite to decide the fate of Tacna and Arica had never been carried out. The people of Tacna, in particular, still felt Peruvian. Leguía and his Chilean colleague in 1929 opted for a compromise. Tacna was returned to Peru while Chile retained Arica. Peruvian nationalists could not forgive Leguía for this concession. With the Depression, Leguía was ousted by a military coup in 1930.

At that time, the Aprista party of the young exiles was already taking root in Haya's native country. Indeed, the specific situation on the northern coast, with its frustrated urban middle class and dispossessed proletarianized small farmers was particularly promising for the new creed. The Popular Universities also had provided well-trained cadres. Haya returned from exile in triumph in 1931 to set the tone in eloquent speeches. "Only APRA can save Peru!" Both presidential contenders, he and Colonel Sánchez Cerro, waged country-wide campaigns. Sánchez Cerro won — his crucial margin likely secured through election fraud. He then established a harsh dictatorship outlawing Apristas and Communists alike. An Aprista rebellion broke out in Haya's home town of Trujillo. The military in 1932 had no less than 1500 prisoners shot after having found the bodies of some military officers, presumably killed by the rebels. The following year Sánchez Cerro himself was assassinated by an Aprista, but the dictatorship was maintained by another general, moderate enough to pass some basic social legislation.

During the 1939–45 period, the banker Manuel Prado, as President, opened up a liberalization of Peruvian politics. He was strengthened by upward economic trends and the easy triumph over Ecuador. At the time of the elections of 1945, Haya de la Torre had considerably moderated the program of the legalized Aprista party. No longer was the United States the great enemy and foreign capital, under certain conditions, would now be welcome to help develop Peru. The party was under his complete command. Aprismo now threw its support to an independent liberal lawyer, Bustamante, who then won. Yet harvest times found Apristas ill-prepared for democratic politics. Haya himself never joined the government. Strikes became rampant and Bustamante's efforts to govern were undercut by the Apristas. Congress was paralyzed by the conservatives. In 1948, an Aprista mutiny broke out among Callao sailors. It was suppressed by Bustamante, who then declared the party illegal once again. Nevertheless he was then himself ousted by a military coup.

While taking on an increasingly populist-type approach, Aprismo seemed merely to have strengthened the alliance between the "oligarchy" and the more and more politicized military establishment. As suggested by figure 9.2, military interventionists largely pursued their own vested interests. Ever since the Trujillo events, however, military hatred for the Apristas was also extraordinarily intense.

In Bolivia, the leader of the Republican party coming into power in 1920, David Saavedra, pursued the same type of progressive, authoritarian policy as Leguía. Yet the uncooperative attitude of tin interests caused him problems and his image was hurt by the Uncía massacre and relations with U.S. business. In foreign policy, the Peru – Bolivian border settlement in 1929 made Bolivian hopes for an outlet to the Pacific vanish. A longstanding dispute with Paraguay over the wild, uninhabited lowlands of Chaco, which provided access to the River Plate system, therefore took on greater importance. Both sides built small fortresses and armed clashes took place. Saavedra's successor, Hernando Siles (1925 – 30) avoided open war, however. He fell himself victim of the Depression, and was replaced by Daniel Salamanca (1931 – 1934), a fiery nationalist orator and rival of Saavedra, who took over the presidency and deliberately pushed the nation into war with Paraguay to escape domestic problems. Urban crowds cheered on the Indian *colonos* and *comuneros*, who formed the bulk of those sent down to the hot, barren grounds of Chaco to fight an utterly senseless, poorly managed war. It cost 52,000 Bolivian lives and 21,000 prisoners (a

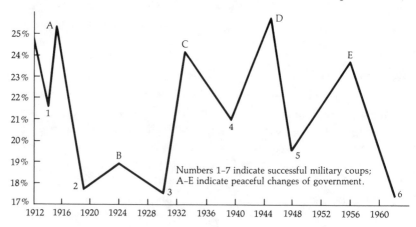

Figure 9.2. The Share of Military Costs of the Peruvian National Budgets. (From: Villanueva 1962: 282.)

fourth of them died, too). Losses totaled about a third of the huge numbers of men drafted for the war. Salamanca was arrested and forced to resign by the army high command. In 1935, an armistice sponsored by Argentina left the Paraguayans with almost all the territory under dispute.

Traditionally the rivalry between two giant oil companies established in Bolivia and Paraguay respectively has been blamed for the war. This seems to be a myth, however; escapist nationalism was undoubtedly the main culprit. The war is a watershed in Bolivia's history. Before, political radicalism had been confined to small groups of intellectuals and union activists. After, embittered war veterans spread radicalism throughout the lower and middle classes.

The military leaders who took over in 1936 aimed to pursue a vaguely worded policy of "military socialism." Colonel David Toro actively promoted labor organization: A Ministry of Labor was set up, an effort was made to eradicate the pongo service to hacendados, and work was started on a new labor code. In 1937, Toro daringly nationalized ESSO holdings (a year before the Mexican President took a similar step). Another, more ideologically confused, "military socialist," Colonel Germán Busch, then pushed Toro aside. The radical constitution of 1938 owed little to Busch, however, and the new labor code was merely enacted under him. In desperate political isolation, Busch took his life in 1939. The military regime now switched drastically to the Right.

Meanwhile new political organizations took shape. Two revolutionary parties, PIR (of orthodox Communist orientation) and PDR (of the Trotskyite brand), vied for worker support. Led by a mild-mannered university teacher, Victor Paz Estenssoro, the *Movimiento Nacionalista Revolucionario* (MNR) appealed to the urban middle class. The slogan of an old revolutionary, Tristán Marof: "The land to the Indians, the mines to the State," gained increasingly wide acceptance. One of the many massacres of striking miners, at Catavi in 1942, helped to destroy government authority. MNR now joined a military faction, strongly tainted by Fascism, to launch a successful coup in 1943. The incompetent new President, Major Gualberto Villarroel, got into a squeeze between the MNR, extreme fascists, miners, and Indian peasants. He resorted to terror tactics against some of his opponents. In 1946, he was dragged out of the presidential palace by a crowd, and hanged from a lamp post nearby. Yet, the ensuing conservative civilian regime could not ensure stability. MNR now turned to POR for support. The tough, experienced miners under a charismatic boss, Juan Lechín, proved valuable allies indeed. Paz Estenssoro actually won the presidential elections of 1951 but the military had the results annulled. Therefore, the people took action, and with considerable bloodshed brought MNR into power the following year, — another crucial divider in Bolivian history. Like APRA, a movement endowed with an eclectic and adjustable ideology, MNR, through populist skill, had been able to mobilize much wider popular political support than any previous movement in the country. Yet the entire social context in Peru and in Bolivia had become increasingly different since the Depression.

From the 1920s onwards, politics in the Andean countries have come to mean much more for greater numbers of people than ever before. To bet on the right political horse has become crucial for swelling groups of public employees and military officers. With the spoils system and corruption, politics also literally came to mean "bread" for an ever wider number of people. Mass nationalism increased. Even in the rural areas, to the degree that traditional isolation broke down, political messages could now be diffused, at times in distorted versions. Top-level political decisions, however opportunistic or abortive they may look in retrospect, therefore had much wider implications than before in the economic as well as social spheres.

d. Social Unrest Within a Tight Economic and Political Frame

Like the rest of the poor countries of the world, the Andean republics underwent crucial demographic change at mid-century (see fig. 9.3). The main cause was a very modest extension of medicine and health care, especially striking in the growing urban sector. In Guayaquil, for example, yellow fever and bubonic plague were eliminated around 1920. In the 1950s, the child mortality rate (those dying before reaching their first year) was still 113 per thousand babies in Ecuador. This was one of the highest figures in the world at that time, and it probably understated reality. The situation in Bolivia also remained very bad. Nevertheless, we must conclude that by 1950 a considerable change for the better had already taken place compared with previous times for which statistics are lacking or exceedingly poor. While mortality rates dropped, in the Andes, as elsewhere in the third world, they remained high. Even so, between 1930 and 1950, the annual growth rates of our three countries remained lower than in Latin America as a whole (see table 9.5). Peru's population grew from about 4.5 million in 1910 to 5.7 in 1930, 9.0 in 1950; that of Bolivia remained about 2.2–2.5 until 1940, and rose to 3.0 in 1950. Ecuador's demographic development was more dynamic: 1.5 in 1910, 2.1 in 1930 and 3.2 in 1950.

Life expectancy increased. In Peru, it was only about 35 years at birth in 1940, which is equivalent to one of the very poorest African or Asian countries today. Between 1950 and 1960 an average of 47 years had been reached. There was, however, a difference of several years be-

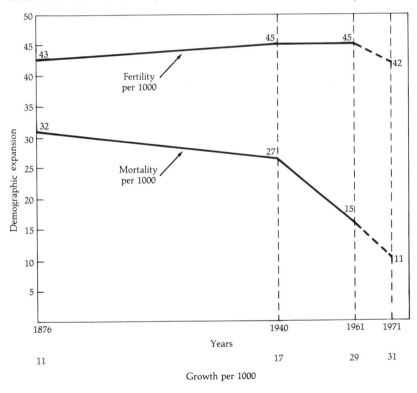

Figure 9.3. The Demographic Evolution of Peru. (From CPED 1970: 152.)

tween the better-off inhabitants of the Coast and those of the Southern Sierra. Similarly, Ecuadoreans, on average had more years to live than Peruvians, Bolivians less.

According to a sociomedical study carried out in the 1940s, the diet of rural highlanders of Peru suffered from a lack of minerals, especially iodine, calcium, protein, and vitamins. This led to deficiency diseases and gastrointestinal infections. In 1950 another research team found the nutritional level of Bolivian miners alarmingly inadequate. Their wages simply were not enough to buy the food required for even a family of three. A sample taken of diets in highland Ecuador in 1948 sugested a worsening of the state of nutrition since an inquiry made in 1934.

In Ecuador and Peru, the share of coastal populations increased. There and in Bolivia, too, urban populations grew more quickly than the national average. Even languid La Paz, which had less than 50,000 inhabitants in 1900, housed more than twice as many in 1950. In Ecuador, the population of the city of Guayaquil, due to natural growth as well as migration, grew from 92,000 in 1919 to 267,000 in 1950. Quito was not far behind. Lima had some 220,000 dwellers in 1920. Thirty years later, Lima – Callao was approaching a million. Here, to a much greater extent than in the other main cities of the Andean region, industrialization helped to promote urban growth.

It is hard to analyze the changes occurring in the ethnic makeup of the population. After all, such changes were not related to differential patterns of vital rates, but were instead the outcome of complex socio-

Table 9.5
Demographic Growth of the Andean Countries
(Thousands of Persons)

	1930	1940	1950	Average Annual Growth Rates 1930/40	1940/50
Peru	5,651	6,681	7,968	1.6	1.6
Ecuador	2,160	2,586	3,225	1.8	2.2
Bolivia	2,153	2,508	3,013	1.5	1.9
Tropical South America	53,832	65,795	83,491	2.0	2.3
Latin America	104,441	126,074	159,312	1.9	2.3

SOURCE N. Sánchez Albornoz, 1974: 184. Latin America's rate of increase between 1900 and 1930 had been 1.7 percent.

economic processes and varying census criteria. In any case, it is worthwhile to point out that in Bolivia in 1950, more than 60 percent of the population were classified as "Indians." Fifty years earlier, less than 50 percent were: a symptom of the increasing rural poverty or just more comprehensive classification criteria? In Peru, on the other hand, the "Indian" percentage in 1940 had dropped to 46 as compared with 58 for the previous census of 1876. Peruvian Indians now formed majorities only in the central and southern highlands. In Ecuador, the vast majority of the rural inhabitants of the highlands were still classified as "Indians" in 1942. That is almost 40 percent of the population of the Republic. From this perspective it is easy to realize that the so called "Indian problem" remained, in fact, the fundamental one in all of the three Andean countries. Yet, notwithstanding increasingly comprehensive and benevolent legislation that was either not implemented at all or merely to a minuscule extent, the depressed situation of the Indians remained very much the same.

In Bolivia, the tenant labor or *colonos* of the haciendas disposed of a subsistence parcel as remuneration for two or three days of weekly labor for the patrón, who supplied their own tools and animals. The peons were even worse off. Through yearly oral contracts, the peon was "required to work continuously and is outside all social protection.... He is a means of transport, a building worker, a farm labourer, a servant, a cook, a messenger for long and tiring errands." The peons could also be hired out to others for days, weeks, or months, a mid-century observer notes.[8] In the southern highlands of Peru, similar systems of tenancy and labor prevailed. In the Ecuadorean Sierra, daywork obligations of Indian tenant labor, the *huasipungueros*, lasted even longer, from Monday to Friday or even Saturday. Also, they received their tiny cash wage with such delay that indebtedness to the hacendado was a foregone conclusion. In the province of Pichincha, Ecuador in 1952, 30 percent of the farmers were huasipungueros but their parcels covered merely 2 percent of all farm land. Still more marginalized than the huasipungueros, the *yanaperos* performed work merely in return for some pasture right or the use of water and wood on the estate. They often lived in nearby communities, but were forced to complement somehow their meager resources there. In fact, life in the communities was hardly better than that on the haciendas. Instead of having one, possibly paternalistic landlord, community Indians were subjected to what González Prada called "the Indian-brutalizing trinity" of the priest, the local administrative officer, and the justice of the peace.[9] All of them normally exacted fees and labor services far beyond or outside the limits set by law. As we have seen, there is a monotonous continuity with respect to all these abuses ever since early colonial times. It is striking, however, that a government commission sent to Puno in 1920 listened to more than 7000 Indian grievances and found that no less than 87 percent of them concerned usurpations of land and another 8 percent abuses committed by the gamonales. This inquiry and other government measures probably had no tangible effect on Indian conditions.

Yet, the period 1920–1950 may have witnessed some slight change for the better, the difference being that even abuses committed in faraway corners of the highlands became more often denounced in both local and national newspapers. At times they were also taken up in the national Congress. At the same time, in Peru at least, the display of some "indigenista" rhetoric became part of the proper political behavior. Thus, bad publicity may have made administrators somewhat more inclined to have the more blatant abuses reduced. More important, though, economic factors occasionally worked in the Indians' favor. The case of the Otavalo Valley in Ecuador is striking. Around 1920, Indians took up weaving for sale on distant markets. They soon sold their produce on faraway journeys in Colombia and Venezuela. In southernmost Peru, on the other hand, the decline in the demand for wool slowed down hacienda aggression and expansion at the cost of Indian communities, a negative kind of blessing.

This latter factor had no immediate effect, however, and Indian uprisings were still frequent and sometimes rather large-scale in the Southern Peruvian Sierra and elsewhere in the Andes during the twenties. As a concrete example, let us take the "Rumitaqe" rising in the southern part of the Cuzco Department in 1921. The intense hatred between the Indians and their Mestizo neighbors comes out with horrifying clarity. Also, in this case, the deep religious attachment of the Indians to their local deities and lands was apparently reinforced by Incaic revivalism diffused by ambulatory members of the Tahuantinsuyo society.

The Indians planned the uprising very systematically; arms were to be brought by contraband from Bolivia, and young men who had performed their military service were to be given key functions. The intention was to kill whites and Mestizos of three parishes, and a city lawyer was to be hired to defend the natives and see to it that Indians should henceforth be named for local administrative positions. After an eloquent exchange of insults in quechua, the two parties clashed. The Mestizo leader was taken prisoner and was put to death with a deliberate, ritualistic cruelty. In the end, of course, the Indians were defeated and many killed. Afraid of a repetition, though, most Mestizos of this area are said to have withdrawn to the cities. The whole story merges traditional and modern elements in Indian resistance.[10]

While Indian uprisings in the Southern Sierra had largely ceased by 1930, in the Central Sierra Indian peasant resistance clearly stiffened from that time on. Huge wool companies (*sociedades ganaderas*), which had been formed with Lima capital, tried to modernize production. In accordance with this aim, Indian shepherds, with their traditional grazing rights for their own sheep on hacienda land, were to be transformed to workers paid in cash only or dismissed. This increased the tension. The companies were able to mobilize more support in Lima than the old gamonales had been; on the other hand, the shepherds showed a striking capacity for passive resistance. Outside pressure on the peasant communities also increased. In the twenties, the establishment of a new smelter at La Oroya by Cerro de Pasco company brought widespread environmental destruction to the cattle and crops of the surrounding communities and haciendas. The company was able to buy some 200,000 hectares at rock-bottom prices. Also, workers dismissed from the mines at the onset of Depression, together with organizers from urban leftist parties, stirred unrest in the countryside. But it was no longer a question of abortive violence. While miners engaged in strikes (without success), a kind of peasant mobilization took place, step by step, with a view to improve living conditions through various means.

While gamonales, indigenistas, and other non-Indians often presented their different views of the Indians, we know much less about how the Indians observed and experienced the changes taking place in the surrounding world. Therefore, the oral autobiography of Gregorio

Condori Mamani, of Cuzco, born in 1908, is exceptionally enlightening. He tells us, for example, about his own reactions and those of other Indians when seeing trains, planes, and cars for the first time and how they tried to reconcile these phenomena with their own cosmos but had to resign themselves to these new triumphs of the *wiracochas*. When describing two normal experiences of the Indian male, a prison term meted out by a corrupt judge and military service, Condori makes clear that the latter was by far the worse. In the faraway world of politicians and intellectuals, military service was often lauded as a means of achieving Indian basic education and integration. Condori shows how the officers tried to make the Indians speak some words of Spanish by prohibiting them from talking Quechua among themselves or simply by knocking them about and insulting them. "Carajo" (Damn it all!), they did pick up. Condori, a city dweller by then, also admirably succeeds in putting political history into a broader and more realistic perspective when summarizing the events of 1948: "When five big loafs of wheat bread cost one *real* and three a half *real*, Odría seized the Presidency from Bustamante.... Those governments always take the Presidency away from one another."[11]

The extraordinary interviews with Condori and his wife present the somber and harsh, albeit profound, world view of the highland Indians. To illustrate the immense variety of the Andean world let us also take up the very different testimony of Candelario Navarro, an 83-year-old black peasant of Nazca, on the southern Peruvian coast. For this sensuous, spirited man "women and cock fights have always been and still are my glory. But, as far as I recall, I never had so many women at my disposal as in the year 1923." Yet Navarro also tells us about how the switch from one crop to another at the command of plantation owners affected the lives and subsistence of their workers adversely. He also speaks about race discrimination, quite outside the law, naturally. In the eyes of all those white bosses, he comments, "Cholos, Negroes, were no people, or, rather, the poor were no people. The bosses, sure, were the people and formed their guild, their society.... decency and chivalry existed for them only."[12]

On the Peruvian coast, sharecroppers (yanaconas) played an important role, especially in cotton plantation labor. There were Indians from the highlands as well as Japanese immigrants and native Negroes or cholos among them. The sharecroppers were usually indebted to the landlord through the company store and thus in a very inferior bargaining position. The law of *yanaconaje*, passed in 1947, guaranteed them tenancy rights and regulated rental fees. Whether or not the law actually improved the yanacona situation is a matter of controversy. Reformist legislation was always notoriously difficult to implement, unless the stronger party found some loopholes. Until the Depression, there was normally a demand for labor in the plantation sector that made the enganche device of procuring labor from the Sierra an important one. After the Depression, enganche ceased and migrant labor became less important.

Beginning in the 1940s, we know more about the inner workings of Andean rural society, thanks to the case studies carried out by pioneer social anthropologists. What they observed around 1950 was the beginning of a process of social change tending toward the integration of rural communities into society. In the small town of Muquiyauyo in the Valley of Mantaro in the Central Peruvian Sierra, an American anthropologist found the demand for workers in the nearby Cerro de Pasco mines and the establishment of rural schools to have been the most important factors of change. At the same time, shortage of land due to population growth also encouraged migration — whether to Lima or the mines. Yet, what made such migration a factor of local change was that Muquiyauyino migrants kept together, maintained contact with their native land and often returned there. Ex-miners, for example, brought the idea of establishing a power plant back to their home town. On the other hand, returnees from Lima who had been radicalized by Mariátegui and the Apristas failed to change general local attitudes to any noticeable degree.

On the coast, also, rural communities used to live rather isolated from the outside world. Such isolation now broke down. In the small coastal town of Moche on the Northern Peruvian coast, with some 3700 people, where the railroad did not stop, the greatest innovation was the frequent bus service to the city of Trujillo. The bus brought passengers as well as supplies, newspapers, and mail. There was a telephone connection, but only for emergency use. As many as 200 newspapers were sold daily.

The Church was losing some of its traditional grip over the minds. The young generation of Moche became interested in soccer and, when in Trujillo, movies. According to the anthropologist who is our source, in this coastal community, with its ethnically heterogeneous population, people felt little local pride and solidarity or cared about the town's historical past (which, in fact, stretched back to a glorious pre-Inca culture).

In the Sierra, as a whole, apparently, psychological continuity and roots were stronger even though differences have been perceived between Mestizo and Indian communities as well as between those of hacienda colonos and members of the *comunidades*. Among the latter, as we touched upon in connection with the 1921 Rumitaque uprising, the presence of pre-Spanish beliefs has been especially noticeable.[13]

We have just observed the social impact of mining from the perspective of a nearby town. If one takes a look at the mining camps themselves, the most striking observation is that the workers remained very much peasants and only passed short periods there. Their nostalgic, melancholic songs reflected their alienation. Occasionally they deserted their jobs at harvest, so that the powerful foreign-owned enterprise was obliged to pay better wages to maintain the labor force, thus widening the gap between its pay and rural wages. But the mining sector as such was far from stable. Between 1929 and 1932, Cerro de Pasco cut its labor force from 13,000 to 4000 workers; by 1950, the number was back to 13,000. (Interestingly, in the 1920s, eight out of ten of the young workers of one of the mines were literate.)[14]

From the viewpoint of the occasional visitor, the most striking features of the large cities were naturally the impressive public buildings, monuments to national heroes, banks, hotels, and plush upper class residential areas. Yet by far most of the swelling urban populations were artisans and workers who lived rather miserably. Some had grown up in the same city; others, in increasing numbers, arrived from outside. In Lima, between 1900 and 1930, about two-thirds of working class children were born out of wedlock, often they never knew their fathers. Migrants, on the other hand, often came from closely knit communities and stayed together.

The city-born were better educated. By 1930, less than 10 percent of Lima's population was illiterate. Until the Depression there was much demand for labor. Yet the opportunities for getting permanent employment and promotion were few inside the artisan sector. Beginning in World War I, manufacturing absorbed growing numbers of workers. Unions, established in some branches, were able gradually to improve the working conditions and wages of their members. Yet the steady rise in the cost of living made it hard for all workers, but especially those outside unions, to subsist. A nonunion construction worker in Lima during the twenties used some 60 percent of his paycheck for food and nearly 25 percent on always very inadequate housing. The increased inflow of migrants and a boom in the construction of middle class homes further deteriorated the standard of workers' dwellings. Poor water and toilet facilities caused frequent illnesses. In the absence of any kind of health insurance, illness easily brought a worker's family to disaster.[15]

With World War I, unionization, already quite advanced in Latin America's leading countries, also became a factor in the Andean countries, despite their low level of industrialization. From the cities, the unions spread both to extractive industries and plantations. Railroad workers also formed an important force in early unions. In Lima, the cost of living almost doubled between 1913 and 1919. A general strike in the capital in that year forced the government to grant union members an eight-hour day. Yet another general strike, later that year, backed up by radical students, tried to force the government to lower the cost of living; it finally failed.

Unionism spread to the mining, petroleum, and plantation sectors. In 1921 and 1932 there were, for example, violent strikes in the sugar producing Chicama Valley, suppressed only with considerable bloodshed. During the twenties, the Leguía government, initially pro-labor, soon switched to a hostile, repressive stance. With Leguía's overthrow in 1930, unions appeared on the scene once again. Communists and Apristas vied for leadership. By 1932, another dictatorship repressed the unions once again. Only in the forties were Peruvian labor organizations able to expand and function more normally. Yet, their percentage of the total labor force (outside the near-subsistence sector) appears to have been low.

In the case of Ecuador, we have already mentioned the dramatic general strike in Guayaquil in 1922. For another few years, anarchosyndicalists led the movement. Later communists gradually gained control, after competition with socialists. In 1928, unions pressed the government to see to it that the first labor legislation was passed.

In Bolivia, organized labor remained numerically small and politically it was divided among Anarchists, Communists, Socialists, and

Trotskyites. Yet, railroad and mining workers proved admirably militant in their fight for more decent conditions. In 1923, for example, miners in the Uncía district of Oruro challenged both the Patiño management and other patróns by organizing a federation. To suppress it, government troops massacred large numbers of workers. Yet, belatedly, the government saw fit to have Congress pass a modest amount of labor legislation. In the early thirties, Depression and the Chaco War forced unions to lie low. Toward the end of the decade, however, they emerged not only as a major force on the labor market but in national politics as well, as we shall soon see.

Thus, key labor unions were struggling to obtain better conditions, gradually leaving the rest of the lower strata farther behind. At the same time, the middle class, recruited from above as well as below, continued its expansion in all three countries. It should be noted that when we use the term "middle class," it does not mean entirely the same thing as in the United States or Western Europe. In Latin America, this class has less cohesion and fewer values in common. After the first political interventions by the professional armies, a military career became a vehicle by which to achieve upward mobility.

Even in the most backward of the countries, Bolivia, there was a considerable degree of structural social change between 1900 and 1950. Literacy grew from 17 to 31 percent; that of urban dwellers (in centers of 5000 people and more) increased from 14 to 23. The number of those with higher education also grew, although in 1950, they still constituted less than 8 percent of the total population. More interestingly, there was a change in the composition of this educational elite. Clergy and lawyers declined in both absolute and relative terms, doctors at least in the latter respect, while the number of middle-rank employees, such as teachers and engineers, swelled. Whether employed in the public sector (as the former) or in the private (as most of the latter) these groups would suffer greatly from inflation and other evils caused by a monocultural economy in serious trouble. They also shared such problems with the upper levels of the working class such as the members of urban, railroad, and mining unions. For these middle and working class people, the continued reliance by the traditional elite on its vast, inefficiently used landholdings must have appeared increasingly anachronistic. Even as late as 1950, almost entirely old-fashioned agriculture employed as many as 72 percent of the economically active population while its contribution to the GNP was less than half as large. It was increasingly unable to provide the food supplies the city dwellers and miners needed. Also, the authority of the most powerful economic interests, with Patiño as their main figure, suffered from being largely absentee, represented by subordinates only. Thus, class structure in Bolivia, from the 1930s onward, certainly suggested that serious social and political problems lay ahead.

Peru, with its much more varied geo-economic base continued to have a more complex social structure. Ever since the guano boom, however, the national elite was based on the coast. This trait had been reinforced, as we have seen, by the export boom from the late nineteenth century onward. The social structure of the Sierra became increasingly subordinated to that of the capital and the coast. In the Sierra, as in Bolivia, traditional landholding — often coupled with a profession—remained a crucial indicator of local or even regional high status. It did not carry with it admission to the national elite, however. Also, middle class status in the Sierra was by definition closed to the Indians, in the south usually the majority. Only by means of individual acculturation, that is by becoming a *cholo*, would a person of dark skin and Indian features be able to achieve a very limited social ascent. On the coast, ethnic borders were more diffuse. Income and occupation were more immediately important there as social class criteria. On the coast the continuing concentration within the plantation sector drastically reduced the number of middle-sized producers and transformed many tenants and sharecroppers into wage-earning workers. The same process was very disadvantageous for the entrepreneurial segment of the provincial cities and towns. In Lima, however, the ambitious, expansionist policy of the Leguía government, backed up by United States loans, increased greatly the number of jobs available in the public sector. For the lower middle class, in Lima and other cities, higher education increasingly took on the function of a vehicle for upward social mobility. It seemed to open up excellent opportunities, in administration as well as in the professions. The number of students matriculated at the San Marcos University increased from 789 in 1907 to 1331 in 1917; from 2510 in 1938 to 10,422 in 1957. At this last date, at least 12 percent, and probably many more, had a working class background.

The start of this development provides the background of the university reform of 1920. In turn, that reform, by making class attendance optional, made it easier for poor students (the majority) to combine work with their studies. Thus, very naturally university students became radical. In their later careers, some continued to feel bitterness and frustration while probably most adjusted comfortably to upper middle class positions in administration, private employment, or the professions. For the sector of small businessmen, the Leguía period looked especially promising. After all, he was one of them himself. Most of the middle class obviously supported his challenge against the "oligarchy," the top clique who until 1919 had been the undisputed arbiters of national affairs.

Yet, the "oligarchy," whether defined in terms of wealth or social perception, whether consisting of 44 or 30 families, would show a surprising capacity for survival. The concept of oligarchy has been much discussed and also abused; the reality of the concentration of a very great amount of wealth and power in very few hands can hardly be dismissed, however. A small number of families continued to control by far most of the plantation sector, banks, insurance companies, industries and mass media. Interestingly, the composition of this group, most of the members of which had been recruited around 1900, would remain virtually unchanged and closed from 1919 until the late sixties. Yet, the analysis of the "oligarchy" should not be a static one. The degree of their control over the whole economy was clearly conditioned by the changing importance of the foreign-owned sector (mines, petroleum) and the varying composition of foreign trade. Thus, paradoxically, the Andean country where the challenge against the traditional social and political order was first and most clearly articulated, would also be the one where that same order proved to be most difficult to shake.

According to an analysis of the Ecuadorean census of 1950, the middle class made up about 20 percent of the population. Two-thirds were city dwellers. By a generous definition, urban population comprised 44 percent of the total. By comparison, the upper class was estimated at merely 1 percent of all Ecuadoreans. The most salient feature of Ecuadorean society by the mid-twentieth century was the heterogeneous character of the middle class. On the bottom there were shopkeepers, white collar employees, and skilled laborers linked in most respects to the lower class. In the middle, civil service and other white collar employees and academics were torn between a very modest income and cultural values as well as consumption patterns linking them to the upper class. The insecurity of government employment obviously increased their frustration and their inclination for politicking to gain their livelihood within this class. On the very border of the upper class were found military officers, bureaucrats, merchants, middle-size landowners, members of the traditional upper class families with declining income — all of whom, as a matter of course, were even more closely tied to the upper class. As in Peru, the latter was formed by a number of large landowners, bankers, industrialists, and top-level bureaucrats.

What sets Ecuador apart from the other Andean countries, in this regard, is the relative regional balance between the Guayaquil and Quito based segments of the upper class. To be sure, that balance had been threatened during the period of liberal ascendancy tied to the cocoa boom of 1895 – 1925, but with the revolution of the latter year it was restored. As a result, the upper class found itself more torn than ever between divergent economic interests and linkages. Thus, as we shall see, they were forced to allow a greater participation in politics by other groups, from middle class and the military particularly.

Under closer scrutiny, current terms of social analysis such as "oligarchy," "bourgeoisie," and "proletariat" appear less than useful in the effort to clarify the fluid, complex, and subtle social reality of this period. Beneath the strata usually designated as "proletarians" and "peasants," that is, wage earners and independent minifundists, there are in both the urban and rural sectors growing amorphous groups hard to classify. On a higher level, the border between skilled labor and low-level white collar workers is rather blurred. The pretension of "whiteness" is a subtle division line, cutting across the entire spectrum of the middle strata. Finally, it is usually very hard to separate the upper middle class from the elite. It is a boundary that individuals, at least in Ecuador and Bolivia, often crossed, up or down, temporarily or for good. The varying impact through time of external economic trends and the general lack of class solidarity go far in explaining the otherwise bewildering political process of the Andean countries for most of the twentieth century. They help us to understand the absence or very slow pace of true socioeconomic development.

X.

The Fight for an Andean Revival: Act II

Since the mid-twentieth century, the world community, as well as articulate people in countries like Bolivia, Peru, and Ecuador have started to define new ambitious and exacting goals for the economic policy. The poor countries of the world were supposed to rise step by step from a stage called "underdevelopment," understood as the opposite to the advantageous socioeconomic situation enjoyed by the old industrial countries and quickly restored there after the destruction of World War II. In the sixties, most economists agreed that, in order to "develop" the poor countries had to carry out thoroughgoing institutional and structural reforms while maintaining a high export volume and reasonably sound finances. Whereas outside economic interests wanted the poor countries to continue to offer good conditions for foreign capital, an increasingly vociferous domestic opinion favored the reduction of external "dependency." In relation to the extremely high level of ambition of "developmental" policy, it would be easy to dismiss the actual performance, at least of Bolivia and Peru, as a failure. Yet, if economic developments are placed within a more realistic framework, including world market trends and unhampered demographic growth, a change for the better is seen actually to have taken place, especially if one takes the long view.

a. The Economic Straitjacket

In all the three countries, manufacturing, foreign trade, and the consumption of energy experienced a notable increase (see table 10.1). The communication network greatly improved, thus knitting together many areas hitherto isolated and neglected. In Ecuador, for example, a total of 4000 km of paved roads in 1978 meant a sixfold increase since 1960. What has been achieved, however, is far less than the hopes of Bolivians and Peruvians when the valiant structural reforms were carried out, or those of Ecuadorians when the oil boom set in. The results attained by the Andean countries are also below the average for Latin America, as a transitional region between the "developed" and the "underdeveloped" world. Formidable obstacles remain in the way of any attempt to improve living conditions in the Andean countries.

The case of Bolivia is especially sad. Stagnating agricultural production, inflation, administrative inefficiency, and the rising production costs of tin helped to trigger the Movimiento Nacionalista Revolucionario (MNR) revolution of 1952. The tin content of the ore had dropped from some 15 percent in 1900 to 2 to 3 in 1950. The MNR takeover led to the nationalization of the tin mines and a drastic land reform. Especially during the first period the land reform merely meant the splitting up of haciendas among the colonos. Between 1955 and 1965, about 6 million hectares were handed out to about 170,000 families. Very little money and knowhow were available to make the reform work economically. Rural production for sale, at least, hit an even lower level.[1] Food imports swelled. Inflation was speeded up even more.

Table 10.1
Foreign Trade and Energy in the Andean Countries, 1960 – 1978

	Bolivia	*Ecuador*	*Peru*
a. Exports in millions of US dollars			
1978	627	1.494	1.949
b. Imports			
1978	768	1.627	1.960
c. Average annual growth rate of exports (percent)			
1960 – 70	9.7	3.7	1.9
1970 – 78	1.7	9.5	-3.8
d. The share of fuels, minerals and metals of total exports (percent)			
1960	—	0	49
1977	79	50	47
e. Energy consumption per capita (kgs of coal equivalents)			
1960	147	201	445
1978	368	505	649

SOURCE: World Bank, 1980

When a state enterprise for tin production (COMIBOL) was set up, foreign engineers left, and "featherbedding" became the norm. All this, combined with the drop in tin prices after the Korean war and the continued deterioration in the tin – ore ratio, resulted in conditions even worse than those in the rural sector.

In 1954, an injection of United States aid (to help prevent a "Communist" takeover) made it possible to avoid national bankruptcy. In 1957, a program of economic stabilization, urged by the International Monetary Fund (IMF) and the United States, was begun. From 1961 onward Bolivia received massive United States economic assistance under the Alliance for Progress. Per capita, Bolivia received more aid than any other country up to 1970. After the fall of the MNR government in 1964, the new regime sought by whatever means possible — including the violent suppression of the miners' rights—to prevent tin production from crumbling. Some economic growth and a better regional distribution of benefits now took place. In the lowland Santa Cruz area, the production of cotton, rice, and cattle quickly increased. Petroleum production, which had gone through several ups and downs since the MNR revolution, was nationalized in 1969. The government of General Banzer in 1971 was able to survive until 1978. During this period of relative political stability, some economic expansion once again took place. The public sector increased its share of the GNP from 18 to almost 25 percent. Exports expanded. However, external indebtedness was also allowed to grow virtually unhampered. By 1978 debt service absorbed almost half of export earnings.

After the fall of Banzer, there could hardly have been more political instability. All the old structural weaknesses are manifesting themselves with increased severity. Inflation is soaring. From a purely economic point of view the preparation of cocaine from coca leaves and the contraband traffic destined for the United States has been one of the very few bright spots. Yet, paradoxically though hardly surprisingly, this principal export income (at least during the dictatorship of 1980 – 81, when it involved major government figures) is not officially recorded. Rather conservative estimates in 1980 put total annual Bolivian earnings from drug traffic at $600 million — that is, two-thirds of those derived from legal exports.[2] It can be argued that traditional tin ore export monoculture has been considerably reduced due not only to cocaine smuggling but also to a considerably more diversified legal export pattern. Yet, considering the great role of smuggling until at least a couple of years ago, all recent economic statistics on Bolivia possess an unreal—indeed ghostlike—quality.

Endowed with a much more varied geoeconomic potential for development than Bolivia, Peru nevertheless faced some of the same structural obstacles in trying to rise from backwardness. The economic rhythm and the sequence of development strategies pursued differed, however. After the failure of state interventionism in the mid-forties, General Odría's government from 1948 resolutely opted for a laissez faire policy, allowing foreign capital virtually free hand. The state did support costly irrigation schemes on the coast, however, and cotton and sugar exports soared. So did those of mining, which in addition to copper, lead and zinc, now included iron as well. From the mid-fifties onward, fishmeal also emerged as a new, major import staple in response to an almost explosive rise in world demand for animal feed products. Yet the benefits of this export-induced prosperity were shared in a glaringly uneven way, perhaps even more so than those of guano a hundred years earlier. Also, Peruvians benefited less than foreign economic interests. Denationalization advanced particularly rapidly in mining. In 1950, five foreign firms controlled 42 percent of the entire mining output; twenty years later their share had grown to 66 percent. In 1950, 30 percent of exports were derived from foreign-owned enterprises, in 1967 no less than 50 percent. Most of the banking sector was in foreign hands. Industrialization and concomitant urbanization advanced very quickly but without any rational planning. Manufacturing's share of a growing GNP increased from 14 percent in 1950 to 20 percent in 1968. In this sector, too, foreign capital became most conspicuous. The remittance of profits to home countries, often in illegal ways, and the light taxation actually contributed by foreign firms in Peru could only attract hostile attention which could no longer be ignored by policymakers. Nor could one be completely blind to the continued misery and lack of infrastructure in most of the highlands. A severe drought in the southern Sierra in 1956 – 57 caused massive starvation. Even in Lima, with its dynamic manufacturing industries, about a third of the labor force was jobless or clearly underemployed. In coast agriculture, mechanization forced many out of work.

In the fifties, the United Nations Economic Commission for Latin America, led by innovative economist Raúl Prebish in Santiago de Chile, launched its call for institutional, structural reforms as a prerequisite for Latin American development. In the sixties, more radical social scientists would directly demand the end of Latin American "dependency" on the old industrial countries, especially the "imperialist" United States, through drastic socialist policy measures. Also in conservative Peru, politicians had at least to pay lip-service to new political demands when Odría was succeeded by two consecutive constitutional governments. The pace of economic expansion, quite high until 1967, was slowing down in the late sixties. In 1964, President Fernando Belaúnde pushed through a land reform which, however, did not at all affect the powerful, profitable agroindustrial sugar and cotton sector. The law was also full of loopholes for negligent large landowners. In the interior, the government in practice gave priority to road building along the *ceja de montaña*, aimed at stimulating lowland colonization.

In the late sixties, the glaring inequity of Peruvian society and the failure of economic policy to produce development could no longer be hidden by, for example, the continued fishmeal boom. The GNP per capita took a downward turn. Income distribution in Peru was clearly even more skewed than in other Latin American countries, with the possible exception of Colombia. The poorest 20 percent of the population held no more than 3.5 percent of the total individual income. While those employed in the modern sectors of the economy and administration had seen their income grow by about 4 percent yearly since 1950, the income of those engaged in the traditional rural sector did not increase at all. Urbanization proceeded with extreme speed. Lima's population grew from 500,000 in 1940 to two million in 1961. Thus, traditional agriculture became increasingly unable to satisfy food demand, even though some cotton areas were turned back to food production. By 1963, food constituted 24.5 percent of total import value, ten years later as much as 35.4.

The military takeover in 1968 was directly triggered by the conciliatory stance taken by President Belaúnde in an agreement with International Petroleum Company. The petroleum sector is always very touchy from a nationalist point of view. Yet the exceptionally forceful and ambitious economic policy of General Juan Velasco's military Junta can be understood only against the backdrop of what was seen as the ultimate socio-economic failure of the "liberal" policy initiated in 1948.

The Junta boldly started a number of drastic policy measures with a view to opening up a new path toward development. The expropriation without compensation of the International Petroleum Company's holdings and the reorganization of an existing state company into the all-powerful PETROPERU were followed by the new and comprehensive land reform in 1969. According to this law all larger properties were subject to expropriation in favor of permanent farm workers organized in cooperatives though with a rather generous provision of compensation to the former landlords. The reform was immediately put into effect in the case of the huge agroindustrial sugar complexes on the Northern coast. In 1970, foreign mining companies were deprived of their undeveloped concessions and a new state company, MINOPERU, took over all mineral-export marketing. Later, the Cerro de Pasco mining company was nationalized. In 1970, also, the Industrial Reform Law gave workers in manufacturing plants a progressively larger share in the management, ownership, and profits of the enterprises. Whenever it was dominant, foreign capital was requested to withdraw to a minority position. The fishmeal industry had reached a peak in 1971, but soon suffered a disastrous drop due to overfishing and the recurrence of the "El Niño" phenomenon in 1972. It was then nationalized. So were a number of foreign owned banks. Thus, the state share of ownership within the modern sector of the economy grew from 11 to 26 percent while that of foreign capital shrank from 21 to 8 and that of domestic private capital from 30 to 22. The political implications were great, of course. The "oligarchy" had suffered a severe blow. Foreign capital had to accept very strict limits for its penetration. The nationalist stance of the Junta was reflected also in the tough new rules for the control over foreign investments (Paragraph 24) agreed upon by the Andean Group. This ambitious organization of regional economic integration on the customs union level was set up in 1969 within the looser framework of the Latin American Free Trade Association by Peru, Bolivia, Ecuador, Colombia, and Chile.[3] In the beginning, the Group, with headquarters in Lima, and with Peru as a driving force, was quite successful. Later it lost much of its original momentum.

By and large, Peru's economic performance from 1970 through 1975 looked very promising. Favorable price trends on the Peruvian staples helped the per capita GNP to grow at an impressive rate (see fig. 10.1). In retrospect, though, the many reforms initiated by the Velasco Junta appear not to have been well enough prepared nor duly coordinated. Also, the expectations of the Junta and of those who believed in government promises that the redistribution of property and income within each economic sector would be sufficient to trigger a takeoff soon proved illusory. Last but not least, the traditional pro-urban bias of policy continued to characterize government actions, if not rhetoric. Indeed, compensations awarded to former landowners implied a net transfer of capital from the traditional rural to the urban sector, when a flow in opposite direction would have been sorely needed.

At first glance, the proportions of land redistribution were impressive. In 1975, half of the agricultural land had been redistributed, mainly to cooperatives of former permanent workers and colonos — a total of some 400,000 families. Yet the poorest rural population, another million families (seasonally employed farm hands and members of Indian communities) probably saw their situation deteriorate. They

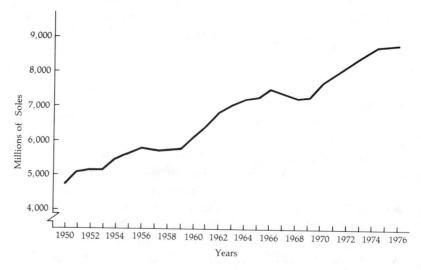

Figure 10.1. Peru's Gross National Product Per Capita, 1950–1976. Prices of 1963. (From Coyuntura Andina 1977: 2:160.)

were excluded from participation in the cooperatives and received, at the most, marginal benefits from larger units, the so-called SAIS. With demographic growth (almost 3 percent yearly), the arable land per inhabitant in Peru was merely 0.18 hectare in 1971, one of the very smallest in Latin America and equal to that of China. Without adequate rural credit and improved distribution networks, without improved labor intensive agriculture through systematic training programs, the Peruvian land reform simply could not succeed in backward areas. In fact, the entire redistribution program of the Junta tended to favor merely the upper levels of the rural and urban working classes alike. However authoritarian and proud of the land reform, the military government were now city dwellers, above all concerned with the price of food.

The economic crisis came in 1975. The per capita decline of agricultural production for domestic consumers was a major bottleneck. The real income of the urban working class declined by 40 percent between 1973 and 1978. Annual inflation had grown from 17 percent in 1974 to 58 in 1978. Foreign indebtedness grew alarmingly. After Velasco had been removed in 1975 the new, more cautious members of the Junta slowed down the tempo of reform. With the blessing of the IMF, they initiated an economic program of austerity and stabilization while preparing for a gradual return to constitutional civilian government to face the apparently overwhelming economic problems.

In 1980, when Belaúnde returned to power, the financial crisis had already become less acute. Mining and manufacturing were expanding; fishing had recovered somewhat. The per capita rise of the GNP in 1981 (see table 10.2 and fig. 10.2) was quite impressive, especially when regarded against the very somber backdrop of general Latin American stagnation. Interestingly, a special agency has been set up to guide development projects through the morass of bureaucratic red tape and intra-agency rivalry that have so often hampered execution. Reversing Velasco's policy, the gvernment is about to determine how large a part of the extensive, mostly unprofitable public sector will be turned over to private enterprise. Also, the programs of employee sharing in profits of private manufacturing had already been undermined during the last phase of Junta government. Just as in Belaúnde's first term, the plight of land reform and the whole rural sector of the

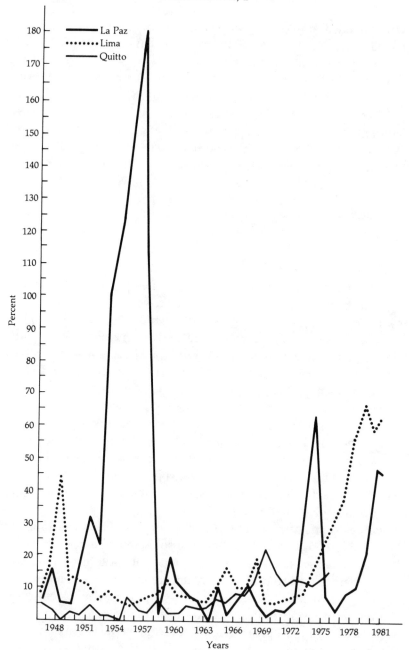

Figure 10.2. Yearly Consumer Price Variations in Percent, 1946–1980. (Source: SALA.)

highlands appear to have drawn little government attention compared with the renewed hope of colonization and oil exploration in the *ceja de montaña*. Once again, the hopes of Peruvian policymakers are set to outward oriented economic expansion, led by free enterprise in alliance with foreign interests. This somehow is expected to produce socioeconomic development. The declining Andean Pact is given little attention.

Tremendous structural problems remain to be resolved in Peru. Real wages are still 25 percent lower than in 1974. The unemployment rate is 8 percent of the labor force, those patently underemployed are estimated at no less than 52 percent. Inflation has soared to new heights, 72 percent in 1981. "Traditional" agriculture lies in shambles. Admittedly, the average per capita GNP of Peru in 1980 was far superior to that of Bolivia. It was also considerably higher than that of Ecuador and only somewhat below the Latin American average. Yet, this statistical figure has little to do with the way in which most Peruvians live.

In comparison with Bolivia and Peru, Ecuador's economic performance since mid-century appears to offer more space for development. Its economic growth rate since 1960 is clearly superior. Yet institutional and structural bottlenecks prove hard to unclog.

By the late forties, the rice export boom made possible by the high level of war and war reconstruction demand was fading, but cocoa exports continued to grow until the mid-fifties. Thanks to a plague ravaging Central American banana plantations, however, Ecuadoreans were now able to launch their own quickly expanding banana crops on the world market. In 1955 bananas were responsible for 41 percent of Ecuadorean exports, seven years later for as much as 61 percent. Cultivation spread throughout the coastal interior, pushing beyond the borders set by cocoa producers. Middle size holdings (from 26 through

Table 10.2
Rates of Inflation in the Andean Countries, 1960 – 1978

	AVERAGE ANNUAL RATES		ANNUAL RATES	
	1960-70	1970-78	1980	1981
Bolivia	3.5	22.7	47.2	32.3
Ecuador	–	14.8	13.1	16.0
Peru	9.9	22.2	59.2	71.8

SOURCES: *1960-78*: World Bank 1980; *1980*: IDB; *1981*: CEPAL 1982

499 hectares) accounted for 75 percent of banana production, which mostly remained in Ecuadorean hands. The banana boom helped to raise the level of the GNP, which in 1950 – 60 grew at 5 percent yearly. Later, competition with other banana producers sharpened and the monocultural export economy revealed its usual weaknesses.

The first agricultural census of 1954 laid bare some of the structural inequities long suspected by social and economic critics. Owners of latifundia (of 500 hectares and more) constituted merely 0.4 percent of all landowners but held 45.1 percent of all agricultural land. The poorest peasants, with less than 5 hectares, formed 73.1 percent of all landowners with merely 7.2 percent of the agricultural land. Furthermore, while the peasants, however primitively, used 85 percent of their parcels, not more than 16 percent of the latifundia areas were actually used either for cultivation or as pastures. Naturally, the glaringly backward highland agriculture was largely responsible for this somber national picture.

In 1964, an Agrarian Reform Law was enacted. It basically pursued the modernization of the whole agrarian sector. The abusive huasi-pungo system was abolished. Inefficient haciendas would be expropriated but owners were given a three-year respite to avoid this by improving productivity. This clause ought to have diminished some of the extensive decapitalization which took place in the case of, for example, frightened Peruvian landowners. A second agrarian reform law in 1973 had the same general goal. The Agrarian Reform Institute (IERAC) proceeded to redistribute land at a rather slow but steady rate. In the highlands, some 315,000 hectares had been distributed in 1977, on the coast, 120,000. More important, about one million hectares of virgin lands had also been colonized. Land reform measures, together with various social and market developments on the coast and in the Sierra respectively, did modify agrarian structure. While, in 1954, latifundia covered 41 percent of the agricultural lands of the coast, in 1968 the share was down to 22. In the highlands the respective figures were 49 percent in 1954 27 in 1968. Market-oriented, middle-sized holdings increased. The haciendas of the Sierra, to a considerable extent, were now modernized. They have turned from extensive pastoral activities in traditional forms to, for example, dairy production. Milk production grew by about 7 percent a year between 1954 and 1978. (see table 10.3)

Meanwhile, growing export deficits and other signs of economic malaise in the late sixties signaled that the export-led economy was heading for trouble. Once again, however, the Ecuadorean economy was almost miraculously saved by a new staple. Almost overnight, the country became a great producer and exporter of crude petroleum in 1972. Furthermore, next year as a consequence of the Middle Eastern War, oil prices soared. Momentarily, Ecuador became Latin America's second largest producer (after Venezuela) but by 1981 it had dropped to the seventh place. While export agriculture in 1970 – 71 had been responsible for 94 percent of the total export value (44 percent bananas), in 1976 – 77 crude oil took 51 percent, leaving only 44 percent for agricultural products. In current dollars, the result was a sevenfold increase in total export values (see table 10.4.)

Step by step, the government assured itself control over this giant resource, until then exploited by foreign companies. In 1976, a state agency for petroleum, CEPE, had reduced Texaco to a minor partner. While not overly pleased, foreign interests finally gave in. Thanks to oil money, Ecuadorean industrialization made a significant advance. It comprises only about a sixth of the GNP, however, and some 11 percent of the labor force. The meager purchasing power of the rural population in particular, which still forms some 60 percent of the total, reduces the

Table 10.3
Ecuador's Gradually Changing Agrarian Structure

A. Farms Broken Down by Hectare			
Year *under 10 hectares*	*10.1 – 50 hectares*	*50.1 – 500 hectares*	*over 500 hectares*
1954 16%	12%	23%	49%
1974 18	22	28	32
B. Farms Broken Down By Unit			
1954 90	7	2	720 units
1974 87	10	3	599 units
C. Land in Hectares Distributed Under Agrarian Reform			
Period	*Highland*	*Coast*	*Total*
1964 – 66	68,447	17,514	85,961
1967 – 71	72,189	21,102	93,291
1972 – 75	72,725	43,297	116,022
1976 – 77	98,293	37,353	135,646
TOTAL	314,654	120,266	431,920

NOTE: in 1954, there were 3,020,400 hectares; 259,579 farm units; in 1974, there were 3,074,274 hectares; 322,586 farm units
SOURCE: Archetti 1980: 41,58.

domestic market for national industrial consumer goods. At the same time, the well-off have been responsible for rapidly growing imports of luxury goods. Oil as a rule offers extremely few employment opportunities, while other economic activities are often hampered by the competition with imports. In Ecuador the production of wheat in 1979 was only a fourth of the 1970 level, while wheat imports reached a much higher level. Some 40 percent of the urban adults are estimated to be underemployed and in the countryside, the proportion reaches 60 percent. Inflation rose, although not nearly to the Bolivian or Peruvian levels.

A new, ambitious civilian government came to power in 1979. It claimed finally to use oil profits wisely. Oil reserves were estimated to last for another twelve years only, and the level of exports of crude was lower than in the early years. The government launched programs of social investment on a massive scale. Thanks to a huge literacy campaign, illiteracy is about to be wiped out even in hitherto monolingual Indian areas. About 400,000 school children have become able to enjoy free breakfasts. The housing problem has been met by large-scale construction. A fairly realistic development plan for the period 1981 –

Table 10.4
Ecuador's Exports, 1970 – 77: An Example of Structural Change
(Millions of US dollars)

	1970-71	*1976-77*
Crude petroleum	*1.5*	*51.2*
Main agrarian products	*93.7*	*44.1*
Bananas	44.2	11.4
Coffee	22.1	14.0
Cocoa	11.9	3.4
Timber	3.4	0.7
Fish	3.5	2.6
Processed cocoa	1.9	9.2
Processed fish	1.3	2.1
Sugar	5.4	0.5
Processed coffee	-	0.2
Minor and non-traditional exports	5.8	4.7
Exports, excluding petroleum	*99.0*	*48.8*
Total exports	*100.0*	*100.0*
Total exports, Millions US$	(194.5)	(1.354.0)
Total exports, Millions US$ excluding petroleum	(193.5)	(660.1)

SOURCE: From Archetti 1980: 61.

84 was adopted, but was soon disturbed by the short border war with Peru. The GNP for 1981 fell below expectations and recent government efforts have had to focus on the reduction of public spending.

Notwithstanding the banana and petroleum booms, Ecuador remains a poor and largely underdeveloped country but, from an economic perspective and in comparison with its Andean neighbors, its developmental prospects are reasonably good.

b. Politics of Underdevelopment

The recent political history of the Andean countries eloquently illustrates the enormous difficulty of conducting a coherent political strategy favoring economic growth and national strength under conflicting external and internal pressures. Any experiment in democracy in a real sense is fraught with uncertainties; yet, neigher can dictatorships afford too blatantly to hurt nationalist feelings or the interests of the international business community. Thus the result necessarily becomes an ambivalent, winding political course. Notwithstanding the appearances it is usually compatible with rather than a challenge to underdevelopment. In the political reality, the fight for an Andean revival has been repeatedly betrayed and confined to the chimeras of rhetoric.

By the mid-twentieth century, striking political changes had taken place in all our three Andean countries, though in different directions. This was the time of the beginning of the Cold War, when first President Harry Truman and then Secretary of State John Foster Dulles engaged the United States in the struggle for world supremacy with the Soviet Union. The Latin American countries were supposed to give their support in return for U.S. private investments, — that is, the blessings of private-enterprise-led development.

In Ecuador, a dynamic businessman embodying this spirit, Galo Plaza, was elected President in 1948. Exceptionally, he as well as his successors, the ever-present Velasco Ibarra and a conservative were able to complete their terms. The backdrop of this unusual political stability was obviously provided by the banana boom. The old political opposition between Guayaquil and Quito was partly transcended by Velasco Ibarra, with his countrywide demagogical appeal.

In Peru, on the other hand, the experiment in democracy was abandoned that very year, 1948, when General Manuel Odría established a dictatorship. His main opponent, Haya de la Torre, found asylum at the Embassy of Colombia in Lima; even at the risk of war the Colombians did not hand him over. Odría cleverly combined internal repression with largesse toward foreign economic interests and rode the waves of economic prosperity until 1956, when he let the country revert to constitutional rule. The pliable conservative Manuel Prado as a President once again provided a gradual liberalization of politics.

The most dramatic political change, however, was that taking place in Bolivia after the MNR revolution of 1952. The new President, Víctor Paz Estenssoro, quickly fulfilled his main political promise, the nationalization without compensation of the "big three" tin producers (Patiño, Aramayo, Hochschild). They were replaced by a state agency, COMIBOL. The MNR regime, under the pressure of spontaneous peasant actions, particularly in the fertile Cochabamba Valley, also decreed the land reform of 1953 which abolished the huge haciendas (see fig. 10.3). Through a very slow-working judicial procedure, most of the land was redistributed. Peasants now received the property rights to the same parcels that had already been at their disposal, as usufruct, when they were still colonos. Little was done to improve the process of production and marketing. The Indian communities were simply left to their fate.

It was mainly urban workers and miners who benefited from revolutionary redistribution, and their benefits were soon largely annulled by inflation. Replacing the old army, peasant, and miners militia, students and other leftist activists displayed considerable revolutionary fervor. Yet what saved the MNR regime, increasingly shaky in financial terms, was United States economic aid. Paradoxically, this happened at the same time as Dulles succeeded in overthrowing a less radical regime in Guatemala, accused of being Communist. To understand the difference it has to be kept in mind that United States investments in Bolivia were far less important than in Guatemala and that the MNR leadership soon showed themselves ready to listen to American advice. Thus, from an American point of view, the threat of Communism in Bolivia was removed. Yet, the main effect of American aid, exceptional in Latin

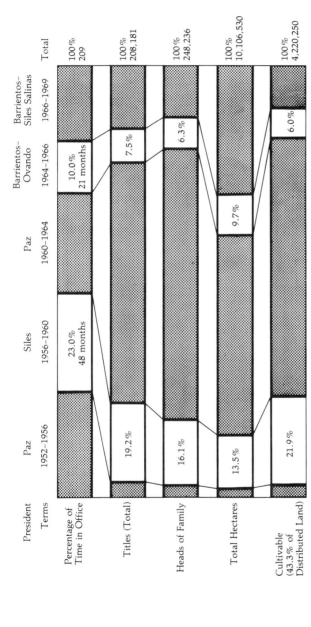

Figure 10.3. Bolivian Land Reform Data by Presidential Period. (From Wilkie 1974: 38.) The statistical data are unreliable, however, as stressed e.g. by José L. Havet in his PhD diss. (cited below p. 283), pp. 68–72.

America during the Dulles era, was simply to keep the MNR establishment in power, despite its many weaknesses, without producing any
major social change. Within MNR ranks, the split grew between Paz
and union boss Juan Lechín on the one hand and Hernán Siles Zuazo,
at that time the leader of the MNR wing (President, 1956–60), on the
other. The latter managed to curb inflation drastically, and in addition,
under him a new professional army also came into being.

From 1959 onward, Fidel Castro's revolution would introduce a new
element of threat/hope in Latin American politics and increase the
tension and urgency of hemispheric relations. Unable to crush the
Cuban revolution by force, the new liberal administration of John F.
Kennedy launched the so-called Alliance for Progress, a massive aid
program aimed at promoting Latin American economic and social
development within a framework of political democracy to counter
"Castroite subversion." The lip-service paid to such ideas was not hard
to obtain. CIA agents, provided with ample funds, did their best to
prevent any revolutionary attempts among members of leftist parties
and union rank-and-filers. Yet some of the young radicals, enthralled
by Castro's fiery message, proved immune to corruption and preached
and planned revolutionary action. Beginning in 1964 (the time of the
Sino-Soviet split), the Cuban regime committed itself to support such
attempts. At the same time, in the Andean countries, a new generation
of military officers was now emerging, some of them sincerely concerned about the social ills besetting their nations and full of nationalist
pride. Against this general background it becomes a little easier to
understand the varied political scenery of the 1960s.

In Bolivia, the increasingly incompetent MNR regime, once again
headed by Paz Estenssoro, was ousted in 1964 by the Vice-President,
General René Barrientos. This charismatic leader was backed by the
army and the urban middle class. He could converse with Indian
peasants in their own tongue, which helped him to gain wide rural
support. Military and peasant organizations, in fact, formed a durable
alliance. Thus, Barrientos easily crushed minor opposition and also the
pathetic guerrilla attempt led by Castro's Argentine-born aide, "Che"
Guevara, in Southeastern Bolivia in 1967. Brutally killed after surren-
dering, however, Che would provide Latin America's revolutionary
cause with a martyr, and a whole young generation all over the world,

with an enduring symbol. Barrientos himself died in a helicopter crash in 1969.

In Ecuador, Velasco Ibarra, when initiating another presidential term in 1960, opted for a flirt with Castro to improve his image among youth. He was then ousted by a military coup in 1961; so was his alcoholic successor in 1964. A moderately progressive military Junta now took over. It initiated more serious developmental planning, started to reduce the almost 50 percent illiteracy rate, and (as discussed already) decreed a cautious land reform along the lines of the Alliance for Progress. Faced both with declining banana export as well as rightist and leftist civilian opposition, they returned the country to constitutionalism in 1966. The incredible popular appeal of old Velasco Ibarra, as a candidate for the presidency, brought him into power once again in 1968.

In Peru, under Prado, party politics had revived toward 1960. Odría, the ex-dictator rallied conservative groups around him while also trying to appeal to the poor; the Apristas under Haya de la Torre followed a right-of-center course while retaining some of their old leftist rhetoric; originally a splinter group from APRA, the *Acción Popular* party threw its support to a young liberal architect, Fernando Belaúnde Terry. According to the Constitution, if presidential elections did not result in a clearcut victory for any candidate, the decision would be made by Congress. Belaúnde won the election of 1962, but not by a margin sufficient enough to allow him to take office directly. Congressional confirmation was required. When in a strikingly opportunistic way the old arch-enemies Odria and Haya agreed to forestall this mildly reformist politician from gaining power, the military intervened. Thus Belaúnde's victory was assured in elections held next year. Yet he had to cope with a sizable, hostile, Aprista–Odriista majority in Congress. This helps to explain his rather bleak performance. The land reform of 1964 merely conformed with the moderate prerequisite set by the Alliance for Progress to initiate some change in the outrageously skewed land tenure pattern.

By this time, however, not all Peruvians were content with waiting for government decisions on this increasingly debated issue. Revolutionary minded youngsters from Lima formed "fronts" (MIR, ELN) with a view to stirring the long-suffering peasant masses into action. Misled by Castroite theory that the conditions for Revolution "will mature in the process of struggle," they took up arms as rural guerrillas without having assured themselves of peasant support. Many did not even know the Quechua language. After a short period of fighting, most of the guerrillas were wiped out by the military in the mountains of Ayacucho and Cuzco in 1965. A more constructive movement had developed since 1958 in the *ceja de montaña* province of La Convención in the North of Cuzco, led by Trotskyite lawyer Hugo Blanco. The lands, cultivated with plantation crops, were taken over by tenants (*arrendires*) and sub-tenants (*allegados*), while the peons remained relatively passive. Blanco was imprisoned in 1953, but the status quo was not restored. Instead, La Convención was declared a zone of Land Reform. Those who gained most of it were the *arrendires*. In some highland areas, also, haciendas of the traditional type or some of their terrains were invaded, more often than not, peacefully by peasants who at times were able to keep the land for good. Thus, uncertainties surrounded Belaúnde's reformist policy, from both right and left. The government tried to improve education and to open up the *ceja de montaña* for colonization to relieve increasing population pressure in the Sierra by means, for instance, of the *carrerera marginal*, a pet road-building project of Belaúnde's. His compromise deal with the International Petroleum Co. (IPC) in the long-standing issue over company debts to the state finally proved fatal for the administration. Military leaders, outraged on nationalist grounds, and fed up with slow-moving reformism, overthrew Belaúnde in 1968 and immediately occupied the IPC oilfields and nationalized its assets.

This military coup inaugurated the most ambitious attempt at structural change in Peru so far and also influenced events in both Bolivia and Ecuador. Yet, by 1975 the forces of change had already been weakened and the return to constitutional civilian rule in 1980 so far implied the adoption of more limited development goals. The strength as well as the limitations of the military establishment as an instrument of social change is highlighted by the Peruvian experiment. Their very campaign experience against the guerrillas made the military more aware of the glaring poverty of the rural masses. Radical theoretical explanations of national problems were also offered at the Center for Advanced Studies (CAEM) of the National War College. Under the dynamic leadership of General Juan Velasco Alvarado the 1968 Junta quickly proceeded to change Peru's economic and social structure by fiat (see fig. 10.4). The land reform of 1969, different from that of 1964, brought about a massive change in land tenure, as we have seen. The nationalization of Cerro de Pasco, of the fishmeal industry, and of numerous banks enormously swelled the public sector. The industrial law of 1970 introduced profit sharing and employee participation in management; the concept of "social property," ominous to the propertied classes, was also launched. The state's share of gross investments had increased from 13 percent in 1965 to 50 percent in 1975. The national bureaucracy, with generals conspicuous among its upper ranks, was overwhelmed by its many tasks. While the first nationalist measures were hailed by popular enthusiasm, it proved increasingly difficult to mobilize the masses in favor of a revolution from above. The organization set up for this very purpose, SINAMOS (National System in Support of Social Mobilization) soon suffered from bureaucratic ills.

The government-led Peasant Confederation (CNA) faced opposition from the left. In the unions, both Communists and Apristas retained much of their strength, even though industrial workers belonged to those particularly favored by the new policy. When the economy took an adverse turn by 1975, discontent and unrest increased. The police forces themselves rebelled in Lima, inciting a riot which was suppressed only with much loss of life. Soon the ailing Velasco was ousted by his fellow generals.

Leadership in the military Junta was now taken over by Francisco Morales Bermúdez, much more moderate and cautious than Velasco but also facing rapidly growing economic problems. The reformed agrarian sector did not receive the economic and educational support that would have helped it to function. Government economic policy was increasingly dictated by the IMF, leading to the drastic reduction of public expenses, rising of taxes, and the withdrawal of basic food subventions. Strikes and riots became the order of the day. The teachers (SUTEP) showed especially great militancy: on the other hand, CNA and SINAMOS, having failed to fulfill their purpose, were dissolved. Yet, CNA, radicalized from within, has managed to survive as a living force. Unemployment increased; inflation soared. Under these circumstances, the military, many of whom had already filled their pockets at

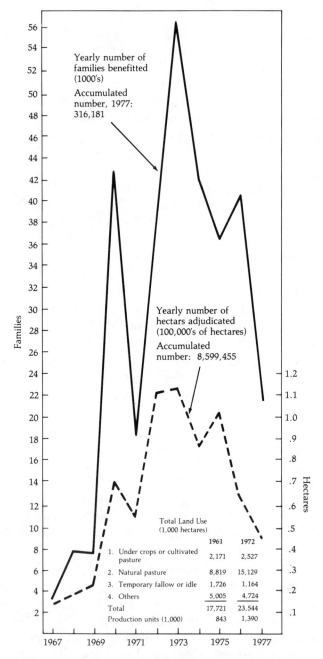

Figure 10.4. Peru's Agrarian Reform, 1967–1977. Families Benefited and Hectarea Adjudicated (Based on Alberts 1981: 176 f., 214.)

public expense, became increasingly fed up with governmental responsibility. Thus, they decided to call elections for a Constituent Assembly in 1978 to prepare for a return to constitutional rule. While Belaúnde's party, Acción Popular, boycotted these elections APRA, the conservatives, and the radical left each took about a third of the vote. With 80-year-old Haya de la Torre as chairman, the assembly miraculously produced a constitution on schedule. Shortly thereafter, in early 1979, the venerable founder and leader of the APRA Party died. With his passing, the party split into right and left wings. Thus, the presidential elections of 1980 were won by Belaúnde, who gathered almost half of the vote in a contest with, among others, the candidate of APRA's left wing. The radical sector of the electorate, which in 1978 had garnered the support of a third of the electorate, now did only half as well. At the end of 1980, however, the left made a better showing in municipal elections. At any rate, the left has been characterized by lack of collaboration and squabbles between its various factions.

When Belaúnde started his second presidential term, economic recovery was already on its way, even though it was too soon to have been noticed by people in general. It is too early to make a balance sheet for Belaúnde's policy. Clearly, for better or worse, many of the innovations of the military era have been formally or informally undone. Press liberties have been restored; so has private ownership in some sectors previously deemed "of national interest." Many cooperatives in the countryside are being split up into individual parcels. The brief war with Ecuador in 1981 as usual helped to bring about some amount of national unity. As in Belaúnde's first term, though, guerrilla activities have been stepped up in recent years. An extreme leftist group, *Sendero Luminoso* ("The illuminated path") usually takes credit (or is blamed) for this phenomenon. The stronghold of this apparently Maoist faction is the Department of Ayacucho in the high Sierra. The government long tried to suppress the guerrillas by police action, but in vain. In early 1983, Belaúnde reluctantly let the Armed Forces take over the task. Few would see a new national leader in the terrorist leader, Abimael Guzmán, but if successful in their campaign, the military might, of course, opt for getting rid of the President himself, as they did in 1969.

As had the second Military Junta under Morales Bermúdez, the Belaúnde administration represented a turn to the right. A new period of economic "liberalization," led by Finance Minister Manuel Ulloa with a view of attracting foreign capital, set in. It is interesting to notice that the government was able to bring down the military's share of government spending from 15 percent in 1975 to 9 percent in 1981. But is it merely a question of a fairly brief civilian interlude or will Peru's great structural problems be resolved within a lasting constitutional framework?

In Bolivia, Velasco Alvarado's example was followed by General Alfredo Ovando, Barrientos' successor, when in 1969 he decreed the nationalization of the assets of Gulf Oil. He also approached organized labor. In 1970 another coup brought a clearly more leftist general to power, Juan José Torres. Presided over by Juan Lechín, a "People's Congress" was convened to replace the parliamentary institution. Private enterprise fell victim to destructive strikes. With Torres' radical if confused politics, a showdown was soon inevitable. The reaction came primarily from the lowland area of Santa Cruz, a center of dynamic colonization and business activities ever since the 1950s. From this base, Colonel Hugo Banzer in 1971 overthrew the Torres regime and reintroduced free enterprise economics. Brazilian economic and political interests could be discerned behind him.

A modest amount of economic expansion helped Banzer to prolong his rule until the elections scheduled for 1978 when his handpicked candidate, a general, faced Siles Zuazo, now backed by the MNR left. While the outcome was still in doubt the general simply ousted Banzer, removed Siles, and established a repressive regime. After two more coups, popular elections took place in 1979, probably the most honest ones in Bolivian history. No less than 1.6 million people went to the polls. A partly new party system could be discerned where peasants no longer lined up behind the sitting government.

A caretaker president named by Congress, Lydia Guiler, made a remarkable effort at stabilizing the chaotic economic and political situation, but in 1980 she was ousted, too. The dictatorship now established by General Luis García Meza established a high record for political repression and corruption — even by Bolivian standards. The regime was so deeply involved in the thriving narcotics export business that not even its anti-Communist zeal could make it acceptable to President Reagan's administration. The ruling Mafia was replaced as usual by coup and a somewhat more reputable Junta set up in late 1981.

Faced by a worsening economic situation and growing union opposition, a year later the military opted for a return to constitutional rule. Congress, which had been closed by García Mesa, made Siles Zuazo President. His task, to restore democracy while trying to lead the country through an acute financial crisis, could hardly have been more difficult. Even if his valiant effort should deserve the support of international credit institutions and the patience of his compatriots, it may be undone any moment. Yet from a longer perspective, social change, however modest its positive results so far, will, it is hoped, bring about less chaotic and more decent political conditions.

In Ecuador, the fifth Velasco Ibarra term was characterized by an even greater amount of leftist verbal demagoguery than usual. Another, somewhat younger, Guayaquil-based populist leader, Asaad Bucaram, was also threatening the establishment. Under these circumstances the military, who as usual had removed Velasco Ibarra in 1972, hoped to bring about structural change similar to their Peruvian counterparts, without committing themselves either to Marxism or capitalism. The reform program of the Junta, led by General Guillermo Rodríguez Lara, appeared less than utopian thanks to the sharp rise of oil exports. Yet, after Velasco Alvarado's fall in Peru, the Ecuadorean military too opted for a more rightist course. They appeared to be inspired, rather, by the example of the Brazilian military.

Rodríguez Lara was toppled in 1976. A gradual return to constitutional government now took place. The permanent contender, Velasco Ibarra, finally vanished from the scene in 1979 at 86 years of age. Bucaram was denied the right to run as a presidential candidate because his parents (Lebanese) were foreign-born. He then threw his mighty support to the husband of his niece, Jaime Roldós. In 1979 the attractive Roldós won the elections on an ambitious socialist reformist platform. Bucaram, however, controlled Congress and very soon the two split on, for example, the issue of constitutional reform. Economic problems also emerged. They were compounded by the short border war with Peru. In May 1981, the young, ambitious president was suddenly killed in an air crash. Soon thereafter, his uncle by marriage, Bucaram, also passed away. The Vice President, Osvaldo Hurtado, a Christian Democrat, took over. The author of a scholarly work, *Political Power in Ecuador,* Hurtado has so far managed to remain in office despite acute economic problems, drastic price rises, and violent strikes. Under Roldós and Hurtado, an efficient campaign reduced illiteracy from nearly 25 to less than 15 percent. A better trained electorate will surely demand more from Ecuadorean politicians than they have so far.

In the context of Latin American cooperation and international law, the Andean countries have made significant contributions. Particularly important has been the policy of Peru and Ecuador with respect to the question of their territorial waters. In the late forties and early fifties, together with Chile, they started to claim a 200 nautical mile limit off shore, for exclusive fishing rights. When clashing with American fishing interests around 1970, they vigorously enforced their claims despite economic sanctions. In so doing they set an example for other third world countries and helped to bring about the new law of the sea, a matter of utmost importance. In the Falkland Islands – Malvinas war of 1982, the Andean countries were among Argentina's most active supporters against Britain. At the same time, the South Atlantic war gave the new Secretary General of the United Nations, Peruvian Javier Pérez de Cuéllar, a tough trial.

At a moment of general economic frustration and more often than not repressive political regimes in Latin America (with Central America as an open wound) Peru and Ecuador, and at the moment of writing Bolivia, present relatively decent political conditions. Yet for how long we do not know. Structural problems remain enormous. The general prospects of the United States and Western Europe, on which the Andean countries remain clearly dependent in so many ways, are far from bright. With the advent of Ronald Reagan's archconservative administration in the United States, any kind of reform policy can count on much less United States undestanding than before. At the same time, an economic policy on the Milton Friedman model would simply spell social and political disaster in this environment. As far as the vision of a final redeeming socialism is concerned, the record of leftist parties so far and the danger of the creation of even more unwieldy and powerful bureaucracies that would impose such solutions leave the observer in doubt.

c. Whither the Swelling Masses?

The process of social change in the Andean countries since the 1950s is above all a change in demographic terms. From 1950 to 1980 the population more than doubled (see table 10.5). By the year 2000, the smallest country, Ecuador, will house 14 million people, — as many as the three countries together in 1950. The decline of the infant mortality rate is obviously an important factor. In Peru, it dropped from 100 per thousand in 1950 – 54 to 70 in 1972. In Ecuador it fell from more than 100 to 63 in 1977. In Bolivia the census of 1976 revealed it to be a tremendously high 202. In 1940, in Peru life expectancy at birth was still about 35 years — the same as in the very poorest African countries today. In 1980 it reached 56 — slightly higher than that of Algeria. (By contrast, U.S. life expectancy was 73 in 1978.)

If lifespan increased, what about living conditions? As we have already seen, the GNP growth on the whole managed to keep considerably ahead of that of population even if the stagnation since the late seventies should be noted. More crucial, however, the trends that can be discerned with respect to income distribution favor the better-off. In the case of Peru, the per capita GNP annual growth rate in 1950 – 66 was rather high, 2.5 percent. Yet the rate of the better-off fourth of the population was 4 percent while that of the rural dwellers in general was only 1.3 percent. The income of the peasants, even during this period of growth, remained the same. (See table 10.6 for more information on the evolution of the gross national product.)

Simply to measure nutritional standards in terms of national per capita food supply is far from sufficient to get a grasp of this vital problem. Yet even so, the tip of the iceberg can be seen. While a daily calorie intake of 2850 is considered sufficient for an adult male, the Ecuadorean average was merely 2050 in the early fifties and about the same in the late seventies. Bolivia had raised its average from a very low level in 1961 – 63 (1630) to about the same as Ecuador in the late seventies, while Peru attained 2286 at that time. Peru also showed the highest apparent per capita protein intake of the three in 1975–79 (58.7 grams). This, however, was less than in 1961 – 63 (61.6). Bolivia and

Table 10.5
Recent Social Development of the Andean Countries

	Bolivia	Ecuador	Peru
Population (thousands):			
1950	3,013	3,225	7,968
1980	5,600	8,000	17,624
Average yearly Population growth (%):			
1950-60	2.0	2.9	2.3
1960-70	2.5	3.1	2.8
1970-80	2.6	3.3	2.7
Projected population for 2000 (thousands)	9,000	14,000	29,000
Crude birth rate per 1000 people:			
1960	48	47	47
1978	44	44	39
Crude death rate:			
1960	23	14	19
1978	15	10	12
Life expectancy at birth:			
1960	43	51	48
1980	52	60	56
Percentage urban population:			
1960	24	34	46
1980	33	45	67
Percentage urban population, cities over 5 million inhabitants:			
1960	0	0	38
1980	44	52	44
Percentage of literate adults:			
1950	32	58	47
1976	63	–	–
1980	–	79	80
Population per physician (thousands)			
1960	3,660	2,600	2,250
1978	1,850	1,570	1,560

SOURCES: IDB, 1968, 1980-81; World Bank, 1980; Sanchez Albornoz, 1974: 184.

Ecuador, on the other hand, both raised their protein consumption somewhat.

What really matters, however, is the situation of the poorest half of the population. In an Andean context, this largely means the "Indians." In 1976, 46 percent of Bolivia's population still had Quechua, Aymara, or some other native language as their only or main tongue. Many poor Indians live in the cities nowadays. Samples recently taken in Puno in Southern Peru suggest that both calorie and protein intake are lowest —and clearly below recognized requirements—in the highland towns. Poor traders and artisans as well as rural workers exhibit calorie, protein, calcium, and vitamin A deficits. Within the family, children between weaning and school age as well as pregnant women are especially likely to get less than their need. In the rural sector, also, seasonal nutritional variations are great. Both sheer lack of food and poor diet

Table 10.6
The Evolution of the Gross National Product

a. Andean countries. 1980 dollars per capita.

	1980	Average annual variation in percent, 1960-80	Variation 1981
Bolivia	566.7	2.0	-3.3
Ecuador	789.2	3.2	1.1
Peru	1.137.3	1.3	1.1

b. Debt service as percentage of GNP (1) and of exports of goods and services (2)

	1. 1970	1978	2. 1970	1978
Bolivia	2.2	8.5	10.9	48.7
Ecuador	1.5	2.8	9.1	11.7
Peru	2.4	7.4	11.6	31.1

c. Agriculture's percentage of the GNP and its annual growth rate

	1960	1978	1960-70	1970-78
Bolivia	26	17	3.0	3.6
Ecuador	33	21	–	4.6
Peru	26	14	1.9	0.7

d. For comparison: Latin America. 1980 dollars per capita.

Average annual variation			Annual variation	
1960	*811*	*1961-70*	*5.7*	*1980*	*3.2*
1970	*1.082*	*1971-75*	*6.6*	*1981*	*-1.3*
1979	*1.423*	*1976-80*	*5.2*		

SOURCES: *1960-78*: World Bank 1980; *1980*: IDB; *1981*: CEPAL 1982.

habits produce diseases. Goiter, caused by the lack of iodine, is especially widespread. Samples taken, for example, in Ecuadorean highland
communities also suggest a high incidence of mental retardation and
other pathologial traits apparently related to malnutrition.

Notwithstanding the misery of the urban poor, in global terms the
urban – rural cleavage is what basically determines the conditions and
chances of life. To judge from the rhetoric of politicians advocating
land reform, their aim was, above all, to improve the standards of the
rural poor and thus make migration to the cities less imperative. In fact,
no government — least of all that of Peru, with more than 50 percent
urban dwellers in the late 1960s, — could afford to let rural producers
have a larger and fairer share of the pie. With about a fourth of Peru's
population, Lima in the late 1970s consumed half the nation's food.
Limeños earned about twice as much as the national average and four
times as much as the rural inhabitants of the Sierra throughout the
period. Also, the compensation paid to ex-hacendados augmented the
net transfer of funds *from* the rural *to* the urban sector.

Under these conditions, nothing is more natural than the rapid
increase of urbanization since the 1950s. In Peru the proportion of
urban population grew from 45 percent in 1960 to 67 percent in 1980;
the rates of urbanization were similar in Ecuador and Bolivia, even
though by 1980 slightly less than half the Ecuadoreans and a third of
the Bolivians were still classified as "rural." In Peru, the census of 1981
gave Lima a total population of more than 4 million compared with 1
million in 1950. Yet, the growth rate since 1972 (3.8 percent) was lower
than that for the previous decade (5.9). In the case of Ecuador, the gap
between Guayaquil, with a population set at 1 million in 1978 and that
of Quito (740,000) narrowed since 1970. In 1950 neither had more
than about a quarter of a million. In Bolivia, the growth of La Paz was
relatively slow, from 300,000 in 1950 to 700,000 in the late 1970s.
There the striking feature was instead the urban explosion of Santa
Cruz, the lowland center which had merely 43,000 inhabitants in 1950,
compared with 237,000 in 1976.

Thus, the process of urbanization is by no means reduced to the
principal city of each nation. Nor is the phenomenon of shantytowns.
Almost everywhere they form a growing part of urban agglomerations.
Nowhere, however, are the shantytowns more conspicuous than in the
desert surrounding the core of Lima. In 1957 there were 56 *barriadas*,
with 120,000 people (some 10 percent of the city's population); in 1978

there were 360, now comprising a third of all Limeños. While nowadays euphemistically termed *"pueblos jóvenes"* (young towns), and often enjoying some degree of social cohesion, poor housing, and lack of appropriate sewage and water facilities continue to characterize the Lima barriadas.

Thus, the glaring contrasts of urban life have grown steadily more ingrained since mid-century. I have had ample opportunity to observe this phenomenon in my visits to Lima, beginning in 1958. On one side are the glamorous hotels, restaurants, costly public buildings, broad avenues and highways, and the cool dignity of the residential areas of Miraflores and San Isidro, with their ample spaces of lawns and trees. Yet their splendid isolation is not complete—at least not in psychological terms. In their fear of the poor, the well-off people defend themselves by turning their residences into virtual fortresses, equipped with fierce watch dogs, and barbed wire or crushed glass on walls or roofs.

However, most urban dwellers have no such safeguards against the drastic rise of crime, the foul smells, the dirt and dust, and the growing traffic noise and air pollution where they live. In the big cities of the Andes — as in all of Latin America — the ills of under- and of over-development combine to make human existence increasingly miserable (see figs. 10.5 and 10.6). Also, with both immigration and internal growth, unemployment and underemployment have become especially visible. There is a heterogeneous, diffuse sector of people eking out a marginal existence: beggars (both children and old people), criminals, invalids, and itinerant street vendors. Their numbers are growing from year to year.

In Peru, as in most other Latin American countries, social security in the main functions mostly for the benefit of the generals and high bureaucrats down to the skilled workers with permanent industrial jobs, who are privileged in comparison with the mass of unemployed and underemployed people. Basic welfare easily gets entangled by red tape. As Gregorio Condori Mamani, the old Indian from the City of Cuzco we have already quoted puts it,

When, due to their old age, those who, with their backs bent, carry loads for a living, barely manage to carry their own bones anymore, they seldom make it to the Homes for Aged. There they would be asked for papers, birth certificates. . . . As they possess no papers of any sort, they are not admitted. Instead, they die when begging for alms anywhere in the streets. . . .

Figure 10.5. Bolivian Tin Miner. (From Nash 1979: 329. Photo by June Nash. Used by permission of the author.)

Figure 10.6. Gregorio Condori Mamani, carrier of the City of Cuzco, an extraordinary informant on Indian ideas and life. (Courtesy of Centrol de estudios rurales andinos, Cusco.)

Yet, for all its grim features, the big city, after all, has a lot of compensation to offer the poor. Compared with the countryside, the chance of getting jobs or even making an income out of domestic service, begging, prostitution, or theft are greater. Servants in 1961 formed almost 10 percent of Lima's economically active population. Nine out of ten were migrants and female, half of them being minors and very poorly paid. Yet their most basic needs were secured. Also, in the cities, schools are within easier reach, so are physicians. Food supply, whether from domestic or imported sources, is better. All the big city dwellers also seem to agree that if whatever changes they want really will occur, the decision-making concerning them will have to take place in the cities. It is there the entrenched elites as well as the labor unionists and leftist agitators make their greatest efforts to defeat each other. The urban setting is still favored in terms of health facilities. Yet the striking expansion of medical centers and personnel has increasingly benefited the countryside as well. Between 1960 and 1978 the number of people served by one physician has been greatly reduced in each of our three countries. They have reached the level of Turkey or Taiwan, but are still far from European standards.

While city dwellers are also clearly favored in terms of access to education, illiteracy has been greatly reduced in the countryside as well. Eighty percent of Peruvian and Ecuadorean adults are by now able to read and write to some extent. In Bolivia the proportion is about 60 percent. Against the backdrop of rapid demographic growth, this is a truly impressive achievement. It was carried out in often very poor schoolhouses by low-paid teachers and children, who at times collapsed from hunger at the end of a long school day. It is hardly surprising that school teachers have formed some of the most militant union federations such as SUTEP in Peru and UNE in Ecuador. Between 1950 and 1961, Peruvian secondary school enrollment trebled. From 1960 to 1977, the percentage of Peruvian youngsters enrolled in secondary school grew from 15 to no less than 52 percent. Even in Bolivia, the percentage has risen from 12 to 26. The number of Peruvian university students more than trebled from 1960, to reach 111,000 in 1970. While in 1960 these students formed only 4 percent of the 20–24 age group, in 1976 their share had risen to 16 percent. In Bolivia the 1976 figure was 10 percent, in Ecuador 28 percent. By comparison — without regarding the difference in quality — the percentage of British university students was merely 19 percent.

Education gets a large share of total government expenditures — necessary, of course, in order to strengthen national development. However, such expenditures have the effect of undermining sociopolitical stability. This is so particularly during periods of economic recession when the post-graduation search for jobs is likely to be hard.

As a consequence, frustration and revolutionary militancy naturally emerge from such a striking educational expansion in an economically unstable setting. As far as the quality of higher education, especially in public schools, is concerned it suffers from the "brain drain" of qualified intellectuals, either because they are attracted to better paying jobs in the United States or, as in Bolivia, become political refugees. Also, better teachers and students often opt for private Catholic univesities where conditions are more calm, thus perpetuating old elite patterns. At state universities, teaching is repeatedly interrupted by strikes, riots, and ensuing government repression. Whatever the reason, these schools are often closed for long periods at a time. In this environment of tear gas and turbulence, young intellectuals naturally adopt revolutionary leftist stances. Tragically, though, this often leads them into scholastic hair splitting along Marxist or pseudo-Marxist lines, which by turn makes for endless internal squabbling. Eventually, some of the radical intelligentsia decide to enjoy the privileges of the establishment. In the higher circles of society, for example in Lima, intellectuals and politicians with a radical past easily blend with members of the traditional upper class, high-ranking military officers, and United States-trained technocrats. At the same time, an incessant struggle is going on inside the establishment between individuals along patron–client rather than social class or party lines for the various positions. As a result they are won or lost by means of intrigues rather than by merit. An increased amount of government activity has opened up many more bureaucratic positions. In Ecuador, for example, the number of bureaucrats doubled between 1970 and 1979.

During most of the time since 1950, organized urban, mining, and plantation labor has been able to function more or less freely in our three countries. In Peru, however, the reorganization of Aprista and Communist unions took place only after the end of the Odría dictatorship in 1956. Within the grand corporativist scheme of the Velasco regime, organized labor was awarded the important but clearly subordinated function of giving substance to the so-called "industrial comunities," composed of all the permanent employees of a firm, whether white or blue collar. Gradually increased worker participation in property, profits, and management was intended as a means of attaining class conciliation. This hope of emasculating the Peruvian labor movement did not succeed, however. From 1972 to 1973 the yearly number of strikes jumped from 409 to 788 (a record since registration began in 1957) involving 3 to 9 percent of the economically active population respectively. More than half involved industrial manufacturing. Although they were outlawed in 1976, strikes on a massive scale (three were intended as general strikes) were designed to oppose the economic austerity program of the Morales Bermúdez regime. In the mining sector labor conflicts were particularly acute. A student of those in Cerro de Pasco (until the nationalization in 1973 they were owned by a U.S. Corporation) finds a cyclical pattern from compromise to confrontation (often violent and bloody) and back again. In the new mining districts in the Southern Sierra, a military proletariat of a more modern type had now emerged, completely cut off from its peasant origins.

In Bolivia unions, spearheaded by the miners, by 1952 had already acquired a high degree of cohesion and militancy. Under the impact of Trotskyite ideas, the miners' federation in 1946 adopted a boldly revolutionary program. Despite their misgivings about MNR's "bourgeois" character, miners took a very active part in the 1952 revolution. Their pressure helped to bring about the nationalization of tin mines and the creation of the state mining corporation (COMIBOL); they also set up a new national labor confederation (COB). Miners made up half of the 50,000 – 60,000 man armed people's militia that was temporarily replacing the army. COB occupied a strong position during the first presidential term of Paz Estenssoro. Yet conflict was bound to erupt when the MNR steered to the right in 1956, and after the military coup of 1964 very harsh government repression set in. Backed up by peasant organizations, the military bloodily repressed minor opposition in 1965 and 1967. After the conspicuous union presence during the short-lived Torres interlude in 1971, fierce repression once again set in.

An important, eloquent human document about life and struggle in the mines is the testimony presented in 1976 by Domitila Barrios de Chungara, a woman leading an organization of miners' wives that sprang out of a spontaneous hunger strike to make the authorities release their captive husbands. As different from the white middle class background of so many Latin American union leaders (for example Lechín) that of Domitila is authentically working class and Indian. She masterly paints the harsh and brutal atmosphere of the mines where the men die young from silicose, and women, as a matter of course, suffer heavy blows from their drunken husbands while starving children are at times abandoned. Yet Domitila and other women left their traditional submissive sex role behind them to join the men in valiantly fighting the corrupt COMIBOL management and heavy-handed military force. While she states her Christian faith and warns for dogmatism, her attitude is deeply revolutionary.[4]

In Ecuador, the extreme fragmentation of organized labor along political party lines clearly reduced its impact and power. In 1977, the suppression of a strike at a sugar mill cost great bloodshed (120 according to the union; 24 admitted by the government). Thus, we can see that laborers, like university students, often provide anti-government martyrs in the course of the political play. Union efforts to obtain modifications of the skewed income distribution pattern have been much less striking. They are undercut by the internal divisions and lack of cooperation, by the corruption of so many leaders (as documented, for example, by former CIA agent Philip Agee) and, not least, by the existence of the swelling sector of unemployed or underemployed masses.

Desperate uprisings by Indian peasants from time to time, as we have seen, have formed part of the Andean tradition. However, from the mid-twentieth century onward, unionization has begun to take root among the *campesinos*. Unions have been launched thanks to outside organizers or natural leaders from among the peasants themselves. Unions usually began by legal procedure. When members tired of waiting for benefits they took direct action — usually but not always without arms or violence. Often they would enter land in dispute in a solemn procession, preceded by musicians. The Indians of the *comunidades* used this means to recover lost lands. On the haciendas, the long-

suffering colonos began to demand better conditions from the hacendados. The efforts of the latter to convert them into wage earners in
order to modernize production usually met with stiff resistance. When
finally faced with concerted peasant action, Andean landlord resistance proved surprisingly weak. In fact, the hacienda structure in the
Andean highlands began to crumble even before the official land reforms. Many hacendados sold out all or part of their holdings to the
colonos.

In Bolivia, the fertile Cochabamba Valley, where large estates were
rather few, has seen the slow but steady building up of peasant unions
since the early forties. Another center of unionization was in the area
bordering on Lake Titicaca. Both comprised considerable commercialization of agricultural produce, making the exploitation of peasant labor
especially rewarding for the landlords. On the whole peasants stayed
outside the MNR revolution of 1952. As soon as it was over, however,
some peasant groups swiftly moved to occupy the lands of their hacendados or, in the case of the communidades, those of their neighbors.
Some peasant bands even attacked small towns where so many of their
exploiters lived. Terrified landowners fled to the big cities. Thus, the
Bolivian land reform of 1953 can largely be seen as a pacification
measure on the part of the new government; Colonos were simply
promised to get legal rights to those parcels which they had often been
cultivating and disposing for generations. Also, by virtue of the law
they were no longer forced to submit to the degrading personal service
they hitherto had to perform for the hacendados and their families.

Like the miners, peasants set up armed militia units. Their world
view was broadened when instead of offering their meager savings to
the priest, they started to buy radios and bicycles. The distribution of
land titles in Bolivia has been extremely slow. Even so, peasants, surprisingly — because they made so few material gains from the land
reform — have proved grateful and loyal to the establishment. Indeed,
they have formed an exceptional element of stability in post-1952 Bolivia. In 1964, peasant leaders easily transferred their loyalty to the
succeeding military governments, as Che Guevara, among others,
would discover. They seem to have accepted the revolutionary myth at
least partly because the land reform, for being so slow, is still going on,
and because the memories of landlord brutalities in the past are kept

alive. At the same time, whites and mestizos retain their traditional disdain for the Indians under the surface of pro-Campesino political rhetorics.

Even so, *some* social change has, indeed, taken place in the Bolivian countryside, and not always for the better. In a district near Potosí, around 1970, a new more hardy and productive brand of potato was introduced by agronomists. Those peasants living close to the road who started marketing this new variety had an astounding success. They were not psychologically prepared for the sudden growth of their income, however. They bought all kinds of articles just for status, even "junk" food of lower nutritional value than their traditional Indian diet. Consequently, by comparison with their poorer neighbors who had not adopted the new potato variety, they had lost in terms of quality of life. Experts have long argued whether or not the traditional Andean peasant custom of chewing coca leaves is nutritionally and psychologically harmful. The immense cocaine smuggling by the Bolivian military and other mafiosi focused international attention also on the use of coca. The authorities characteristically then tried to curb the coca use by the peasants. As peasant spokesmen stated in their protest, "coca is for us a sacred element, a ritual. It is a medicine and helps to feed us. . . . We are not the ones who prepare the poisonous cocaine."[5]

Since the 1930s, the community of peasants around Cerro de Pasco in the central Peruvian Sierra have made systematic efforts to recover lands absorbed by the haciendas. Demographic pressure on their own tiny parcels and pastures had increased when unemployed Indian miners returned home as a result of depression. The slovenliness of legal procedure increased peasant desperation. In 1956, land invasions began to take place in the area. With President Belaúnde's vague talk about land reform four years later, the conflict here as elsewhere in the highlands became acute. One hacienda, Chinche, had been occupied peacefully. When ousting the peasants, however, a military detachment killed 27 people. As soon as soldiers left the area, the hacienda was sacked by the peasants. Pacification in the Cerro de Pasco interior was simply brought about, however, by the government declaring it a zone of land reform priority. It should be strongly underscored that long-suffering endurance and patience are much more characteristic of Andean peasants than the occasional bouts of accumulated bitterness and violence. The famous movement led by Hugo Blanco and market oriented tenant farmers in La Convención in Northern Cuzco was resolved by the government in a similar fashion as in Cerro de Pasco. The much publicized guerrilla attempts by urban revolutionaries in some corners of the Sierra in 1965 probably hampered rather than favored peasant mobilization. Still, by 1968 there were a total of 369 recognized peasant unions in Peru.

Thus, peasant actions showed the inevitability of land reform, but when it came in earnest, in 1969, it was imposed from above, with land transfers on a massive scale. By 1980, about 1000 cooperatives had been establshed, also a few larger units called SAIS. A third of all useful land with more than half of all privately owned rural properties had been affected by the reform. Large landowners usually had time to decapitalize estates before expropriation, however. Furthermore, they usually received handsome compensation while the peasants had to pay for ownership by means of a series of installments. This obligation, plus peasant demand for guarantees of individual ownership of their parcels, caused an anti-government peasant movement in the Sierra province of Andahuaylas in 1974. It was easily suppressed, however, while the Velasco Junta set up a National Peasant Association in defense of the Reform. As in Bolivia, the land reform in the Peruvian highland has suffered from excessive red tape and, above all, from the lack of money to finance adequate training programs and investments to improve infrastructure. In Cuzco department, for example, tourist roads just to the north of the city are excellent and also permit a few cooperatives and a number of small haciendas to sell, even export their high-quality maize. These haciendas are run by their old owners, who are careful to keep their property just below the 30 hectare expropriation limit.

Just south of the town there is a mountainous area with many peasant villages that can be reached only via extremely poor roads or paths. There, as in colonial times, horseback remains the best way to get to them. In that province (Paruro), also, annual fairs related to the three main sanctuaries reflect Pre-Hispanic ethnic patterns and needs for barter between the inhabitants of different ecological zones.

The land reform no doubt left great irreversible benefits. The old landlords and the traditional forms of peasant subjugation have vanished. Some cooperatives are more or less efficiently run by collective leaderships. Yet in the Sierra most apparently languish or exist only on paper. The Indian communities have been reorganized by special legislation but on the whole have gained little from the reform.

The land reform, obviously, was a very difficult undertaking, hardly possible to carry out to the entire satisfaction of the various parties concerned. Unfortunately, it owed a lot of inspiration to myths. Following Mariátegui the generals believed that Indian highland peasants were still collectivists at heart as in Incaic times. They also thought in terms of a largely illusory. "Hacienda – Peasantry" dichotomy. In fact, by the late twentieth century peasant minds had become economically individualistic. The hope for profits even made some Indian peasants lose their traditional respect for "Mother Earth" (Pachamama). Thus, "Despachamamización" has been launched as one of the factors explaining increasing erosion. Also, the indiscriminate use of the same term, "hacienda," to designate coastal agroindustrial enterprises and quite modest Sierra farms owned and run by "kulaks" rather than "feudal landlords" obscured the deep cleavage between them. Furthermore, the measure of hectares meant practically nothing in the Sierra, with its sharply accidental terrain and deficient roadnet and marketing facilities.

Also, the cooperatives had been handed over to the former colonos and resident workers. Just like the resident wage laborers who took over coastal plantations, Sierra colonos carefully excluded former occasional dayworkers from the cooperatives. Thus, some 200,000 *eventuales* found themselves in a desperate situation on the coast while Indians of the comunidades who used to find temporary labor on a neighboring hacienda found its gates closed. The SAIS were designed to resolve this problem. These large units were formed around even larger, more dynamic cooperatives that ought to share some of their income with but not allow full participation to the surrounding comunidades. This did not prevent a number of sharp conflicts from taking place between cooperatives and their worse-off neighbors. In this way, the age-old struggle between haciendas and comunidades would be perpetuated even after the disappearance of the hacendados. Also, the persistence, in many parts of the Sierra, of the ancient ayllu organization with a dualist division between an upper and a lower portion (moiety) located in different ecological niches, might complicate land reform. A recent case study by a Norwegian anthropologist from a district in Andahuaylas shows how the lower moiety of the old ayllu was able to monopolize the new cooperative replacing the hacienda, making for bitter tension with the worse-off peasants of the upper half.

The main factors of pre-reform rural poverty in the Sierra were not related merely to the unfair distribution of property and usage of land. To be sure, distribution was perhaps not so skewed as commonly believed. Poverty was also a function of the sheer lack of cultivable land. With 0.16 hectares per rural inhabitant, the highland statistical average was among the lowest in Latin America and about the same as in far more fertile countries like China and India. To this can be added the overwhelming problems posed by topography and low productivity. At the same time, as different from current generalizations, highland peasants did not eke out their meager livelihood from mere subsistence agriculture. On the contrary, according to the results of serious research, they received from 60 to 80 percent of their income, however tiny, in cash. But they entered the market on very unequal terms and still do. The price mechanism has largely favored urban consumers and producers. Middlemen in the distribution of agricultural goods have siphoned off a disproportionate share of peasant compensation.

Against this general background it is understandable that the land reform of 1969, for all the good intentions and energy displayed by the Velasco Junta, managed only to modify very slightly the extremely skewed income distribution pattern prevailing in Peru at that time. Between 1968 and 1975, merely 2 or 3 percent are calculated to have changed places and that mostly within the upper range of income earners. The second Belaúnde government is bent on favoring free enterprise and lowland colonization schemes. It appears simply to be avoiding as much as possible any effort to grapple seriously with the messy problems of highland agriculture and a rural society in flux.

Colonization schemes in the montaña lowlands obviously affect much smaller numbers of native people. Under the Junta, a strikingly generous special land reform was enacted to satisfy the specific needs of lowland tribes dependent on shifting agriculture, fishing and hunting. Difficult to enforce from the start, owing to geographical distance and weak administration, this farsighted protection of the natives and the fragile environment is now being undermined by the government. Large groups of settlers are invited to come from the highlands, and concessions for oil prospecting and other business are handed out to entrepreneurs. In recent years, tribal Indians also managed to unionize and make contact with other native peoples all over Latin America and the world. The Campas, Amuesha, and other tribes are mounting a desperate defense against overwhelming odds. Outside concern for the Indians has been dismissed as "conspiracies" and "pseudo-defense of human rights and the natural world" by the Peruvian President himself.[6]

In Ecuador, also, the time was ripe for the old-fashioned labor obligation of the colonos for their patrons (*huasipungo*) to disappear in accordance with the land reform of 1964. In the rice zone along the Guayas River, a widespread system of sharecropping (*precarismo*) was abolished in 1970. Yet, five years later, only a small portion of some 40,000 ex-precaristas had received titles to their lands. In Ecuador, on the whole, peasant conditions remain far from satisfactory and some 100,000 people yearly leave the countryside for urban shantytowns.

In the Ecuadorean lowlands of the interior, one kind of domination over tribal peoples was recently challenged, and one hopes it will be removed. I refer to the so-called Summer Institute of Linguistics (SIL), a dynamic and well financed American missionary enterprise built up around the task of translating Bibles into the various native tongues. At the same time the missionaries – linguists do provide some health services to the natives, but also promote their acculturation — with tragic psychological and social results. Since 1945 SIL has exercised a great degree of control over tribal Indians in Northeastern Peru (where I have observed the linguists in action); in the fifties they also established themselves in Bolivia and Ecuador. There they helped oil prospectors to persuade the brave Auca Indians to give up their lands. While some of the accusations leveled against SIL, who have airplanes and other extraordinary facilities in the jungle, are probably groundless, this is an ethnocentric alien enterprise of doubtful value to the natives. President Roldós decreed that SIL should get out within a year a few days before he died in 1981.

To predict the future is not the historian's task. Yet in some troubled areas of the world the direction of change appears more than likely.

South Africa, for instance, is no doubt headed for more acute problems. The old industrial countries simply have to undertake some radical structural change in order to stop or slow down their decline. In the case of our Andean countries, about the only certainty is that of their continued demographic growth even though, fortunately, in Peru the most recent statistics suggest a slight slowing down of the rate. Also, natural disasters continue to strike now and then, as in the case of the floods in Ecuador in 1950, which killed 6000 people, or the huge earthquake in Callejón de Huaylas, northeast of Lima, in 1970, which cost at least 50,000 lives.

What will happen next? At times the endurance and patience of the Andean masses appear almost incredible. The middle class elites now running the countries include some competent people who can help to bring about a gradual change for the better if left in peace by the intrigues of ambitious politicians or potential military "saviors." Yet the problems are enormous. Neither nostalgic dreams about the Inca past nor imported social theory will constitute a panacea. In some details, even a foreign observer can discern solutions. Why not try to modernize traditional agriculture in the direction of advanced labor intensive farming on either the Japanese-Taiwanese market oriented or the Chinese collectivistic model? Why not try to restore some of those large abandoned terrace systems and their nets of irrigation which were obviously in intensive use in Inca and perhaps early colonial times? Why not attempt to extend systematically the cultivation of cereals like quinoa and cañihua and the tarwi starch — not just because they are authentically Andean but because of their greater resistance and nutritional value compared with some of the Old World crops, which practically replaced them? Why not restrict the unhampered growth of road-building and unplanned urbanization on some of the best agricultural land, as in the irrigated valleys of the Peruvian coast? Obviously, such measures as these require relatively rational policy making, realistic information for, and active participation by very broad strata of the population. Without idealizing the Incas, they appear to have been the most rational Andean policymakers so far, even though they hardly admitted popular participation. Yet the many centuries of usually inept government by once Spanish-imposed elites suggests that precisely the great and largely untapped popular human potential of the Andean countries has to be searched to find the practical, realistic, leaders that the future requires.

NOTES

1. The Vertical Dimension

1. Throughout, "peasant" will only be used in the general sense of poor rural inhabitant. For a discussion of the problems surrounding the use of the word as an analytical concept see, for instance, my discussion in Kenneth Duncan and I. Rutledge, eds., *Land and Labour in Latin America* (Cambridge: Cambridge University Press, 1977), pp. 456 ff. For the Pachamama myth see Rosalind Gow and B. Condori, eds. *Kay Pacha,* (Cuzco: Centro de Estudios Rurales Andinos B. de las Casas, 1976), pp. 5–8.

2. Ticci Viracocha played an important role in the theories of the Norwegian Thor Heyerdahl about the settlement of Polynesia by an Andean naval expedition. Heyerdahl called the raft with which he set out to prove the feasibility of the theory in 1947 *Kon Tiki.*

3. N. David Cook, *Demographic Collapse: Indian Peru, 1520–1620* (Cambridge: Cambridge University Press, 1981), p. 114 after a series of very detailed and careful estimates. C. T. Smith, in *Current Anthropology* (1970) Vol. 2 estimates the population of the Empire at between 8.8 and 12 million people. W. M. Denovan, in *The Native Population of the Americas in 1492* (Madison: University of Wisconsin Press, 1976) opts for 7.5 (p. 291).

4. See Gregorio Condori Mamani, *Autobiografía,* ed. by R. Valderrama and Carmen Escalante Gutiérrez (Centro de Estudios Rurales Antinos B. de las Casas, Cuzco, 1977), p. 27. This is an exceptionally fascinating book.

5. A student of nutrition in Tahuantinsuyo, Santiago E. Antúñez de Mayolo R., claims that, in most respects, it was superior to that of contemporary Peru. *Etnohistoria y antropología andina* (Lima: Museo Nacional de Historia, 1978), pp. 277–98.

2. Conquest

1. Letter from Gaspar de Gárate, Cajamarca, July 20, 1533, reproduced in translation by James Lockhart, *The Men of Cajamarca* (Austin: University of Texas Press, 1972), pp. 459–61.

2. As told to José María Arguedas in Puquio and reproduced by Franklin Pease G. Y., *El dios creador andino* (Lima: Mosca Azul, 1973), pp. 139–40. The little book also contains other versions of the same tale. Jan Szeminski and Juan Ansión, "Dioses y hombres de Huamanga," *Allpanchis,* (1982) 16 (19) : 187–233 (especially, 190–95).

3. Silver and Mercury

1. B. Lewin, ed., *"Descripción del virreinato del Perú*, Crónica inédita de comienzos del siglo XVII," (Rosario, Argentina, 1958), p. 32.

5. Indian Revolt

1. His body was torn apart by four horses. A recently found document suggests that, ironically, the "enlightened" Spanish judge had taken the model of this savage punishment from France, where an attempted murderer of Louis XV was punished this way.

2. Royal decree of April 21, 1782 reproduced in R. Konetzke, ed., *Colección de documentos para la historia de la formación social de Hispanoamérica, 1493 – 1810*, 3 : 2 (Madrid, 1962), pp. 482 ff.

3. "Concolorcorvo" (pseud.), *El Lazarrillo de ciegos caminantes desde Buenos Aires a Lima (1773)* (Buenos Aires: Solar, 1942), pp. 328 ff.

4. Letter to President Villalengua, October 27, 1787, reproduced in *Biblioteca Ecuatoriana mínima: Precursores* (Puebla, Mexico: Cajica, 1960), pp. 245 – 50. Julio Díaz Arguedas, *Juan Wallparrimachi Sawaraura* (ISLA, La Paz, 1970). Many poems reproduced in Jesús Lara, *La poesía quechua. Ensayo y antología* (Cochabamba, 1947).

5. Quoted by J. Lynch, *The Spanish American Revolutions, 1808 – 1826* (London: Weidenfeld & Nicolson, 1973), p. 50.

6. G. Mendoza, ed., *Diario de un soldado de la Independencia altoperuana en los valles de Sicasica y Hayopata.* (Sucre, Bolivia, 1952).

7. J. F. de Abascal y Sousa, *Memoria de gobierno*, V. Rodríguez Casado and J. A. Calderón Quijano, eds. (Seville: Escuela de Estudios Hispano-Americanos, 1944), p. 113.

8. Very unpopular with the Peruvians, Monteagudo was also driven out himself in 1822 while San Martín was away in Guayaquil to meet Bolívar.

9. *Selected Writings of Bolívar*, (New York: Colonial Press, 1951), 2:448.

10. Quoted by Lynch, *Revolutions*, p. 163.

11. *Selected Writings*, 2 : 511.

6. The Hope of Liberalism

1. W. B. Stevenson, *Historical and Descriptive Narrative of Twenty Years' Residence in South America*, (London: Hurst, Robinson, 1829), p. 408.

2. Gilbert F. Mathison, *Narrative of a Visit to Brazil, Chile, Peru and the Sandwich Islands, During the Years 1821 and 1822…* (London: C. Knight, 1825), pp. 287 – 89.

3. Carl August Gosselman, *Informes sobre los estados sud-americanos en los años de 1837 y 1838*. M. Mörner, ed. (Stockholm: Biblioteca e Instituto de Estudios Iberoamericanos, 1962), p. 80.

4. Tulio Halperín-Donghi. *The Aftermath of Revolution in Latin America* (New York: Harper, 1973), p. 111.

5. Stevenson, *Descriptive Narrative*, 1 : 422 – 49; Flora Tristan, *Les pérégrinations d'une paria, 1833 – 34* (Paris: Masperó, 1979, pp. 345 – 52). The planter assures his visitor: "Madame, you don't know the Negroes. They let their children die out of laziness. Without the whip you can't obtain anything from them." Similar discussions have taken place ever since between "experienced old-timers" and fresh, liberal visitors from abroad, on all aspects of labor and race relations all over Latin America.

6. Gosselman, *Informes sobre los estados*, p. 91.

7. J. D. Choquehuanca, *Ensayo de estudística completa de todos los ramos económico-políticos de la provincia de Azángaro...* (Lima, 1833); Mörner, *Historia social latino-americano. Nuevos enfoques*. (Caracas: Universidad Católica Andrés Bello, 1979), pp. 179 – 221; José María Dalence, *Bosquejo estadístico de Bolivia* (Chuquisaca, 1851), pp. 223 ff.; new ed., La Paz, 1975, pp. 210 ff.; Michael T. Hamerly, *Historia social y económica de la antigua provincia de Guayaquil, 1763 – 1842*, Guayaquil: Archivo Histórico del Guayas, 1973, *passim*.

8. Joseph Andrews, *Journey from Buenos Ayres through the Provinces of Cordova, Tucuman, and Salta, to Potosí*, (London: 1827), 2 : 144.

9. José María Blanco, *Diario del viaje del Presidente Orbegoso al Sur del Peru*, F. DeNegri Luna, ed. (Lima: Instituto Riva-Agüero, 1974), 1 : 109.

7. Export Boom

1. See especially Erwin P. Grieshaber, "Survival of Indian Communities in Nineteenth-Century Bolivia: A Regional Comparison," *Journal of Latin American Studies*, (1980), 12(2) : 223–69.

2. L. Gibbon as quoted by T. Jones, *South America Discovered*, 1949, p. 179 (Minneapolis: University of Minnesota Press, 1949), p. 179.

3. In the 1860s, however, according to Friedrich Hassaurek, *Four Years Among the Ecuadoreans*, C. H. Gardiner, ed. (Carbondale: Southern Illinois University Press, 1967), p. 12, "there has been a great falling off in this article, owing to the introduction of other hats of greater cheapness. This has led to great poverty and distress in the hat-making districts, which, for want of water, are almost without agriculture."

4. *Ibid.*, p. 111.

5. G. E. Church as quoted by Lewis Hanke, "A Note on the Life and Publications of Colonel George Earl Church," *Books at Brown*, (Providence, R.I.: Brown University Press, 1965), 20 : 143.

6. The quote from Guillermo Lora, *A History of the Bolivian Labour Movement, 1848–1971* (Cambridge: Cambridge University Press, 1977), p. 26. There is a fairly extensive listing of nineteenth-century revolutionary attempts in Nicanor Aranzáez, *Las revoluciones de Bolivia* (La Paz, 1918).

7. As quoted by Heraclio Bonilla, "The War of the Pacific and the National and Colonial Problem in Peru," *Past & Present*, (1978), No. 81 : 98.

8. *Ibid.*

9. In a thorough recent study, *Campesinado y nación: Las guerrillas indígenas en la Guerra con Chile* (Lima: Centro de Investigación y Capicitación, 1981), Nelson Manrique criticizes Bonilla severely as far as the character of the Indian resistance is concerned. I am very much obliged to Brooke Larson and Enrique Amayo for having drawn my attention to this controversy.

10. As quoted by William W. Stein, "Town and Country in Revolt: Fragments from the Province of Carhuaz on the Atuspharia Uprising of 1885 (Callejón de Huaylas, Peru)," *Actes du XLIIe Congrés International des Américanistes... 1976* (Paris, 1978), 3:183.

11. Jorge Basadre, "La aristocracia y las clases medias civiles en el Perú republicano," *Libro Jubilar de Víctor Andrés Belaúnde en su octogésimo aniversario* (Lima, 1963), pp. 461–71.

12. We refer to the articles on rural labor in Spanish America by Arnold J. Bauer and Brian Loveman in the *Hispanic American Historical Review* (1979), 59 : 34–63, 478–85 and by Peter Blanchard on the enganche in *Inter-American Economic Affairs* (1980), 33(3) : 63–83. Michael J. González, "Capitalist Agriculture and Labour Contracting in Northern Peru, 1885–1905," *Journal of Latin American Studies*, (1980), 12(2) : 291–315, shows how the system actually combined coercion, violence and economic incentives.

13. We refer to *Aves sin nido* ("Birds Without Nests") by Clorinda Matto de Turner.

14. Church as quoted by Hanke, "A Note on Colonel Church," p. 141.

8. World Market Domination

1. In 1950, I met an elderly German-born mason at a "hotel" on the Uruguay River. He proved to be one of the very few, out of a shipload of people dispatched from Hamburg to work on this railroad, who survived.

2. See C. F. S. Cardoso and H. Pérez Brignoli, *Historia económica de América Latina*, Barcelona: Editorial Crítica, 1979), pp. 136–41.

3. For the quote from Montes, see Frederick B. Pike, *The United States and the Andean Republics: Peru, Bolivia and Ecuador*, (Cambridge: Harvard University Press, 1977, p. 155).

4. Dan C. Hazen, "The Awakening of Puno: Government Policy and the Indian Problem in Southern Peru, 1900–55," PhD diss, Yale University, 1974, p. 7.

5. The figures on land sales taken from a paper read by Nils Jacobsen in 1979 on the "Wool Export Economy of Peru's Altiplano and the Region's Livestock Haciendas, 1850 – 1920." In his 1982 Ph.D. dissertation, "Land Tenure and Society in the Peruvian Altiplano: Azángaro Province, 1770–1920" (University of California, Berkeley), Jacobsen goes into much more detail as far as one of the Puno provinces is concerned. For the number of Puno haciendas, see Alberto Flores-Galindo, *Arequipa y el sur andino: ensayo de historia regional (siglos XVIII-XX)* (Lima: Editorial Horizonte, 1977), p. 101. For Cuzco, Luis E. Valcarcel, *Memorias* (Lima: Instituto de Estudios Peruanos, 1981), pp. 83 ff.

6. Quote from Hazen, "The Awakening of Puno," p. 40, who, in turn, took it from a book by Manuel González Prada referring to a local paper.

7. H. Bingham as quoted by P. Blanchard, "The Recruitment of Workers," *Inter American Economic Affairs* (1980) 33(3) : 72.

8. Quotes from J. V. Fifer, "The Empire Builders: A History of the Bolivian Rubber Boom and the Rise of the House of Suárez," *Journal of Latin American Studies* (1970) 2(2) : 138–39

9. Andean Revival, 1

1. The quote from Vallejo's poem (1922) in Jean Franco, *The Modern Culture of Latin America: Society and the Artist* (London, 1967), p. 150; that on the Mexican revolution from Pedro Henríquez Ureña, *A Concise History of Latin American Culture* (New York: Praeger, 1966), p. 113.

2. Quote from his posthumous *Horas de lucha*.

3. His name was Albert A. Giesecke, President of the University of Cuzco from 1910 to 1923. José Tamayo Herrera, *Historia del indigenismo cuzqueño. Siglos XVI-XX* (Lima, 1980), pp. 170 ff.

4. Refers to Pío Jaramillo Alvarado, *El indio ecuatoriano* (1922). See John D. Martz, *Ecuador: Conflicting Political Culture and the Quest for Progress* (Boston: Allyn & Bacon, 1972), pp. 47 ff. for an assessment.

5. Quote from newspaper summary in 1930 in Dan C. Hazen, "The Awakening of Puno," p. 196.

6. Quote from José Carlos Mariátegui, *Seven Interpretive Essays on Peruvian Reality*. (Austin: University of Texas Press, 1971), p. 22.

7. Quote from Jesús Chavarría, *José Carlos Mariátegui and the Rise of Modern Peru, 1890–1930* (Albuquerque: University of New Mexico Press, 1979), p. 172.

8. Quoted from Rafael A. Reyeros, *El pongueaje. La servidumbre personal de los indios bolivianos* (La Paz, 1949), pp. 156 ff. as quoted in *Indigenous Peoples.*

Living and Working Conditions of Aboriginal Populations in Independent Countries (International Labour Office, Geneva, 1953), pp. 344 ff.

9. M. González Prada as quoted by Thomas M. Davies Jr., *Indian Integration in Peru. A Half Century of Experience, 1900 – 1948* (Lincoln: University of Nebraska Press, 1974), p. 38.

10. Abraham Valencia Espinoza, "Las batallas de Rumitaque. Movimientos campesinos de 1921 en Canas," in Jorge Flores Ochoa and A. Valencia, eds., *Rebeliones indígenas quechuas y aymaras* (Cuzco: Centro de Estudios Andinos, 1980), pp. 62 – 131. The Indian rebellion in Chayanta, north of Potosí, in 1927 exhibits similar features. Tristan Platt, *Estado boliviano y ayllu andino. Tierra y tributo en el Norte de Potosí* (Lima: Instituto de Estudios Peruanos, 1982), pp. 145 ff.

11. Ricardo Valderrama Fernández and Carmen Escalante Gutiérrez, eds., *Gregorio Condori Mamani. Autobiografía* (Cuzco, 1977). Quote from p. 83.

12. Gregorio Martínez, *Canto de Sirena* (Lima, 1977). Quote from pp. 102, 137. My friend Heraclio Bonilla drew my attention to the historical interest of this "documentary novel."

13. Richard N. Adams, *A Community in the Andes: Problems and Progress in Muquiyauyo* (Seattle, 1959); John Gillin, *Moche: A Peruvian Coastal Community* (Washington, D.C.: Smithsonian Institution, 1947).

14. Heraclio Bonilla, El minero de los Andes. *Una aproximación a su estudio* (Lima, 1974).

15. Steve Stein, "Máximo Carrasco — or Working Class Life in Lima, 1900 – 1930," in *Historia, problema y promesa. Homenaje a Jorge Basadre*, (1978) 1 : 583-600.

10. Andean Revival, 2

1. Estimates of agricultural production from 1950 to 1959 are incomplete and differ widely as shown by J. G. Wilkie, *Measuring Land Reform*, (Los Angeles: UCLA, 1974), pp. 58 ff. According to one, crops of potatoes, rice and corn dropped drastically from 1954 onward, while another estimate suggests a strong rise for all basic crops between 1950 and 1958. Possibly, increased consumption by peasants themselves helps to explain the discrepancies.

2. *Latin America. Regional Reports. Andean Group* (London, August 29, 1980), p. 5. One of these *mafiosi* was the Minister of Education, Colonel Ariel Coca, a most appropriate name.

3. Chile withdrew from the Andean Group in 1976, partly for disagreeing on the interpretation of paragraph 24. Venezuela, on the other hand, joined the Group in 1973.

4. Valderrama Fernández and Escalante Gutierrez, *Condori*, p. 88.

5. Moema Viezzer, *"Si me permiten hablar..." Testimonio de Domitila, una mujer de las minas de Bolivia* (Mexico City: Siglo XXI, 1977).

6. I am grateful to Bolivian social scientist David Montesinos for his account. He also prepared, at the University of Pittsburgh in 1980, an unpublished paper on the impact of this "Papa Sani Imilla" in the area of Lequezana. On coca and cocaine see William E. Carter et al., *Coca in Bolivia.* (La Paz, 1980), quote, p. 170.

7. "Peru: President Belaúnde's Amazon Policy," *IWGIA Newsletter,* (Copenhagen, Oct. – Dec. 1981) no. 28/9. See also various references in *Latin America. Regional Reports. Andean Group* (1981).

8. For an interesting critical evaluation see Søren Hvalkof and Peter Aabye, eds., *Is God an American? An Anthropological Perspective on the Missionary Work of the Summer Institute of Linguistics* (Copenhagen: IWGIA, 1981). I visited the Yarinacocha base in 1958. I was kindly received by SIL founder William C. Townsend (d. 1982) and his collaborators, but got a very mixed impression of SIL activities.

BIBLIOGRAPHICAL NOTES

Chapter I: The Vertical Dimension and the Growth of Andean Civilization

a. The Geo-ecological Framework

Apart from the geographical surveys, two works deserve special mention. Paul T. Baker and M.A. Little, eds., *Man in the Andes: A Multidisciplinary Study of High-Altitude Quechua*, (Stroudsburg, Pa.: Dowden, Hutchinson & Ross, 1976) analyzes the ecology and human adaptation in the Southern highland community of Nuñoa (above 4000 m.a.s.l.); Daniel W. Gade, *Plants, Man and Land in the Vilcanota Valley of Peru* (The Hague: W. Junk, 1975) is an excellent case study of the river valley of Cuzco, also known as Urubamba.

b. Early Societies

More recent surveys of pre-Inca archeology include E. P. Lanning, *Peru before the Incas* (Englewood Cliffs, N.J.: Prentice-Hall, 1967); F. A. Engel, *An Ancient World Preserved: Relics and Records of Prehistory in the Andes* (New York: Crown, 1976); George Bankes, *Peru Before Pizarro* (Oxford: Phaidon, 1977); Rogger Ravines, *Panorama de la arqueología andina* (Lima: Instituto de Estudios Peruanos, 1982); David L. Browman, ed., *Advances in Andean Archeology*, (The Hague and Paris: Mouton, 1978) provides up-to-date information on many controversial issues. R. Ravines, ed. *Tecnología andina*, (Lima: Instituto de Estudios Peruanos, 1978) is also very useful. Betty J. Meggers, *Ecuador* (London: Thames & Hudson, 1966) forms part of the series "Ancient Peoples and Places." Jorge E. Hardoy, *Pre-Columbian Cities* (London: Allen & Unwin, 1973); Michael Edward Moseley, *The Maritime Foundations of Andean Civilization* (Menlo Park, Calif.: Cummings, 1975), and R. A. Donkin, *Agricultural Terracing in the Aboriginal New World* (Tucson: University of Arizona Press, 1979) cover important aspects. See also B. J. Price, "Prehispanic Irrigation in Nuclear America," *Latin American Research Review* (1971) 6(1) : 3–60. For ridged fields see an article by W. M. Denevan et al. in *Geographical Journal*, (1968) 134 : 353–67. For herding see Jorge A. Flores Ochoa, ed., *Pastores de puna*, (Lima: Instituto de Estudios Peruanos, 1977).

c. The Inca Empire

Literature on the Incas is enormous. For a standard account, John H. Rowe, "Inca Culture at the Time of the Spanish Conquest," J. H. Steward, ed., *Handbook of South American Indians*, (Washington: Smithsonian Institute, 1946) 2 : 198 – 410. His use of the sources and his chronology have been convincingly criticized, however, by Åke Wedin, *El concepto de lo incáico y las fuentes* (Uppsala, Sweden: Akademieförlaget, 1966. The present state of research owes very much to John V. Murra. See his "Current Research and Prospects in Andean Ethnohistory," *Latin American Research Review* (1970) 5(1) : 3–36. Murra's own main work has so far appeared in Spanish only: *Formaciones económicas y políticas del mundo andino* (Lima: Instituto de Estudios Peruanos, 1975) and his Ph.D. dissertation from 1955: *La organización económica del Estado Inca* (Mexico: Siglo XXI, 1978). Murra's thesis on verticality was also examined in L. Millones and H. Tomoeda, eds., *El hombre y su ambiente en los Andes Centrales*, the National Museum of Ethnology in Osaka, Japan, 1980. Important contributions to Inca history have been published in Peru by Franklin Pease and María Rostworowski de Diez de Canseco among others. The comparison between Cuzco and Tenochtitlán in the text is based on an article by Friedrich Katz in *Atti del XL. Congresso Internazionale degli Americanisti* (1972) (Geneva, 1976) 4 : 23–31. See also Burr C. Brundage, *Two Earths, Two Heavens: An Essay Contrasting the Aztecs and the Incas* (Albuquerque: University of New Mexico Press, 1975). The fascinating chronicle of Guamán Poma de Ayala has finally appeared in English: *Letter to the King*, ed. by C. Dilke (New York: Dutton, 1978). There are also English editions of some of the writings of Cieza de León, Bernabé Cobo (1653), Inca Garcilaso de la Vega and Pedro Sarmiento de Gamboa.

Chapter II: Conquest: New Men, Animals, Plants and Diseases

a. The Events

John Hemming's excellent survey, *The Conquest of the Incas* (London: Sphere Books, 1972) was mentioned in the text. It also covers the history of the Neo-Inca state. James Lockhart's *The Men of Cajamarca: A Social and Biographical Study of the First Conquerors of Peru* (Austin: University of Texas Press, 1972) provides exhaustive detail. To understand the theoretical nature of the Conquest, no single work in English is better than Mario Góngora's *Studies in the Colonial History of Spanish America* (Cambridge: Cambridge University Press, 1975). The scarce Indian testimonies on the Conquest are gathered in Edmundo Guillén Guillén, *Versión inca de la Conquista* (Lima: Milla Batres, 1974). The role of the Huancas and Cañaris are dealt with in W. Espinoza Soriano, *La destrucción del Imperio de los Incas* (Lima: INIDE, 1977), and in an article by Udo Oberem in *Journal de la Société des Américanistes* (Paris, 1974–76) 18 : 263–74 (in Spanish).

b. Structural Changes

The psychological impact is dealt with by Nathan Wachtel, *The Vision of the Vanquished* (Hassocks, Sussex: The Harvester Press, 1977). The standard account of post-Conquest Indian conditions is George Kubler's "The Quechua in the Colonial World," *Handbook of South American Indians* (Washington: Smithsonian Institution, 1946) 2 : 331 – 410. See also K. Spalding, "The Colonial Indian: Past and Future Research Perspectives," *Latin American Research Review* (1972), 7(1) : 47 – 76. How Conquest transformed the Andean natives into an inferior "Caste" subordinated to the colonizers is very well told by Steve Stern in his recent monograph, *Peru's Indian Peoples and the Challenge of Spanish Conquest: Huamanga to 1640* (Madison: University of Wisconsin Press, 1982). The relationship between encomenderos and curacas is particularly well analyzed. Population decline is explored in great depth by N. D. Cook, *Demographic Collapse...* For Spanish immigration see my survey in F. Chiappelli, ed., *First Images of America: The Impact of the New World on the Old,* (Berkeley: University of California Press, 1976) 2 : 737–82.

Early colonization is also well presented in James Lockhart, *Spanish Peru, 1532–1560: A Colonial Society* (Madison: University of Wisconsin Press, 1968). Frederick P. Bowser, *The African Slave in Colonial Peru, 1524–1650* (Stanford: Stanford University Press, 1974) provides thorough treatment of the subject. See also my book, *Race Mixture in the History of Latin America* (Boston: Little, Brown, 1967). For present Bolivia, see Joseph M. Barnadas, *Charcas. Orígenes históricos de una sociedad colonial* (La Paz: CIPCA, 1973). For the coast: Robert G. Keith, *Conquest and Agrarian Change: The Emergence of the Hacienda System on the Peruvian Coast* (Cambridge: Harvard University Press, 1976).

Chapter III: The Impact of Silver and Mercury on Andean Society

a. The Viceroyalty and its Function

The only biography in English of Toledo is Arthur F. Zimmerman, *Francisco de Toledo, Fifth Viceroy of Peru, 1569 – 81* (Caldwell, Idaho, 1938). The basic documents are well presented in N. D. Cook, ed., *Tasa de la visita general de Francisco de Toledo.* (Lima: UNMSM, 1975), and L. Hanke, ed., *Los virreyes españoles en América durante el gobierno de la Casa de Austria. Perú.* (Madrid, 1978), vol. 1. On administration see also John L. Phelan, *The Kingdom of Quito in the Seventeenth Century* (Madison: University of Wisconsin Press, 1967).

b. Mining and Draft Labor

D. A. Brading and H. E. Cross, "Colonial Silver Mining: Mexico and Peru," *The Hispanic American Historical Review* (1972) vol. 52(4) for an excellent survey. See also Lewis Hanke, *The Imperial City of Potosí* (The Hague: Nijhoff, 1956) and B. Arzáns de Orsúa y Vela, *Tales of Potosí* (Providence, R.I.: Brown University Press, 1975).

c. Taxation and Resettlement of the Indians

The demographic history is highlighted in Henry F. Dobyns, "An Outline of Andean Epidemic History to 1720," *Bulletin* of the *History of Medicine,* (1963) vol. 37(6). On taxation, above all, N. Sánchez-Albornoz, *Indios y tributos en el Alto Perú* (Lima: IEP, 1978). The reducción and the policy of racial separation dealt with in M. Mörner, *La Corona española y los foráneos en los pueblos de indios de América* (Stockholm: Almqvist & Wiksell, 1970).

d. Spanish Towns

Two books by John P. Moore: *The Cabildo in Peru under the Hapsburghs* (Durham: University of North Carolina Press, 1954) and *The Cabildo in Peru under the Bourbons* (Durham: University of North Carolina Press, 1961) and Inge Wolff, *Regierung und Verwaltung der kolonialspanischen Städte in Hochperu, 1538 – 1650* (Cologne: Böhlau, 1970) for detailed treatment. In addition to my book on *Race Mixture,* several articles by Karen Spalding, e.g. "Social Climbers: Changing Patterns of Mobility among the Indians of Colonial Peru," *Hispanic American Historical Review,* (1970) vol. 50(4), deal with aspects of stratification.

e. Spread of Culture

Mariano Picón-Salas, *A Cultural History of Spanish America from Conquest to Independence* (Berkeley: University of California Press, 1963) provides brief but excellent treatment. See also Pál Kelemen, *Baroque and Rococo in Latin America,* 2nd ed. (Dover, New York, 1967), vols. 1 and 2; and Gerard Béhague, *Music in Latin America: An Introduction* (Englewood Cliffs, N. J.: Prentice-Hall, 1979), chs. 1 – 2. For the campaign against idolatry, see Pierre Duviols, *La lutte contre les religions autochtones dans le Pérou colonial* (Lima: Institut français d'études andines, 1972).

Chapter IV: Land and Labor in Colonial Andean Society

For a state of research survey, see Mörner, "The Spanish American Hacienda," *The Hispanic American Historical Review*, (1973) vol. 53(2). See also Robert Keith, *Conquest and Agrarian Change: The Emergence of the Hacienda System on the Peruvian Coast* (Cambridge: Harvard University Press, 1976) and two Ph.D. dissertations in history: Keith A. Davies, "The Rural Domain of the City of Arequipa, 1540–1665" (University of Connecticut, 1974) and S. Ramírez-Horton, "Land Tenure and the Economics of Power in Colonial Peru" (University of Wisconsin, Madison, 1977; deals with Lambayeque). In Spanish, among others, Mörner, *Perfil de la sociedad rural del Cuzco a fines de la Colonia* (Lima: Univ. del Pacífico, 1978); V. Roel Pineda, *Historia social y económica de la Colonia* (Lima, 1970), and Pablo Macera, *Trabajos de Historia*, 2 (Lima: Instituto Nacional de la Cultura, 1977), which contains a number of important essays on Andean rural history. For Upper Peru, Brooke Larson's Ph.D. dissertation in history, "Economic Decline and Social Change in an Agrarian Hinterland: Cochbamba (Bolivia) in the Late Colonial Period" (Columbia University, 1978) and her various articles have opened up in depth research. See also chapters 2–3 of Herbert S. Klein's recent survey, *Bolivia: The Evolution of a Multi-Ethnic Society*, Oxford: Oxford University Press, 1982. Conditions in Ecuador are highlighted in Robson B. Tyrer's Ph.D. dissertation in history, "The Demographic and Economic History of the Audiencia of Quito: Indian Population and Textile Industry, 1600–1800" (University of California, Berkeley, 1976) and in Nicholas P. Cushner. *Farm and Factory. The Jesuits and the Development of Agrarian Capitalism in Colonial Quito, 1600–1767* (Albany. State University of New York Press, 1982).

Chapter V: Indian Revolt, Reorganization and Collapse of Colonial Rule

a. Reforms Imposed

My short survey, *La reorganización imperial en Hispanoamérica, 1760 – 1810* (Tunja, Colombia: ed. Nuestra America, 1979) gives reference to literature.

b. Rebellion

An excellent introduction to sources and literature is L. G. Campbell, "Recent Research on Andean Peasant Revolts, 1750 – 1820," *Latin American Research Review*, (1979) vol. 14(1). Among the more stimulating contributions are Jürgen

Golte, *Repartos y rebeliones. Túpac Amaru y las contradicciones de la economía colonial* (Lima: Instituto de Estudios Peruanos, 1980). Juan José Vega, *José Gabriel Tupac Amaru* (Lima, 1969) and O. Cornblit, "Society and Mass Rebellion in Eighteenth-Century Peru and Bolivia," in R. Carr, ed., *Latin American Affairs,* (Oxford, 1970). See also Mörner, *Perfil,* ch. 5. For Ecuador see S. Moreno Yánez, *Sublevaciones indígenas en la Audiencia de Quito desde comienzos del siglo XVIII hasta finales de la Colonia*(University of Bonn, West Germany, 1976).

c. Imperial Reorganization

J. R. Fisher's *Government and Society in Colonial Peru: The Intendant System, 1784 – 1814* (London: Athlone Press, 1970) and articles on mining, e.g. "Silver Production in the Vice-Royalty of Peru, 1776 – 1824," *The Hispanic American Historical Review* (1975) vol. 50(1) are indispensable. The standard work on demography, available, I believe, in German only, is G. Vollmer, *Bevölkerungs-politik und Bevölkerungsstruktur in Vizekönigreich Peru zu Ende der Kolonialzeit, 1741 – 1821* (Bad Homburg, West Germany: Gehlen, 1976). See also D. G. Browning & D. J. Robinson, "The Origin and Comparability of Peruvian Population Data: 1776–1815," *Jahrbuch fur Geschichte...Lateinamerikas* (Cologne, 1977) vol. 14. For Ecuador see R. D. F. Bromley, "Urban-rural demographic contrasts in Highland Ecuador: Town recession in a period of catastrophe, 1778 – 1841," *Journal of Historical Geography* (1979) 5 (vol.3) and Michael T. Hamerly's excellent *Historia social y económica de la antiqua provincia de Guayaquil, 1763 – 1842* (Archivo Histórico del Guayas, Guayaquil, 1973). Enrique Tandeter, in 1980 presented a dissertation in Paris on eighteenth-century Potosí which I hope will soon appear in Spanish. See also his article "Trabajo forzado y trabajo libre en el Potosí tardío," *Desarrollo económico* (Buenos Aires, 1981) vol. 20(80).

d. The Bulwark of Spain; e. Independence Imposed

Published sources and literature on the process of Emancipation is quite extensive. For the Andean countries, the many volumes of the *Colección documental de la Independencia del Perú* (Lima, 1971 –   ) are especially important. H. A. Bierck, ed., *Selected Writings of Bolívar,* 2 vols. (New York: Colonial Press, 1951) offer fascinating reading. An excellent survey is John Lynch, *The Spanish American Revolutions, 1808 – 26* (London: Weidenfeld & Nicolson, 1973), with extensive bibliography. See also Timothy E. Anna, *The Fall of the Royal Government in Peru* (Lincoln: University of Nebraska Press, 1979). The best biography of Bolívar I know of is Gerhard Masur, *Simón Bolívar* (Albuquerque: University of New Mexico Press, 1948). There is no counterpart in English, on José de San Martín. Vol. 1 of Jorge Basadre's monumental work, *Historia de la República del Perú, 1822–1933,* 6th ed. (Lima: Editorial Universitaria, 1969); an anthology of revisionist essays, *La independencia en el Perú* (Lima: Instituto de Estudios

Peruanos, 1981); and Charles W. Andrade, *The Emergence of the Republic of Bolivia* (Gainesville, Fla., 1957) describe the process of formations of these two nations. I know of no survey of that quality on Eduador. For the situation at the end of the wars, see R. A. Humphreys, ed., *British Consular Reports on the Trade and Politics of Latin America, 1824 – 1826.* (London: Royal Historical Society, 1940), and Tulio Halperín-Donghi, *The Aftermath of Revolution in Latin America* (New York: Harper, 1973).

Chapter VI: The Hopes of Liberalism; Realities of Caudillism

a. The External Impact

Using travelogues, Tom B. Jones wrote his entertaining *South America Rediscovered* (Minneapolis: University of Minnesota Press, 1949). Chapters 8–10 deal with Peru and Bolivia, 1810–70.

b. Political Models and Realities

Apart from literature listed for chapter 5, c – e., special mention should be made of Valerie Fifer, *Bolivia: Land, Location and Politics Since 1824.* (Cambridge: Cambridge University Press, 1972); Heraclio Bonilla, *Un siglo a la deriva. Ensayos sobre el Peru, Bolivia y la guerra* (Lima: Instituto de Estudios Peruanos, 1980); and George Kubler, *The Indian Caste of Peru, 1795 – 1940: A Population Study Based Upon Tax Records and Census Reports* (Washington, D.C.: Smithsonian Institution, 1952). There are three as yet unpublished doctoral dissertations on Bolivia: W. B. Lofstrom, "The Promise and Problem of Reform: Attempted Social and Economic Change in the First Years of Bolivian Independence" (Cornell University, 1972); Antonio Mitre, "The Economic and Social Structure of Silver Mining in XIX Century Bolivia" (Columbia University, 1977); and Ervin P. Grieshaber, "Survival of Indian Communities in Nineteenth-Century Bolivia" (University of North Carolina, 1977).

Chapter VII: Export Boom, War and Defeat

a. Export Boom

See J. Levin, "Peru in the Guano Age" in his book *The Export Economies: Their Pattern of Development in Historical Perspective* (Cambridge: Harvard University Press, 1960), pp. 27 – 123; Heraclio Bonilla, *Guano y burguesía en el Perú* (Lima:

278   *Bibliographical Notes*

Instituto de Estudios Peruanos, 1974); and W. M. Mathew, "Anthony Gibbs & Sons, the Guano Trade and the Peruvian Government, 1842–1861," in D. C. M. Platt, ed., *Business Imperialism, 1840–1930: An Inquiry Based on British Experience in Latin America* (Oxford: Clarendon, 1977), pp. 337–70; on Bolivia, A. Mitre's dissertation referred to above and his book, *Los patrarcas de la plata: Estructura socioeconómica de la minería boliviana en el siglo XIX* (Lima: Instituto de Estudios Peruanos, 1981). See also Bonilla's recent book, *Un siglo a la deriva...* mentioned for chapter 6. Bibliography on Ecuadorean economy during the period is scarce.

b. The Growing Ambitions of Government

J. Basadre, *Chile, Peru y Bolivia independientes* (Barcelona and Buenos Aires: Salvat, 1948) (Historia de América y de los pueblos americanos, XXV) and Frederick B. Pike, *The United States and the Andean Republics: Peru, Bolivia and Ecuador*, (Cambridge: Harvard University Press, 1977) provide useful surveys. On the Ecuadorean leader see Ricardo Pattee, *Gabriel García Moreno e o Equador de seu tempo* (Petrópolis: Vozes, 1956) (though somewhat biased in his favor) and Peter H. Smith, "The Image of a Dictator: Gabriel García Moreno," *The Hispanic American Historical Review* (1965) 40(4): 1–24.

c. The War and Its Aftermath

There exists an enormous literature on the War, but V. G. Kiernan, "Foreign Interests in the War of the Pacific," HAHR, (1955) 25: 14–36 and H. Bonilla, "The War of the Pacific and the National and Colonial Problem in Peru," *Past & Present* (1978), No. 81, pp. 92–118 deserve to be singled out. On Bolivia see Ramiro Condarco Morales, *Zárate, el temible, Willka, Historia de la rebelión indígena de 1899* (La Paz, 1965) and Herbert S. Klein, *Parties and Political Change in Bolivia, 1880–1952* (Cambridge: University Press, 1969). On Ecuador, from about this time onward the ambitious work *Political Power in Ecuador* (transl.) (Albuquerque: University of New Mexico Press, 1980), by the present President of that republic, Osvaldo Hurtado, can be consulted.

d. Society During a Period of Economic Change

For Bolivia see Danièle Demelas, *Nationalisme sans nation? La Bolivie aux XIXe-XXe siecles* (Paris: CNRS, 1980) and Silvia Rivera Cusicanchi, "La expansión del latifundio en el Altiplano boliviano," *Allpanchis Phuturinqa* (1979) 12: 189–218. A fascinating account of Indian conditions in Ecuador in Udo Oberem, "Contribución a la historia del trabajador rural de América Latina: 'Conciertos' y 'huasipungueros' en Ecuador" Universitet Bielefeld, Universitets-Schwerpunkt Lateinamerikaforschung: Arbeitspapiere, nr. 11 (Bielefeld: GFD, 1977). For Peru see Janet E. Worrall, "Italian Immigration to Peru: 1860 – 1914," Ph.D. dissertation in History (Bloomington: Indiana University, 1972); Peter Klarén, *Modernization, Dislocation, and Aprismo: Origin of the Peruvian Aprista Party, 1870 – 1932* (Austin: University of Texas Press, 1973); Jean Piel, "The Place of the Peasantry in the National Life of Peru in the Nineteenth Century," *Past & Present* (1970) No. 46, pp. 108 – 33 and Margarita Giesecke, *Masas urbanas y rebelión en la historia. Golpe de estado: Lima, 1872* (Lima: CEDHIP, 1978).

Chapter VIII: World Market Domination Reinforced

a. Economic Dynamics

For the general framework see W. Arthur Lewis, *Growth and Fluctuations, 1870 – 1913* (London: Allen & Unwin, 1978). On Peru, Rosemary Thorp and Geoffrey Bertram, *Peru, 1890 – 1977: Growth and Policy in an Open Economy* (New York: Columbia University Press, 1978). The leading entrepreneur of Bolivia is portrayed in Herbert S. Klein, "The Creation of the Patiño Tin Empire," *Inter American Economic Affairs* (1965) 19(2) : 3–23. L. Weinman wrote a Ph.D. dissertation in 1970 at UCLA: "Ecuador and Cacao: Domestic Response to the Boom – Collapse Monoexport Cycle." It has appeared as a book: *El Ecuador en la época cacaotera* (Quito: Editorial Universidad, 1980). The author's name is now given as Lois Crawford de Roberts. On the same topic, Manuel Chiriboga, *Jornaleros y gran proprietarios en 135 años de exportación cacaotera (1790 – 1925)* (Quito: Consejo Provincial di Pichincha, 1980) and Andrés Guerrero, *Los oligarchas del cacao* (Quito: El Conejo, 1980). For a general view including the highlands, see: Y. E. Saint-Geours, "Quelques aspects de la vie économique d'Equateur de 1830 à 1930," *Bulletin de l'Institut français d'études andines,* (1980) 9 (3–4) : 69–84.

b. Politics

A general survey in F. Pike, *The United States and the Andean Republics...* On Bolivia, H. Klein, *Parties and Political Change...* on Ecuador, Hurtado, *Power...* The border problems are dealt with by J. V. V. Fifer, *Bolivia...* and in the comprehensive work, *Boundaries, Possessions and Conflicts in South America* (Cambridge: Harvard University Press, 1938).

c. Elite Pleasures and Popular Misery

Apart from some of the works listed under (a) see Demelas, *Nationalisme...*,
A. Flores Galindo, *Arequipa...*, and Silvia Rivera Cusicanqui, "La expansión
del latifundio en el Altiplano boliviano," *Allpanchis Phuturinga*, (1979) 12 : 189–
218. The 1982 Ph.D. dissertation at the University of California, Berkeley, by
Nils Jacobsen, "Land Tenure and Society in the Peruvian Altiplano: Azángaro,
1770–1920," is an extraordinary effort at quantification with penetrating analysis of rural structure and change. Among other works to be noted are Dan C.
Hazen, "The Awakening of Puna: Government Policy and the Indian Problem
in Southern Peru, 1900–55," (Ph.D. dissertation, Yale University, 1974), José
Tamayo Herrera, *Historia del indigenismo cuzqueño. Siglos XVI-XX* (Lima: Insti-
tuto Nacional de Cultura, 1980) and Jesús Chavarría, "The Intellectuals and the
Crisis of Modern Peruvian Nationalism," *The Hispanic American Historical
Review*, (1970) 50 : 257–78, focus on the attitudes towards the Indians.

Chapter IX: The Fight for an Andean Revival: Act I

a. Economic Vulnerability Revealed

For Peru we have the standard work already cited for chapter 8: Thorp and
Bertram, *Peru, 1890 – 1977: Growth and Policy in an Open Economy...*; for
Ecuador until 1925 those of Roberts and Chiriboga, also mentioned above.
Otherwise historical overviews are unfortunately lacking. One has to track the
economic development of Ecuador and Bolivia until 1950 using a variety of
sources and literature.

b. The Intellectual Awakening

A comprehensive overview of official indigenism in Peru is Thomas M.
Davies Jr., *Indian Integration in Peru: A Half Century of Experience, 1900–1948*
(Lincoln: University of Nebraska Press, 1974). See also François Chevalier's
article on "official *indigenismo*" in Magnus Mörner, ed., *Race and Class in Latin
America* (New York: Columbia University Press, 1970), pp. 184 – 196, and D.
Hazen, "Awakening..." Much has been written on the ideas of leading "indigenista" thinkers. A recent thorough biography on Mariátegui should be especially noted: Jesús Chavarría, *José Carlos Mariátegui and the Rise of Modern Peru,
1890–1930* (Albuquerque: University of New Albuquerque, 1979). For a short
account of Ecuadorean indigenism see John D. Martz, *Ecuador: Conflicting
Political Culture and the Quest for Progress* (Boston: Allyn & Bacon, 1972),
pp. 45–52.

c. Revolutionary Challenges and Populist Solutions

Very useful as a survey stressing the important relations with the mighty Northern neighbor is Frederick B. Pike, *The United States and the Andean Republics*...(1977), already mentioned. On Ecuador there is George Blanksten's classical *Ecuador: Constitutions and Caudillos* (Berkeley: University of California Press, 1951); Oswaldo Hurtado, *Dos mundos superpuestos: Ensayo de diagnóstico de la realidad ecuatoriana* (Quito, 1969); and his more recent *Political Power*; Agustín Cueva, *The Process of Political Domination in Ecuador* (Transl.: New Brunswick & London: Transaction Books, 1982); and Armando Abad Franco, *Parteiensystem und Oligarchie in Ecuador* (West Berlin, 1974). Focusing on APRA, there are, among others, Francois Bourricaud, *Power and Society in Contemporary Peru* (New York & Washington: Faber & Faber 1970); Peter Klarén, *Modernization, Dislocation and Aprismo: Origins of the Peruvian Aprista Party, 1870 – 1932* (Austin: University of Texas Press, 1973); and Jeffrey L. Klaiber, "The Popular Universities and the Origins of Aprismo, 1921–1924," *The Hispanic American Historical Review* (1975) 55(4) : 693–715. On Bolivia, the standard work is Herbert S. Klein, *Parties and Political Change...*, cited above. For the Peru – Ecuadorean conflict and the Chaco war see Bryce Wood, *The United States and Latin American Wars, 1932–1942* (New York: Columbia University Press, 1966).

d. Social Seething Within a Tight Economic and Political Frame

An excellent overview of the Andean Indian situation toward mid-century is provided by the International Labour Office's comprehensive work: *Indigenous Peoples: Living and Working Conditions of Aboriginal Populations in Independent Countries*, (Geneva, 1953). An important Ph.D. Dissertation should be mentioned here: Florencia E. Mallon, "The Poverty of Progress: The Peasants of Yanamarca and the Development of Capitalism in Peru's Central Highlands, 1860–1940" (Yale University, 1980). Even though she covers a longer period, the author focuses on the twenties, believing them to be the most crucial moment for the capitalist breakthrough. For Peru there is a very useful book, Magali Sarfatti Larson and Arlene Eisen Bergman, *Social Stratification in Peru* (Berkeley: University of California Press, 1969). There is nothing comparable on the other two countries.

Chapter X: The Fight for an Andean Revival: Act II

a. The Economic Strait-Jacket

For Bolivia see especially James M. Malloy and Richard S. Thorn, eds., *Beyond the Revolution: Bolivia Since 1952* (Pittsburgh: University of Pittsburgh Press, 1971). For the 1970s Mechthild Minkner, "Wirtschaftentwicklung in Bolivia unter der Regierung Banzer (1971 – 78)" (Hamburg: Institut für Iberoamerika-Kunde, 1981: mimeogr.). For Peru, Thorp and Bertram's fine work covers this period, too, until 1977. The development of Peruvian agriculture before the land reform of 1969 is thoroughly studied by Raúl Hopkins, *Desarrollo desiqual y crisis en la agricultura peruana, 1944 – 1969* (Lima: IEP, 1981), and José María Caballero, *Economía agraria de la Sierra peruana antes de la Reforma agraria de 1969* (Lima: IEP, 1981). There is a vast literature on the Land reform of 1969, but two recent works deserve to be singled out: Tom Alberts, *Agrarian Reform and Rural Poverty: A Case Study of Peru* (Lund: Research Policy Institute, and Stockholm: Institute of Latin American Studies, 1981) and José Matos Mar and J. M. Mejía, *La reforma agrara en el Perú* (Lima: IEP, 1980). Ecuadorean economic problems receive some attention in *Ecuador: hoy* by Gerhard Drekonja and others (Mexico City: Siglo XXI, 1978). The yearbook issued by the Economic Commission for Latin America, *Statistical Yearbook for Latin America* (United Nations); the Inter-American Development Bank's, *Economic and Social Progress in Latin America* and the World Bank's *The World Development Report, 1980,* have been especially useful for recent developments.

b. Politics of Underdevelopment

In his work *The United States and the Andean Republics...* (1977), Frederick B. Pike does not only take up foreign policy issues. He also studies intellectual developments at length. In the present survey, these aspects have received little attention. For Bolivian politics, in addition to the work by Malloy and Thorn, mentioned above, the last two chapters in Herbert S. Klein's recent survey, *Bolivia: The Evolution of a Multi-Ethnic Society* (Oxford: Oxford University Press, 1982) are especially relevant. For the early phase of military government in Peru, see Abraham F. Lowenthal, ed., *The Peruvian Experiment: Continuity and Change Under Military Rule* (Princeton: Princeton University Press, 1975). Among many more recent monographs, Alfred Stephan, *The State and Society: Peru in Comparative Perspective* (Princeton: Princeton University Press, 1978) should be mentioned. For a timely short account of the state of research on the Junta see Luis Pásara, "Diagnosing Peru," *Latin American Research Review* (1982) 17(1). On Ecuador apart from the recent publications of the translations of the works by Osvaldo Hurtado and Agustín Cueva listed in the bibliographical note to the previous chapter, the monograph by John S. Fitch, *The Military Coup d'Etat as a Political Process: Ecuador, 1948 – 1966* (Baltimore: Johns Hopkins University Press, 1977) and John D. Martz, *Conflicting Political Culture and the Quest for Progress* (Boston: Allyn & Bacon, 1973) should be noted. The very useful newsletter, *Latin America. Regional Reports. The Andean Group* (London) has helped trace recent political developments in the three countries.

c. Whither the Swelling Masses?

For demography, urbanization, and education, data are available e.g. in the yearbook *Statistical Abstract of Latin America* (Los Angeles: UCLA) and *World Development Report 1980* (tables 17 – 20, 23). Nutrition is dealt with in Jacques

M. May and Donna L. McClellan, *The Ecology of Malnutrition in Western South America* (London: Hafner, 1974). I have, however, relied rather on a number of unpublished FAO reports. In his work *Social Security in Latin America: Pressure Groups, Stratification and Inequity* (Pittsburgh: Pittsburgh University Press, 1978), Carmelo Mesa-Lago takes up the case of Peru. On unions see e.g. Julian Laite, "Miners and National Policies in Peru, 1900–74," *Journal of Latin American Studies* 12(2) : 317 – 340; and Guillermo Lora, *A History of the Bolivian Labour Movement* (1977). See also June Nash, *We Eat the Mines and the Mines Eat Us* (New York: Columbia University Press, 1979). For the Bolivian peasants from 1952 onwards see James V. Kohl, "Peasant and Revolution in Bolivia, April 9, 1952 – August 2, 1953," *The Hispanic American Historical Review* (1978) 58 : 238 – 59 and José L. Havet, "Rational Domination: The Power Structure in a Bolivian Rural Zone," (Ph.D. dissertation, University of Pittsburgh, 1978). For the account of events in Cerro de Pasco we consulted Wilfredo Kapsoli E., *Los movimientos campesinos en Cerro de Pasco, 1800 – 1963* (Instituto de Estudios Andinos, Huancayo, 1975). The case study from Andahuaylas referred to in the text is Harold O. Skar's *The Warm Valley People. Duality and Land Reform Among the Quechua Indians of Highland Peru* (Oslo: Universitetsforlaget, 1982). On La Convención see e.g. Eric Hobsbawm, "A Case of Neo-Feudalism: La Convención, Perú," *Journal of Latin American Studies* (1969) 1(1) : 1 – 30 and, in more depth, Eduardo Fioravanti, *Latifundio y sindicalismo agrario en el Perú. El caso de los valles de La Convención y Lares, 1958 – 64* 2d ed. (Lima: IEB, 1976). For a study of the social aspects of land reform in the rice belt along the Guayas River see M. R. Redclift, *Agrarian Reform and Peasant Organization on the Ecuadorean Coast* (London: Athlone Press, 1978). Colonization in the lowlands is surveyed by Raymond F. Crist and Charles M. Nissby, *East from the Andes: Pioneer Settlements in the South American Heartland* (Gainesville: University of Florida Press, 1973).

BIBLIOGRAPHICAL NOTE FOR FURTHER STUDY AND RESEARCH

The student is doubtlessly acquainted with standard bibliographical tools and reference works, such as the *Handbook of Latin American Studies, Statistical Abstract of Latin America,* and the *Latin American Research Review,* with its many useful state-of-research articles as well as the *Hispanic American Historical Review* with its comprehensive review section. Nevertheless, there still are some works on the three countries dealt with in this book and not already mentioned in the bibliographical references to each chapter which deserve to be mentioned.

To start with Bolivia, there is a bibliographical yearbook called *Bio-bibliografía boliviana* (Cochabamba: Los amigos del libro, 1975 –). It should be stressed, also, that Herbert S. Klein's very recent *Bolivia: The Evolution of a Multiethnic Society* (New York and Oxford: Oxford University Press, 1982) contains a detailed bibliographical essay. An annotated selection of 100 works is presented in Juan Siles Guevara's *Bibliografía selecta de historia de Bolivia* (La Paz: Los amigos del libro, 1975).

For Peru there is the *Anuario bibliografíco peruano* (Lima: Biblioteca Nacional, 1943–), even though usually lagging behind a great deal. For a brief annotated selection see Franklin Pease G. Y., *Perú: una aproximación bibliografíca* (Lima: Centro de estudios económicos y sociales del Tercer Mundo, 1979). Other useful bibliographies include: Carlos Moreyra y Paz Soldán, *Bibliografía regional peruana* (Lima, 1967) and *Fuentes bibliograficas en las ciencias sociales (1879–1979),* edited by A. Pérez Cáceres (Lima, 1981). For colonial history there are two basic works: Rubén Vargas Ugarte, *Manual de estudios peruanistas,* 4th ed. (Lima: 1959) and Raúl Porras Barrenechea, *Fuentes históricas peruanas* (Lima: UNMSM, 1963). For the period 1822–1933 a work by Jorge Basadre is even more exhaustive. *Introducción a las bases documentales para la historia de la República del Perú con algunas reflexiones,* 1–3 (Lima: Villanueva, 1971). Economic history for the same period is covered in detail by Pablo Macera and Shane J. Hunt in a part (pp. 547–649) of *Latin America. A Guide to Economic History, 1830–1930,* edited by Roberto Cortés Conde and Stanley J. Stein (Berkeley and Los Angeles: University of California Press, 1977). For selective bibliographies see also a recent issue of *The History Teacher* 14(3) (Long Beach, California, 1981) which includes surveys by Leon G. Campbell on Colonial Peru and by Thomas M. Davies on the period 1826–90. See also Hector Maletta's list of U.S. dissertations on Peru, "Cuatrocientas tesis doctorales norteamericanas sobre el Perú, 1869–1976; apéndice: 153 tesis más, 1949–1978," *Estudios Andinos* (Lima, 1979) 8(15) : 57–134.

Ecuador also has a bibliographical yearbook, *Anuario Bibliográfico ecuatoriano* (Quito: Biblioteca general de la Universidad Central, 1975 –). See also the bulletin *Ecuador: Bibliografía analítica* (Cuenca: Banco Central del Ecuador, 1979 –). For history, fortunately, there is a special bibliography, Robert E. Norris, *Guía bibliográfica para el estudio de la historia ecuatoriana* (University of Texas, Austin: ILAS 1978).

A good coverage of the official publications of all the three countries is given by Rosa Quintero Mesa in her series *Latin American Serial Documents* (Ann Arbor, Michigan: University Microfilms): Bolivia (1972), Ecuador (1973), and Peru (1973). Texts of and comments on the various constitutions of each country can be found in the series *Las constituciones hispanoamericanas* (Madrid: Ediciones Cultura Hispánica): 1, *Ecuador* (1951); 4, *Perú* (1954), and 13, *Bolivia* (1958).

For general reference there is the *Diccionario enciclopédico del Perú ilustrado*, vols. 1 – 3 (Lima: Mejía Baca, 1966 – 67), edited by Alberto Tauro and with an Appendix published in 1975. Francisco Terán's *Geografía de los países del Grupo Andino* (Quito: Casa de la Cultura Ecuatoriana, 1975) is useful for all the three countries. The slim volumes of the series of *Historical Dictionaries* by the Scarecrow Press, Metuchen N.J. can be used for quick elementary reference and also contain short bibliographies: *Bolivia* by D. B. Heath (1972); *Ecuador* by A. W. Bork and G. Maier (1973); *Peru* by Marvin Alisky (1979). On Peru there is an impressive cartographic work with more than 700 pages of maps, photographs, and high-quality text of great usefulness: *Atlas histórico, geográfico y de paisajes peruanos* (Lima: Instituto Nacional de Planificación, 1970).

For research in the archives of the three countries and Chile there is an excellent recent handbook: John J. TePaske, ed., *Research Guide to Andean History: Bolivia, Chile, Ecuador, and Peru*, (Durham, NC: Duke University Press, 1981).

For the historiography of Bolivia see an article by Charles W. Arnade, "The Historiography of Colonial and Modern Bolivia," *The Hispanic American Historical Review* (1962) 42(3) : 333 – 84 and Valentin Abecia Baldivieso, *Historiografía boliviana* (La Paz, 1965); for Ecuador, Adam Szászdi, "The Historiography of the Republic of Ecuador," *The Hispanic American Historical Review* (1964) 44(4) : 503 – 50. Peruvian historiography is presented by Vargas Ugarte, Porras Barrenechea and Basadre in their works listed already. For an idea about the present trends see Heraclio Bonilla, The New Profile of Peruvian History," *Latin American Research Review*, (1981) 16(3) : 210 – 24.

WORKS CITED IN TABLES AND ILLUSTRATIONS

Alberts, Tom. 1981. *Agrarian Reform and Rural Poverty: A Case Study of Peru*. Lund, Sweden: Research Policy Institute.

Archetti Eduardo P. 1980. "Haciendas and Peasants: The Process of Agrarian Change in Ecuador." Conference paper from Bellagio, Italy.

Avellaneda Mollinedo, I. G. 1956. *Aspectos generales de la población boliviana*. La Paz.

Bankes, George. 1977. *Peru Before Pizarro*. Oxford: Phaidon.

Bonilla, Heraclio. 1980. *Un siglo a la deriva. Ensayos sobre el Perú, Bolivia y la guerra*. Lima: Instituto de Estudios Peruanos.

Brading, D. A. and Harry E. Cross. 1972. "Colonial Silver Mining: Mexico and Peru." *The Hispanic American Historical Review*, 52:4.

Carbo, L. A. 1953. *Historia monetaria y cambiaria del Ecuador desde época colonial*. Quito.

Cardoso, Ciro Flamarion S. and Héctor Perez Brignoli. 1979. *Historia económica de América Latina*, I–II, Crítica, Barcelona.

Castedo, Leopoldo. 1969. *A History of Latin American Art and Architecture. From Pre-Columbian Times to the Present*. New York: Praeger.

CEPAL. 1982. "La evolución económica de América Latina en 1981." *Notas sobre la economía y el desarrollo de América Latina*. Comisión económica para América Latina, Santiago de Chile (Nr. 355/356).

Cisneros Sanchez, Manuel. 1975. *Pancho Fierro y la Lima del 800*. Lima: García Ribeyro.

Cobo, Bernabé. 1979. *History of the Inca Empire*. Transl. and edited by R. Hamilton. Austin: University of Texas Press.

Cole, J. P. 1975. *Latin America. An Economic and Social Geography*. London: Butterworth.

Cook, N. David. 1977. "Estimaciones sobre la población del Perú en el momento de la conquista." *Histórica*, 1:1 (Lima).

Cook, N. David. 1981. *Demographic Collapse. Indian Peru, 1520–1620*. Cambridge: Cambridge University Press.

CPED. 1972. *Informe demográfico—Perú 1970*. Lima: Centro de estudios y de desarrollo.

Crawford de Roberts, Lois. 1980. *El Ecuador en la época cacaotera. Respuestas locales al auge y colapso en el ciclo monoexportador*. Transl. Quito: Editorial universitaria.

Demelas, Danièle. 1980. *Nationalisme sans nation? La Bolivie aux XIX–XX siècles*. Paris: Centre National de Recherches Scientifiques.

Erneholm, Ivar. 1948. *Cacao Production of South America. Historical Development and Present Geographical Distribution.* Gothenburg: University of Gothenburg.

Escobedo Mansilla, R. 1976. "La alcabala en el Perú bajo los Austrias," *Anuario de Estudios Americanos,* 33 (Seville).

Fifer, Valerie. 1972. *Bolivia: Land, Location and Politics Since 1824.* Cambridge: Cambridge University Press.

Fisher, John R. 1975. "Silver Production in the Viceroyalty of Peru, 1776–1824." *The Hispanic American Historical Review,* 35:1.

Gade, Daniel W. 1975. *Plants, Man and the Land in the Vilcanota Valley of Peru.* The Hague: Junk.

Golte, Jürgen. 1980. *Repartos y rebeliones. Túpac Amaru y las contradicciones de la economía colonial.* Lima: Instituto de Estudios Peruanos.

Hamerly, Michael T. 1973. *Historia social y económica de la antiqua provincia de Guayaquil, 1763–1843.* Guayaquil: Archivo Histórico del Guayas.

Helmer, Marie. 1955/56. "La visitación de los yndios chupachos—inka et encomendero." *Travaux de l'Institut français d'études andines,* 5 (Paris & Lima).

Historia. 1948. *Historia de América y de los pueblos americanos.* 25. Barcelona: Salvat.

Humphreys, R. A. 1952. *Liberation in South America, 1806–1827. The Career of James Parpissier.* London: Athlone.

Humphreys, R. A., ed. *British Consular Reports on the Trade and Politics of Latin America. 1824–1826.* London: Royal Historical Society.

IDB. 1968. *Socio-Economic Progress in Latin America. Social Progress Trust Fund . . . Report 1968.* Washington: Inter-American Development Bank.

IDB. 1980/81. *Economic and Social Progress in Latin America. 1980–81 Report.* Washington: Inter-American Development Bank.

Jara, Alvaro. 1966. *Tres ensayos sobre economía minera hispanoamericana.* Santiago: University of Chile.

Klaren, Peter. 1978. "The Rise of Modern Capitalism in Peru: The Case of the North." Conference paper at Lima.

Lewis, W. Arthur. 1978. *Growth and Fluctuations, 1870–1913.* London: Allen & Unwin.

Lockhart, James. 1968. *Spanish Peru, 1532–1560: A Colonial Society.* Madison: University of Wisconsin Press.

Lofstrom, W. B. 1972. "The Promise and Problem of reform: Attempted Social and Economic Change in the First Years of Bolivian Independence." PhD. diss. Cornell.

Lopez, Rivas, Eduardo. 1955. *Esquema de la historia económica de Bolivia.* Oruro: Univ. Técnica.

Lynch, John. 1973. *The Spanish American Revolutions, 1808–26.* London: Weidenfeld & Nicolson.

Meggers, Betty J. 1966. *Ecuador.* London: Thames & Hudson.

Mitre, Antonio. 1981. *Los patriarcas de la plata. Estructura socio-económica de la minería boliviana en el siglo XIX.* Lima: Instituto de Estudios Peruanos.

Mitre, Antonio. 1977. "The Economic and Social Structure of Silver Mining in Nineteenth-Century Bolivia," Ph.D diss., Columbia University.

Morales Padrón, Francisco. 1975. *Historia general de América*. 2d ed. Madrid: Espasa Calpe.

Mörner, Magnus. 1967. *Race Mixture in the History of Latin America*. Boston: Little, Brown.

Mörner, Magnus. 1978. *Perfil de la sociedad rural del Cuzco a fines de la colonia*. Lima: Univ. del Pacífico.

Morris, Craig. 1976. "Master Design of the Inca." *Natural History*, 85:10.

Nash, June. 1979. *We Eat the Mines and the Mines Eat Us*. New York: Columbia University Press.

PAU. 1911. *Pan American Union Country Booklets: Bolivia, Ecuador, Peru*. Washington.

PAU. 1952. *The Foreign Trade of Latin America Since 1913*. Washington: Pan American Union.

Peñaloza, Luis. 1953. *Historia económica de bolivia*. 1–2. La Paz.

Platt, D. C. M. 1972. *Latin America and British Trade, 1806–1914*. London: Adam & Black.

Poma de Ayala, Guamán. 1978. *Letter to the King*. Ed. by C. Dilke. New York: Dutton.

Ravines, Rogger, ed. 1978. *Tecnología andina*. Lima: Instituto de Estudios Peruanos.

Rippy, J. Fred. 1949. *British Investments in Latin America, 1822–1949*. Minneapolis: University of Minnesota Press.

SALA. 1981. *Statistical Abstract of Latin America*. No. 21. UCLA Latin American Center.

Sanchez-Albornoz, Nicolás. 1974. *The Population of Latin America. A History*. Berkeley: University of California Press.

Shafer, Robert James. 1978. *A History of Latin America*. Lexington, Mass.: D. C. Heath.

Slicher van Bath, B. H. 1979. "Economic Diversification in Spanish America Around 1600: Centres, Intermediate Zones and Peripheries." *Jahrbuch für die Geschichte von Staat, Wirtschaft und Gesellschaft Lateinamerikas*, 16 (Cologne).

Thorp, Rosemary & Geoffrey Beatram. 1978. *Peru, 1890–1977. Growth and Policy in an Open Economy*. New York: Columbia University Press.

Tord, Javier. 1977. "Sociedad colonial y fiscalidad." *Apuntes*, 14:7 (Lima).

Vicens Vives, Jaime, ed. 1961. *Historia de España y América*. vol. 4. Barcelona: Editorial Vicens Vives.

Villanueva, Victor. 1962. *El militarismo en el Perú*. Lima.

Villavicencio, Manuel. 1858. *Geografía de la República del Ecuador*. New York.

Wilkie, James W. 1974. *Measuring Land Reform*. UCLA: Latin American Center.

World Bank. 1980. *World Development Report, 1980*. Washington.

INDEX